HARDY AND THE LADY FROM MADISON SQUARE

HARDY AND THE LADY
FROM MADISON SQUARE

By

CARL J WEBER

❧

"We talked with open heart, and tongue
Affectionate and true,
A pair of friends, though I was young,
And he was seventy-two."

WORDSWORTH: *The Fountain*

WATERVILLE, MAINE
COLBY COLLEGE PRESS
1952

18,061

Colby College Monograph No. 20

Printed in the United States of America by
The Anthoensen Press of Portland, Maine

To the Memory of the late

CARROLL A. WILSON

who, shortly before his death in 1947, purchased

and generously presented to the

COLBY COLLEGE LIBRARY

the entire Thomas Hardy Collection of

REBEKAH OWEN

CONTENTS

PREFACE

LESS than a year before Hitler marched his troops into Poland, a parcel of books was sold at auction at Sotheby's in London, and early in 1939 they reached the library of Colby College. Their arrival led shortly afterward to the discovery that there were, in the Lake District home in England from which the books had come, other volumes *not* offered for sale at the auction, volumes and papers and albums and letters which belonged with the original lot of books. By the time that arrangements had been made for the purchase of these additional volumes and for their transfer to Colby, World War II was in full swing. In order to minimize the risk on an ocean infested with German submarines, the books were sent in a series of small parcels, only one of which was lost. These shipments continued over a period of two years after "Pearl Harbor"; then they stopped, not to be resumed until the end of hostilities in Europe. In 1946 further additions were made to the re-assembly line at Colby College; and at last, in the summer of 1950, the final arrival put in its appearance. Not until then could it be said that the Hardy Collection of Miss Rebekah Owen was once again a unit and, miraculously, a unit preserved almost intact—only two books having been lost in the war-time shipments.

After the expenditure of more than a dozen years in this transatlantic transfer, it seemed wise not to extend the close examination of the books, and of Miss Owen's activities in bringing them together, over another dozen years. The President and Trustees of Colby College therefore granted the present writer leave of absence, a welcome relief from normal duties, which has permitted him to complete this study within two years of the date of the arrival of the last Owen parcel in the Colby library. "For this relief much thanks." Grateful acknowledgment must also be

made of help received from a large number of friends, col-
leagues, librarians, and officials in various parts of the world, who
have patiently answered questions, looked up old records, and in
other ways contributed to easing the work of the investigator.
Chief among those to whom the writer feels indebted is one who,
alas, did not live to see these words in print. This book is accordingly dedicated to the memory of that ardent Hardy "fan"
whose generosity to the Colby College Library accounts for its
possession of the Owen Collection.

Without Rebekah Owen's books the world might never have
known who the Americans were to whom Hardy was referring
when, in one of his prefaces, he wrote about "some good judges
across the Atlantic," or who the ladies were who called at Max
Gate two days before the death of the first Mrs. Hardy, a mysterious pair about whom the second Mrs. Hardy wrote merely:
"two ladies called." Without Rebekah Owen's help, we might
never have known why "Susannah" vanishes after two appearances among the "Interlopers at the Knap," to have her place
thereafter taken by a "Rebekah," and why Hardy was "provoked" with Grace Melbury in *The Woodlanders*. Rebekah
Owen's Hardiana have not only provided answers to these and
many other similar questions, but have disclosed her own un-
heralded and previously unsuspected rôle as the original Hardy
Perennial. James Boswell never shadowed Johnson's footsteps
with greater zeal than that shown by Rebekah Owen in her devotion to Thomas Hardy. "Devotion" is the right word; she
wrote quite frankly about it, calling Hardy "the adored one." In
spreading knowledge of him and interest in his works among
readers on both sides of the ocean, her Boswellian services to the
Wessex novelist were of such magnitude that this book about her
might quite truthfully have been called "Hardy and his Female

Boswell," for the similarity between Rebekah Owen and James Boswell is, in many ways, a striking one.

She never carried out the idea which had, at one time or another, occurred to her—that of writing the life of Thomas Hardy. It was an idea that had been urged upon her by friends, and if she had ever carried it out, she might have used the exact words with which Boswell began his *Life of Johnson*. Boswell wrote:

As I had the honor and happiness of enjoying his [Dr. Johnson's] friendship for upwards of twenty years; as I had the scheme of writing his life constantly in view; as he ... from time to time obligingly satisfied my enquiries, by communicating to me the incidents of his early years; as I ... was very assiduous in recording his conversation ... ; and as I have spared no pains in obtaining materials concerning him, from every quarter where I could discover that they were to be found, and have been favored with the most liberal communications by his friends; I flatter myself that few biographers have entered upon such a work as this, with more advantages. ...

As Rebekah Owen "had the honor and happiness of enjoying his [Hardy's] friendship for upwards of twenty years," and as "the scheme of writing his life" was specifically suggested to her by friends who knew both her enthusiastic admiration for the Wessex novels and her ability to wield a fluent and effective pen, and "as he ... from time to time obligingly satisfied her enquiries, by communicating to her the incidents of his early years, as she ... was very assiduous in recording his conversation ... and spared no pains in obtaining materials concerning him ... and was favored with the most liberal communications by his friends" as well as by both his wives, she might, had she ever applied herself resolutely to the task for which she was so well equipped, have entered upon it with Boswellian advantages.

Miss Owen died, however, without having achieved a book on Hardy. After the reader has heard her story, he will, I think, understand why she remained silent after spending half of her life in zealous study of the Wessex writings. Fortunately, she preserved her Hardiana; they survived her and they speak for themselves. They provide a solid foundation on which the following pages are based. The letters of Thomas Hardy are printed by special permission of Miss Irene Cooper Willis, Trustee (with Lloyds Bank, London) of the Hardy copyrights under the will of Mrs. Thomas Hardy. These letters and the pages which accompany them are here offered to the public with the hope that they will not only help to keep Rebekah Owen's memory alive, but will also help readers to understand why that memory deserves to be kept alive and why Hardy referred to her and her sister as those "good judges across the Atlantic."

C. J. W.

HARDY
AND THE LADY
FROM
MADISON SQUARE

Chapter I

Henry Owen, Merchant

IF, like Mark Twain's Connecticut Yankee, you had been hit on the head with a crowbar—or, what is not only more possible but also more likely, if you had been run down by a taxicab while you were crossing the street and had been knocked senseless—and if you had awakened to find yourself, not in King Arthur's England as the Connecticut Yankee found himself, but in Queen Victoria's England—not the England of the gray-haired Queen, mother of Edward the Seventh and Empress of all India, but the England of the young, unmarried and newly crowned girl-queen—if, in short, you had awakened to find yourself miraculously transported back in history into the world into which Thomas Hardy was born three years after Queen Victoria had acceded to the throne, how long do you think it would take you to tell that you had been bumped backwards a hundred and ten or twelve years? What things do you think you would notice at once as evidence that you were no longer living in the U. S. A. in 1952 but in a very different world? Certainly the great number of horses would attract your immediate notice, and as soon as your head had cleared you would note the absence of letter-boxes and the paucity of schools. The large quantity of horses and the small number of schools may, indeed, be taken as the positive and negative poles of a metaphorical electric current which will throw light on the lives and careers which we are about to follow in this book. The horses were important; schools were not. Queen Victoria came to the throne in 1837, and shortly thereafter the British Parliament made certain appropriations. It voted £70,000 for the construction of stables for the horses of the young queen, and in that same year appropriated only £30,000 for the education of the children of all England—three million of them—fully one-half of whom were growing up in a state of utter ignorance. Prior to 1839, the annual appropriation for public education had been only £20,000. No wonder the England into which Thomas Hardy was born on June 2, 1840, was an England in which great masses of the people were living in ignorance and degradation.

Conditions were particularly wretched among the factory workers of the North and Midlands, and the extreme misery of their lives made these workers listen all the more readily to the revolutionary agitators of the Chartist movement. During the summer preceding Hardy's birth, torchlight meetings of workingmen were held at night in many industrial regions of the North—meetings at which armed insurrection was openly advocated. In Lancashire and Yorkshire, the fires of revolt merely smouldered, but in Monmouthshire an armed attack was eventually made in November, 1840, by aroused laborers. The uprising was put down, but some months later the Labor leaders called a general strike which resulted in further rioting in Lancashire, Cheshire, and other industrial districts. A petition to Parliament received the surprising number of over 3,300,000 signatures. Since the Chartists believed that all improvement in the living conditions of the laboring classes depended upon political reform, they drew up a five-point *Charter* and presented it for parliamentary approval. What the three million petitioners really wanted, however, was expressed simply enough by one of their writers: "a good house to live in, good clothing to keep one warm and to make one look respectable, and plenty of good food and drink." Parliament, however, rejected the Chartist petition and left the laboring classes with a feeling of hopelessness that any real alleviation of their poverty and of the wretchedness of their working conditions could be soon achieved.

No wonder, then, that Englishmen left the country in increasing numbers throughout the decade that followed Hardy's birth. The American writer Jacob Abbott (creator of *Little Rollo*), who visited England in 1843 and again in 1847, witnessed this large-scale flight from misery and later commented on the fact that in England even the children were being "sent forth to the world alone, to . . . Jamaica, to . . . Hindostan, or to wander about the world. . . ." Among these foreign places, America attracted many an Englishman. By 1830 the number of immigrants who came to the United States annually had already risen to twenty thousand; but during the Chartist agitations in England the average number of immigrants jumped to nearly five times the previous figure. The relatives of Wildeve (in Hardy's *Return of the Native*) migrated to Wisconsin, and (says Hardy in his preface) "the date may be set down as between 1840 and 1850." And at this same time there emigrated from Sheffield, in Yorkshire, four children of a family by the name of Owen.

The head of the Sheffield household had apparently come originally from Wales. By the time of Thomas Hardy's birth, there were three brothers and two sisters in the Owen home; and under the harsh economic conditions that drove Yorkshire workingmen to insurrection, four of the five Owens decided to move. Joseph, the eldest brother, continued to reside in Sheffield; but Henry, Thomas, and their two sisters, all emigrated to New York.

Just what Lorelei attracted them to that spot it is now impossible to say. Certainly it was *not* the song sung by Charles Dickens, who had recently visited New York and found that growing metropolis to be something other than a paradise. Dickens had come to America in 1842 and later reported in his *American Notes* that New York was "by no means . . . clean," that it was terribly hot, that in crossing the street one had to "take care of the pigs . . . , the city scavengers," and that in the "narrow ways diverging to the right and left" where "many of these pigs live," there were inescapable signs of "poverty, wretchedness, and vice." Dickens

would certainly have convinced the Owens—if they read him—
that New York City was no better than Sheffield.

But in 1842 Dickens was of course not the sole source of information to which an Englishman could turn for an introduction
to the New World. Another family group had, like the Owens,
recently fled from harsh conditions in England to seek its fortune in America. Mrs. Frances Trollope had gone to the United
States with three of her children, a son and two daughters. She
had not made her fortune—far from it!—but upon her return
to England Mrs. Trollope had done something else which eventually made her famous. She had (in March, 1832) published
her *Domestic Manners of the Americans,* with its vivid and at times
lurid details about life in these United States. Before the end of
the year in which the book was published, it had sailed gloriously
(scandalously, its American readers thought) through four editions. Obviously, Englishmen were eager to read about life in
America, and many of them were thus made acquainted with the
attractiveness of New York City. For Mrs. Trollope's picture
of New York is quite unlike the scene painted by her country-
man Charles Dickens. Mrs. Trollope's ecstatic account is found
in Chapter 30 of her book:

I have never seen the bay of Naples, I can therefore make no comparison,
but my imagination is incapable of conceiving anything of the kind more
beautiful than the harbor of New York. . . . We seemed to enter . . . upon
waves of liquid gold and . . . New York . . . appeared to us, even when we
saw it [later] by a soberer light, a lovely and a noble city. . . . I must . . .
declare that I think New York one of the finest cities I ever saw. . . . The
extreme [southern] point . . . is converted into a public promenade, and
one more beautiful . . . no city could boast. From hence commences the
splendid Broadway. . . . This noble street may vie with any I ever saw. . . .
I will not . . . attempt a detailed description of this great metropolis of the
new world, but will only say that, during the seven weeks we stayed there,
we always found something new to see and to admire; and were it not so
very far from all the old-world things which cling about the heart of an
European, I should say that I never saw a city more desirable as a residence.

Frances Trollope was fifty years old when she wrote this, and she had more reason to recall "the old-world things which cling about the heart" than Henry Owen perhaps had when he turned his back upon his native Yorkshire. In 1843 he was only thirty-two years old. Whether he crossed the Atlantic with a heavy or a light heart it is now impossible to tell. One would like to know what he would have thought of Charles Dickens's remarks (in Chapter 6 of *American Notes*) about the Yorkshire groom in New York City "who had not been very long in these parts and looked sorrowfully round for a companion," or whether young Owen would have been set a-dreaming by Dickens's description of New York's "great infusion of the mercantile spirit" and its "display of wealth and costly living." In any case, Henry Owen left Yorkshire about 1843, crossed the ocean, and established himself in New York—that "city more desirable as a residence" (if he was to believe Mrs. Trollope) than Sheffield or any other town in strife-torn Yorkshire.

By 1845 Henry Owen had been in New York long enough to have established a "permanent" residence and to get himself into the New York City directory. There he is listed as a "turner," but just what that means is not clear. The word suggests a handicraft and implies that Henry Owen began working in New York at the trade or craft he had learned in Yorkshire. One well-informed English authority remarks that in 1845 a "turner" would be a wood-turner, that is—probably—a handle-maker. Henry Owen's later interests, however, and his business position for the last twenty-five years of his life imply a social rank higher than that of a mere turner. It is perhaps possible that he did not bother to explain the word "turner" to the inquiring agent of the editor of the city directory. Perhaps, to Henry Owen himself, the word meant Member of the Turners' Guild, and it is perhaps possible that he came to New York in the first place as the export-representative, or agent, of a British guild. Certain it is that, if he did not come as such a representative, he eventually became one, and in later issues of the New York City directory Owen was called an "agent." No mention was made of "turner" after 1846.

About this time, then, the young man from Yorkshire effected a marked improvement, if not in his way of earning a living, at least in the manner and style of his living in New York. The presence of his brother Joseph back in Sheffield undoubtedly put Henry Owen in a favorable position, for Joseph was at headquarters, as it were. He was on the spot where information about England's rapidly growing steel industry could be most easily picked up and acted upon. Sheffield had long been famous for its iron works. Smelting from local ore had been carried on there ever since the Roman occupation of Britain, and from the date of the Norman Conquest the town was well known for its iron manufacturing. By Chaucer's time Sheffield had become famous for its cutlery, and The Cutlers' Company was formed in 1624—a "company" which is still doing business today. It is possible (though I have not been able to prove) that Joseph Owen was, in one way or another, connected with this Cutlers' Company.

But there was a new and more cogent reason for Henry Owen's success as an agent in New York City. In 1830 an Englishman named James Perry took out a patent on a steel slip-pen, and it was not long before the manufacture of pen nibs from cast steel became a thriving business. Birmingham was the first home of the steel-pen industry; but whether the company or companies for whom Henry Owen later acted as agent were Birmingham companies, or whether Sheffield continued to be headquarters for him, I have been unable to learn. When asked about Henry Owen, the present secretary of the Cutlers' Company replied confidently: "I am certain he was not sent to America by this Company."

What *is* clear is the fact that Henry Bessemer's new method of steel-manufacture enabled the iron works at Sheffield to make great improvements, so that steel could be made much more cheaply and quickly in the decade following the establishment of Henry Owen's New York agency; and there is, perhaps, no good reason why he may not have had connections with *both* Sheffield and Birmingham. In any case, he had a free field in which to operate, for there was no American manufacture of steel pens for many years, and not until after the Civil War did Camden, New Jersey, begin to offer the British companies any real competition.

For twenty-five years (1847 to 1872) Henry Owen's place of business was 91 John Street, and during this period, when the city directory called him an "agent," it named pens, or steel pens, as his business. In his will Owen called himself a merchant, and there can be no doubt about the fact that he soon proved himself a capable and deservedly prosperous one. The "great infusion of the mercantile spirit" which Charles Dickens had noted in New York, with its resultant "display of wealth," can be well illustrated by the example of Henry Owen. In or about 1848 he married Catherine Ann Sackett. She was an American—a native of Bedford Village, about thirty-five miles north of New York. Owen took his bride to 143 Second Avenue to live, but it was not long before they needed and could afford larger quarters. By 1850 they were established at 259 Tenth Street, and there a daughter was born to them in 1851. They named her Catherine after her mother.

It is significant that, just as soon as Henry Owen's improved financial status permitted, he set about acquiring a library. The present book would never have been written but for Henry Owen's interest in books, for this was an interest that he passed on to his daughters. He began by buying an eight-volume Boston edition of Shakespeare and thus inaugurated the practice of acquiring bulky sets of books—a practice which he continued throughout the remainder of his life and which he bequeathed as a settled habit to his wife and family after his death. Owen's purchases were not those of a man who had grown up with books. He bought few contemporary authors; he read little poetry; he did not deal with London booksellers, and almost all of his purchases were of American editions. Book-collecting just as a hobby held no interest for him. He took no delight in the search for elusive treasures. He owned no first editions, and the "points" of rare books obviously meant nothing to him.

In this respect Owen was quite different from another British *emigré* who was at this same time buying books in New York City. John Allan was a Scot from the "Burns Country" who, on emigrating to America, followed a course that in a number of ways parallels that of Henry Owen. Allan settled in New York and at first worked as a clerk for a firm of merchant tailors. Later, he acted as commission-agent for Scottish wool-exporters and in this way made enough money to have a tidy surplus to invest in books. By the time of the Civil War, John Allan had come to be regarded as one of the leading book-collectors of his time. When James Wynne published his *Private Libraries of New York* (New York, French, 1860), he devoted the whole of his first chapter to the collection of John Allan and gave a detailed description of its missals, illuminated manuscripts, and books printed on vellum. Unlike Henry Owen, Allan took no delight in *sets* of books. He obviously had an eye for rarity and bought with discrimination and skill. When his library was eventually sold, Allan's books brought "wonderfully high prices" (I quote the New York *Herald* for May 5, 1864) and the auction was reported as marking "an epoch in the history of the sale of literary property in the United States." Previous advertising of the Allan library had been achieved by means of an article in the New York *Evening Post* published in the year of Rebecca Owen's birth.

Henry Owen acquired *his* books in a wholly different way. He bought because he wanted to read. For his purposes, a cheap edition of Shakespeare published in Boston was just as good as, or even better than, one that had to be imported from London. Owen's library thus became a sign of his own intellectual vitality and curiosity, rather than a mark of his commercial acumen.

This genuine interest in books was doubtless one of the reasons for the development of friendly relations between the Owen household on Tenth Street and a neighboring family named Drisler. At 226 Tenth Street lived Professor and Mrs. Henry Drisler and (after 1852) their daughter Mary. Henry Drisler was five or six years younger than Henry Owen but he had lived longer with books. After graduating from Columbia in 1839, Drisler had been appointed an instructor in the classics, and about the time of Henry Owen's arrival in New York, he had been promoted to an adjunct professorship at Columbia. He thus had his feet on the second rung of the academic ladder. Mary Drisler and Catherine Owen, who (thirty years later) were to meet so often and have so much in common, lived, then, as close neighbors on Tenth Street for the first few years of their lives; but before the girls were of school age, both families moved farther north in the growing city. The Owens made the shift first.

Henry Owen chose the neighborhood of Madison Square for his home and in 1854 established his family at No. 26 West Twenty-fifth Street. There his daughter Rebecca was born, on February 6, 1858. Although she was eventually to change the spelling of her name to "Rebekah," it was as Rebecca that she was first known, and that is the way her father wrote her name in his will. Miss Owen was, later on, to make one other change in her biographical record: in applying for a passport many years later, she informed the State Department at Washington that she was born in 1868. But this is obviously incorrect. Her father's will mentioned her in 1864, and one of the executors of that will (James M. Bates) filed a petition dated May 30, 1872 (two weeks after Owen's death), in which he stated that Rebecca was at that time known by him to be over fourteen years of age. She apparently found it convenient, later on, to drop ten years of her life. One of her English friends of a much later era reported to me: "My dear old friend is touchy; she won't tell anyone her

age!" One wonders whether Rebecca's father had by any chance
set her an example of such secretiveness. Henry Owen was forty-
seven when Rebecca was born.

The books continued to pile up in the Owen library. A fifteen-
volume New York set of Irving was acquired about the time of
Rebecca's birth; the next year a *fifty*-volume edition of Scott
(Boston, 1859); and in 1860 Owen bought two sets published
in Philadelphia: one, a fifteen-volume edition of Prescott, the
other a sixteen-volume set of Bulwer-Lytton's works. Rebecca
Owen's father also had money for paintings, and among other
works of art he acquired a picture painted by Daniel Huntingdon (1816-1906) called "Roman Charity." Owen prized this
painting highly enough to make specific mention of it in his will,
when he referred to it as "Alms Giving." Huntingdon was a New
York artist who (after 1846) devoted his time chiefly to portrait-
painting. At the time when Henry Owen made his will, Daniel
Huntingdon was president of the National Academy.

Meanwhile, the Drisler family had, like the Owens, moved
farther north on Manhattan. In 1857, when Henry Drisler was
promoted to the Professorship of Latin at Columbia, he and his
family moved to 48 West Forty-sixth Street, in order to be near
the site (then the new site, now the old site) of Columbia College
at Madison Avenue and 49th Street. In the Forty-sixth Street
home, young Mary Drisler soon showed that she had inherited
the professor's linguistic abilities. In time, she not only mastered
her father's special subjects, Latin and Greek, but also acquired
facility in French and German, and was eventually reputed to
be able to read five other languages. By the time that Catherine
and Rebecca Owen had established an adult friendship with her,
Mary Drisler was able to impress them with her intellectual powers, and in time they came to quote her as an authority: "Miss
Drisler says this"; "Miss Drisler says that." She doubtless had
not a little to do with arousing their interest in history and in
travel.

History was already a favorite subject with the Owen girls, for their father liked it. To his fifteen volumes of Prescott, Henry Owen added a seven-volume set of Motley in 1867 and six volumes of Hume and twelve volumes of Froude in 1870. In 1868 he became a member of the New York Historical Society, and from that date on, the publications of the society made their annual appearance in the Owen library. Except for his initial purchase of Shakespeare, Henry Owen bought very little poetry; and except for Scott and Bulwer-Lytton, fiction occupied very little space in the home near Madison Square. When Rebecca was eight years old, her father gave her a gilt-edged copy of Jean Ingelow's *Stories Told to a Child* (Boston, 1866), and as she grew up, her father's serious intellectual interests were successfully grafted upon her retentive young mind.

Henry Owen was fifty years old when the Civil War began. Having no son to be drafted for military service, and enjoying the profits on the sale of steel pens *from* England rather than on the sale of cotton *to* England, Owen found it easier to continue to take quiet delight in the books and pictures he was buying than to get steamed up over the abolition of slavery. One event during the war may, however, have had something to do with moving Henry Owen to act. On May 2, 1864, the sale of John Allan's library began. The recent death of the wool-agent from Scotland may have served to remind the steel-pen agent that it is not only on the battle-field that men die. In any case, Henry Owen decided to write his last will and testament. He then learned what war can do in raising the high cost of everything. On Saturday, December 3, 1864—it was just one week before Sherman, on his march from Atlanta to the sea, reached the outskirts of Savannah—Henry Owen signed his will and, in order to legalize the document, had to affix to it $45 in United States Internal Revenue stamps. Owen willed all his estate, "both real and personal whatsoever and wheresoever," to his wife Catherine

Ann; or, in case she should die before him, to his "two daughters Catherine and Rebecca to be equally divided between them, share and share alike."

Thereafter, events moved rapidly in the lives of both of the former Tenth Street neighbors. At Columbia, Professor Drisler was transferred, in the fall of 1867, to the Department of Greek and made Jay Professor of that language. For a short period in that year he served as Acting President of Columbia College. Henry Owen, too, was making rapid progress—toward retirement. According to the United States Census records for 1870, there were no Owens at 26 West Twenty-fifth Street when the census was taken, and it may be surmised that the entire family was abroad. If this surmise be correct, it was Henry Owen's last chance to see his brother Joseph in England. For Henry survived his will-making by only a little over seven years. On May 14, 1872, he died at the age of sixty-one. I have not learned where he is buried—a failure which, if it had happened years later, might have reminded one of his daughters of Thomas Hardy's lines in *Late Lyrics*—lines in a poem which has, of course, no actual connection with Henry Owen:

> While he was here with breath and bone,
>   To speak to and to see,
> Would I had known—more clearly known—
>   What that man did for me. . . .
>
> Now that I gauge his goodliness
>   He's slipped from human eyes;
> And now he's passed there's none can guess
>   Or point out where he lies.

"What that man did" for Rebecca and her sister is, however, clear enough. In thirty years as a New York merchant, Henry Owen amassed a fortune large enough to educate his daughters, to equip them with a sound literary culture, and to launch them into the post-Civil-War world with generous provision for living lives of ease and comfort—lives strikingly different from that on which he had turned his back in Yorkshire shortly after the birth of Thomas Hardy.

Chapter II

Rebekah Owen Comes of Age

REBECCA Owen was fourteen years old when her father died; her sister Catherine was twenty-one. After Henry Owen's death, Mrs. Owen continued the well-established habit of building up the family library; and, while there is no evidence that Catherine or her mother made any real use of the books, there is abundant evidence that Rebecca not only used them—she studied them diligently and soon acquired a detailed knowledge of their contents and a critical discernment and discrimination in their use. The girl had brains and learned how to use them. In 1873 a five-volume New York edition of Ruskin was bought for the Owen library and in 1879, when Rebecca became of age, a twenty-four-volume set of Thackeray. Of these two purchases, the Ruskin was to play an important part in the determination of future events, whereas Thackeray was to gather dust on the shelf.

At this point in her life Rebecca Owen was busy with Shakespeare. In the course of her studies she came upon a sonnet by Henry W. Longfellow. Those readers who, in earlier years, memorized Longfellow's verses may remember that this poem, entitled "Shakespeare," runs in part as follows:

> A vision as of crowded city streets,
>   With human life in endless overflow;
>   Thunder of thoroughfares; trumpets that blow
> To battle; clamor, in obscure retreats,
> Of sailors landed from their anchored fleets;
>   Tolling of bells in turrets, and below
>   Voices of children . . .
> This vision comes to me when I unfold
> The volume of the poet paramount. . . .

But when Rebecca Owen unfolded *her* copy of the poet paramount, the vision that came to her did *not* include "voices of children." She had read Shakespeare attentively enough to feel convinced that Longfellow was wrong, and on November 18, 1879, she performed a very characteristic act. She wrote to the Cambridge poet to propose that he change the text of his sonnet. This letter from the twenty-one-year-old girl in New York gives us a pre-view of the thirty-four-year-old young lady who was to tackle Thomas Hardy in England and persuade him to change the text of his novel. To Longfellow Miss Owen wrote:

It seems to me that the childish element enters so little into Shakespeare's plays,—I can recall only the slight sketches of Fleance, William Page, Mamillius, Prince Arthur, the little Tower Princes, Coriolanus's son, and a few minstrel-boys, none of them particularly *childish* children,— that, in their stead, might it not be better to recognize his great army of lovers? Read thus, in connection with the following words, is not the picture exquisite?

—and below
Voices of lovers, and bright flowers that throw
O'er garden walls their intermingled sweets!

Does not one at once have a vision of many stately old-time gardens with fitting centre lover-figures—Juliet at her window, overlooking Capulet's orchard; Olivia with her pretty oaths,

by the roses of the spring,
By maidhood, honor, truth, and everything,

wooing Cesario; Beatrice in Leonato's garden, cozened into love; Richard's child-queen, weeping her husband's downfall; the parting of Imogen and Posthumous; that lawn where Orlando

wrestled well, and overthrew
More than his enemies;

meek Desdemona losing the kerchief and Othello's trust; and many another fair pleasaunce, scene of true-love sorrows and joys, not forgetting that modest shepherd's plot where sweetest Perdita did sort her posies to her guests, and lacking flowers, gave to her prince more loving words?

Rebecca Owen thought well enough of her letter to make and keep a copy of it. And well she might! Does she not "sort her posies" well at twenty-one? "With fitting centre-figures . . . and many another fair pleasaunce"! "Is not the picture exquisite?"

Longfellow also thought well of the letter. He answered it at once. Writing from Cambridge on November 19, 1879, he declared: "I am much obliged to you for your suggestion. It is a decided improvement on the line as it now stands, and I wonder the word did not occur to me when I wrote the sonnet." One can imagine the delight with which the twenty-one-year-old girl read the poet's letter when it reached Madison Square on the twentieth. "It is a decided improvement." She—Rebecca Owen —had made "a decided improvement" in a line by the famous Henry Wadsworth Longfellow. She would watch for the next edition of his poems. Meanwhile, she kept on with her reading of the poet paramount. When A. C. Swinburne's *Study of Shakespeare* was published in New York in 1880, Miss Owen promptly obtained a copy of the book and, after digesting its contents, she got out the copy of her letter to Longfellow and, opposite her reference to "the slight sketches of . . . Mamillius," she added the notation: "I had not then studied the *Winter's Tale* with Swinburne."

Longfellow died on March 24, 1882. The next edition of his poetical works appeared in Boston in 1883 and Rebecca Owen promptly bought a copy. It was still in her library fifty-five years later. She was doubtless disappointed to discover that the poet had made no change in the text of his sonnet on Shakespeare. She prized her letter from Longfellow, however, and kept it in her book of his poems. In all probability she never knew that he, too, had kept her letter: it is in the files at Craigie House in Cambridge to this day.

When the twenty-four volumes of Thackeray had joined the fifty volumes of Scott on the shelves in the Owen home, there were no fewer than seventy-four books of fiction which the Owen sisters proceeded to—to ignore! There is no evidence that they disturbed the dust on any of them. This makes it unlikely that Scott's portrait of Rebecca Gratz of Philadelphia, painted in the disguise of the Jewish maiden in *Ivanhoe*, or Thackeray's even more famous portrait of another Rebecca in *Vanity Fair*, had anything to do with Miss Owen's use of the name "Rebecca." But, for some reason or other, she now took to signing herself "Rebekah," spelling the name "the Hebrew way," as she later explained to Mrs. Hardy. One may here suspect the influence of the linguistically expert Mary Drisler. Rebekah's sister Catherine similarly became "Catharine." Perhaps these changes signalize nothing more than the young ladies' emancipation from the dictation of their elders. It is significant that, after 1880, they gave up the habit of buying books in bulky sets. No more fifty volumes in a row! Thereafter they began to pick up individual titles, like the Swinburne book on Shakespeare, and soon thereafter to substitute contemporary authors like Howells for classics like Irving or Scott.

I do not know when Mrs. Owen died and have been unable to find any record on which to base even a guess as to how long she survived her husband; but in any case the sisters were ready to step out "on their own" by 1883, when Rebekah bought her copy of Longfellow. She was then twenty-five; her sister Catharine, whom she called "Tat," was thirty-two. Their school days were over. I write "school days" without implying that either of the girls had ever, in any formal way, gone to school. None of the books in which they wrote their names show any school connection, and in none of their letters is any school, either public or private, ever mentioned. One is forced to the conclusion that, in providing his daughters with an education, Henry Owen had used the good old English method of hiring governesses who had come to the Madison Square home to give private instruction to the girls. This was the method used at this same time in London with Beatrix Potter, who is to appear on some later pages of this book. She afterwards remarked: "I was never sent to school. In those days parents kept governesses and only boys went to school in most families." Beatrix Potter's father and Rebekah Owen's father probably saw eye to eye on this matter.

Although Rebekah was Catharine's junior by seven years, it was Rebekah who took the lead in everything. She had the brains, the vivacity, and the charm. "Tat" was a humble follower. The sisters did everything together; but whatever they did, and wherever they went, it was Rebekah who made the decisions. She chose the books; she hired the servants; she decided on the travels; she paid the bills; she invited the guests; she did the talking; she "made people laugh." When there were trips to be taken, "Tat" went where Rebekah wanted to go, and the sisters were always accompanied by their childhood nurse and (later) maid, Caroline Ash. In private they called her "Ashy," but in public they often amused outsiders, when there were any present, by the formality (and—one might add—the genuine American democracy) with which they addressed their elderly maid as "Miss Ash." She was sixty years old in 1880.

It is interesting to speculate on how different the lives of the Owen sisters might have been if Rebekah had been the older of the two, or if Catharine had been the forceful leader instead of the undemanding follower. Catharine became twenty-one in 1872, and in the very next year Thomas Hardy made his first appearance as an author in the United States. On June 2, 1873, Henry Holt published *Under the Greenwood Tree*—the first book ever printed to bear the magic words "by Thomas Hardy" on its title-page, for his books previously published in London had been anonymous. A month later Holt published *A Pair of Blue Eyes* and before the year 1873 had run its course the New York *Tribune* was bringing this same novel to the attention of additional thousands of American readers. Throughout the eighteen-seventies, this publicizing of Hardy went on. In 1874 Holt issued *Desperate Remedies* and *Far from the Madding Crowd*; the New

York *Times* printed "Destiny and a Blue Cloak" on the fourth of October, and the *Tribune* later serialized *Far from the Madding Crowd*. The *Eclectic Magazine* duplicated this serialization, and in 1875 the *Times* published *The Hand of Ethelberta* by installments. In 1876 Henry Holt issued this novel in book form. In 1877 the pirates began their attacks on Wessex shipping, and George Munro made *Under the Greenwood Tree* available to American readers at a price of ten cents. In 1878 and 1879, the Hardy titles came closer together and in greater variety and appeal than ever before, and Americans were thus introduced to "The Impulsive Lady of Croome Castle," "An Indiscretion in the Life of an Heiress," "The Distracted Preacher," and (best of all) *The Return of the Native*. This last-named title appeared first as a serial in *Harper's Magazine* and then as a book published by Henry Holt. All of this feverish publication of an English author by American firms, both by authorized publishers and by pirates, by newspapers and by magazines, made Hardy known to an immense audience all over the United States. Curiously enough, the wave of printer's ink rolled by the home just off Madison Square without washing up a single scrap of paper. Catharine snapped up none of these unconsidered trifles, and during the eighteen-seventies Rebekah was not yet old enough to assume the leadership which she shortly came to exercise.

The Owen sisters had not been long in possession of their father's estate before they discovered its usefulness in enabling them to get away from the increasingly noisy traffic of New York City. They soon developed a great fondness for travel. Their love of flowers drew them south in the early Spring of 1883 and they apparently spent Easter at Charleston, South Carolina. This port was of easy access by ship from New York City. In view of the fact that, in later years, a love of flowers was the one thing that challenged the love of Hardy's books in Rebekah Owen's mind, it is curiously if not miraculously appropriate that the famous gardens near Charleston should have been the attraction

that lured Miss Owen to the spot where (apparently) she met
the work of Thomas Hardy for the first time. For in the *Charleston Sunday News* for April 1, 1883—the Sunday after Easter—
Rebekah first came upon the name that was to change the whole
course of her life.

As every reader of the Wessex Novels knows, Hardy was a
great believer in Chance and constantly emphasized in his writings the part that accident and co-incidence play in human life.
In view of this fact, Rebekah Owen's presence in Charleston on
that spring Sunday is a chance event worthy of a typical Hardy
"irony." For, in view of the part that he himself was later to
play in the lives of these two American ladies, the month of
March, 1883, was just about the most *in*opportune time for them
to absent themselves from New York City. For just at that moment the agencies were multiplied in the metropolis on the Hud-
son whereby the Owens might have been introduced to Hardy's
work. But they were not there to take advantage of any of them.
Early in the month of March, "The Three Strangers" (first published in *Longman's Magazine* in London) was printed in two installments in *Harper's Weekly*. Rebekah Owen was, later on, to
call this story Hardy's best; she placed it "far above all his and
other people's short stories." But when it appeared in New York
in *Harper's Weekly*, she was apparently not on hand to see it. No
sooner was the second installment in print than the New York
Evening Post, knowing that the "Three Strangers" could not be
copyrighted, reprinted the entire text in its issue for March 10,
but Rebekah was (apparently) not on hand to see it. One would
have guessed—unless he had been brought up on Hardy's fiction
and had been thus trained to expect the unexpected—one would
have guessed that there was little likelihood of Rebekah's meeting, while travelling in the South, what she had failed to meet
in New York City. But that is just what happened; for on April
1, 1883, the Charleston *Sunday News* printed "The Three Stran-

gers," Rebekah Owen saw it, she clipped the story from the paper, and the die was cast.

It all happened so quietly that Miss Owen had no way of knowing that an event of immense importance to her future life had taken place. She knew from her study of Shakespeare that Desdemona's handkerchief drops to the ground quietly and unobserved; only later is the tragic import of its loss fully realized. But in her own case, Rebekah knew no more than that she had read an excellent short story by an unknown author. Yet, when she clipped "The Three Strangers," she had come face to face with the work of the writer to whom she was to devote herself for the next half-century.

Sometimes such meetings create a great stir. Keats knew instantly, on first looking into Chapman's *Homer*, that something had happened to him.

> Then felt I like some watcher of the skies
> When a new planet swims into his ken.

When Rebekah Owen first looked into Hardy's "Strangers," she sensed no new planet. When Robert Louis Stevenson was asked to write an essay on "Books Which Have Influenced Me," he declared:

The most influential books, and the truest in their influence, are works of fiction. . . . Shakespeare served me best. Few living friends have had upon me an influence so strong for good as Hamlet or Rosalind . . . nor has the influence quite passed away. Kent's brief speech over the dying Lear had a great effect upon my mind.

When Rebekah Owen stumbled upon "The Three Strangers," she was aware of no such strong influence. She had merely happened upon an inviting little stream on which, like some Jacques Marquette, she launched her boat and let it follow its own course, only to discover to her later amazement that the stream she had chanced upon was the head-water of a mighty river—one of the great rivers of the earth.

Nor did Rebekah Owen know how extremely appropriate it was that her meeting with Hardy's work should take place in Charleston, for it was that city that had provided Hardy with an amusing passage in one of his most recently published books. A chapter in *The Trumpet-Major* (1880) contains a passage of several hundred words which would not be there if an Englishman named John Lambert had not visited Charleston, South Carolina, many years before. Although the story of Lambert's relationship to Hardy's novel is an extremely complicated one, that story is worth outlining briefly here, if only to make clear to the reader why Charleston was an appropriate place for Rebekah Owen to have met the "Strangers" in. John Lambert had been travelling through Canada and the United States in 1807. Like Rebekah Owen, he sailed from New York for South Carolina and landed at Charleston on January 23, 1808. There he picked up in a book shop a little pamphlet containing what he called an "excellent satire" on the American militia. It was an amusing sketch, published anonymously but now known to have been written by one Oliver Hillhouse Prince (1787-1837), describing how a certain Captain Clodpole conducted a drill of his raw militia soldiers. This sketch had appeared originally in a Georgia newspaper, the *Washington Monitor*, on June 6, 1807, but it was immediately reprinted in various places, and in various forms and even under various titles, in other parts of the country. In 1808, then, John Lambert happened upon a copy of "The Militia Company Drill"; he carried it from Charleston back to England; and when, in 1810, he was preparing to publish an account of his *Travels through Lower Canada and the United States*, he transcribed the entire sketch, saying: "As it may afford my readers some amusement, I have taken the liberty to lay it before them." Among those who were thus afforded some amusement was C. H. Gifford, then at work upon an ambitious *History of the Wars Occasioned by the French Revolution.* He too "took the liberty," and Lambert's "excellent satire" from Charleston was copied out of the *Travels* into the *History of the Wars.* This last-named work was published in London in 1817. It was consulted by Thomas Hardy when, more than sixty years later, he came to write *The Trumpet-Major.* Hardy, too, found Prince's sketch of the militia drill amusing, and without acknowledging his source, Hardy lifted the drill scene out of Gifford into Chapter 23 of *The Trumpet-Major*—an act of plagiarism that was to prove very annoying later on. Rebekah Owen, clipping Hardy from the Charleston *News,* was blissfully unaware that the same Thomas Hardy had laid piratical hands on a Charleston sketch only three years before.

Although the South Carolina meeting was a first contact for Rebekah, it was (as we have seen) far from being the first time that Hardy's work had appeared in America. As has been already explained, Hardy's name had been printed on the title-page of book after book all through the eighteen-seventies—in New York, in Boston, and in Chicago—but Catharine Owen had seen none of them, and Rebekah was too busy with her Shakespeare and with reading Swinburne, writing to Longfellow, perusing Ruskin, studying French and otherwise busying herself. Thus it came about that neither of the Owen sisters had as yet become acquainted with Henry Holt's Leisure Hour series of Hardy books —a series which (by 1883) included *Under the Greenwood Tree, A Pair of Blue Eyes, Desperate Remedies, Far from the Madding Crowd, The Hand of Ethelberta, The Return of the Native, The Trumpet-Major, A Laodicean,* and *Two on a Tower.* Henry Holt could take pride, not only in his sponsorship of these nine novels, but also in the fact that through them he had made Hardy's name known to Americans at a time when Hardy was still an anonymous question-mark in his own country. Thanks to the help that Henry Holt had received from a young English friend, Frederick Macmillan, he had been able to penetrate behind the anonymity of the first Wessex Novels to be published in London; and by acting with promptness and boldness, Holt became Hardy's first American publisher. Many years later, when Holt was seventy years old and had nearly forty years of success as a publisher behind him, he was able to boast, with truth as well as with pride: "I introduced Hardy here."

Curious, then, that with all this "authorized" activity going on in their own City of New York, the Owen sisters should have completely missed Hardy there throughout an entire decade. All the more curious that, upon their return to New York from their South Carolina visit, they should discover that, during their absence, "The Three Strangers" had been printed there and had been noticed by one of their friends. This was, presumably, Mary Drisler, for (as we shall shortly see) she was the first person outside of the Owen home to whom Rebekah began to read Hardy aloud, and she was the first person to be enlisted by Rebekah Owen in the league of Hardy admirers which she was shortly to organize. Although it cannot now be proved, it is plausible to think that Miss Drisler was Rebekah's source of information regarding the appearance of "The Three Strangers" in the Saturday Supplement of the New York *Evening Post* (March 10, 1883).

Rebekah learned, also, that a full-length novel by the same Thomas Hardy had been recently published by Henry Holt, for *Far from the Madding Crowd* had been re-issued in his thirty-cent Leisure Moment Series. This discovery led Miss Owen, not only to make the acquaintance of this novel, but also to learn to keep her eyes open for further publications by Henry Holt. When *A Pair of Blue Eyes* appeared in his Leisure Moment Series in 1885, Rebekah Owen promptly got a copy, and this novel, more than any other, served to transform her into one of Hardy's most devoted admirers.

A Pair of Blue Eyes has indeed had an amazing history—both as a magnet for attracting readers to Hardy and as magic incantation for their enslavement afterwards. In his autobiography William Lyon Phelps declared: "Nearly fifty years ago I read

my first novel by Thomas Hardy . . . , a novel with the agreeable title *A Pair of Blue Eyes*. . . . Within a year I had read every
one of his books." William Dean Howells made a similar confession: "Thomas Hardy I first knew in *A Pair of Blue Eyes*. After I had read this book, I wished to read the books of no other
author, and to read his books over and over. I could not get
enough of them." Rebekah Owen was affected the same way.
Having read *A Pair of Blue Eyes* once, she promptly set about
reading it a second time. She demonstrated the wisdom of the advice Hardy had received from his London publisher, William
Tinsley. After publishing Hardy's first two novels, both anonymously, Tinsley advised Hardy to put more "sentiment" into
his writing. The publisher thought that *Under the Greenwood Tree*
was "the best little prose idyll" he had ever read, "but strange
to say, it would not sell. It just lacks the touch of sentiment that
lady novel-readers most admire." Hardy took Tinsley's advice
and the history of *A Pair of Blue Eyes* proved the soundness of
Tinsley's judgment. Among the early American admirers of this
novel was the actress Julia Marlowe, and the testimony of Phelps
and Howells, just quoted above, shows that it was not only "lady
novel-readers" like Rebekah Owen and like Julia Marlowe who
liked Hardy's book: it received just as warm applause from men.
Reginald Brooks, the son of the editor of *Punch*, finished reading *A Pair of Blue Eyes* one rainy January day in London and then
remarked: "Very good indeed: worth all the other novels I have
read for a long time."

That is exactly what Rebekah Owen thought, and hers was not
a judgment based on a narrow reading-list or on a restricted experience. Her expanding horizon was not limited by the bound-
aries of Madison Square or of Hardy's Wessex. She was widen-
ing her circle in New York City, where her association with Mary
Drisler resulted in her acquiring a certain degree of familiarity
with the academic world. In the eighteen-eighties, that of course
meant a familiarity as an outsider, as a spectator rather than as a

participant, for in New York City the academic world was still almost exclusively masculine. Barnard College did not open its doors to admit women students to Columbia until 1889, when Seth Low became president. At this time Henry Drisler was senior professor, and for nearly two years before Seth Low assumed office, Dr. Drisler served as Acting President. He had recently found in his classes a brilliant young student, Nicholas Murray Butler by name, who had won three Columbia degrees in three years: the B.A. in 1882, the M.A. in 1883, and the Ph.D. in 1884. When young Dr. Butler married a year later, his bride (née Susanna E. Schuyler) was soon welcomed into Mary Drisler's circle of friends. Mrs. Butler thus became acquainted with Rebekah Owen, and it was not long before "darling Sue" was on intimate terms with the Owen household—and eventually with the writings of Thomas Hardy.

This friendship with Mrs. Butler provided Rebekah with a means for hearing about Columbia University from a new point of view. "Darling Sue" could not conceal the fact that her brilliant young husband stood in no great awe of Dr. Drisler's dawdling way of teaching Greek. Years later, long after Dr. Butler had become the president of Columbia University, he recalled (in *Across the Busy Years*) that his old teacher Henry Drisler was "so given to insistence upon the minutest details of grammar that our eyes were kept closely fixed on the ground and we hardly ever caught any glimpse of the beauty and larger significance of the great works upon which we were engaged. For example, I recall that during the first term of the sophomore year we were to read with Dr. Drisler the *Medea* of Euripides and that when the term came to an end we had completed but 246 lines. In other words, we never came to know what the *Medea* was all about or to see either the significance of the story or the quality of its literary art."

This sort of picture of Columbia classrooms would not have attracted Rebekah Owen, even if Barnard College had been open in 1886, and it wasn't. But there *was* a new college for women, just then about to open its doors—St. Hugh's College at Oxford University, England. This college did not provide for the first appearance of women in that city of spires, for Lady Margaret Hall and Somerville Hall had both been founded in 1879. But St. Hugh's was the first women's institution at Oxford to be admitted to the full dignity of being called a college, and the news that there was to be such a place reached Rebekah Owen's ears and aroused a desire to see the place. She "hankered" after it— to use a word that turns up in one of the letters of her Oxonian days. She had no desire to go to Oxford like some gaping tourist, just to look at the outside of the Gothic buildings. She wanted to go to stay a while, to read and to study. Not that she wished to enroll at St. Hugh's College: she was too old for that (she was twenty-eight in 1886); but Oxford attracted her with an irresistible pull. One would like to know whether Rebekah's interest in Ruskin, whether the fact that Ruskin had been an Oxford student and that he had later lectured at Oxford, had anything to do with the magnetic power of the place. One thing at least is clear. Rebekah wanted very much to go to Oxford; and of course if Rebekah went, "Tat" would go. "Ashy" too!

So plans were made at Madison Square for spending the summer of 1886 at Oxford. The Owens sailed in April, and *A Pair of Blue Eyes* went with them. On the steamer's passenger-list the entry reads: "Miss Owen, Miss R. Owen, and maid." It may avoid confusion and ambiguity in the following pages of this book, if the statement is made here at once that—no matter what the steamship practice was, or similar practice on land—"Miss Owen" and "Rebekah" are to be regarded by our readers as synonymous. Whenever reference is to be made to Miss Catharine Owen, that fact will be made clear by the use of her name "Catharine," or by quoting Rebekah's affectionate designation of her sister as "dear Tat."

Chapter III

The Owens Discover England

WHEN Rebekah Owen and her sister embarked at New York in April, they of course had expectations that the summer of 1886 would do something more than merely provide them with a glimpse of Oxford. They had relatives in England—or had had until recently (I do not know when their Uncle Joseph died)—and through their relatives they had made, and had the prospect of soon making, many new friends. Among the places that the Owens visited frequently in England was a home in the cathedral city of Worcester—the home of the Reverend George Oliver (1817-1894) and of his wife Emma. From the fact that both the Olivers addressed Rebekah by her first name, and the fact that Mrs. Oliver showed that she was informed about birthdays in the Owen home in New York, together with the just-mentioned fact that the Owen sisters visited the aged Olivers at Worcester over and over again and continued such visits after Mr. Oliver had died, I hazard the guess that Mrs. Oliver was related to the Owens. Perhaps she was Rebekah's Aunt Emma—a younger sister of Rebekah's father. If this unproved guess should be true, it would explain why the Owen sisters not only visited the Olivers but paid them more than a brief call, no mere how-do-you-do and goodbye.

In 1886 the sisters went directly to Worcester as soon as they had set foot on English soil. Whatever the relationship, the Owens found the Olivers to be an interesting old couple. The Reverend George was seventy years old, but he was an alert and active member of the Worcester Diocesan and Archaeological Society, and Rebekah's interest in ancient lore and history was genuine enough to enable her and Mr. Oliver to get on well together. The Worcester Archaeological Society proved to be an excellent preparation for Rebekah's later contact with the antiquarian interests of the Dorset Field Club.

Early in May the Owens were settled in Oxford. It proved to be a delightful month, and the boat races on the "Isis" and the University ceremonies—which Rebekah was later on to find described in *Jude the Obscure*—crowded all thought of study out of her mind. There was so much to see and do in Oxford, and even the environs of the city proved attractive. The Owen notes for this summer contain references to Botley, to Amy Robsart's Cumnor, to Oseney, and to Iffley. Apparently, both summer and autumn rushed by without Rebekah's making any attempt to gain admittance to the Bodleian Library. The knocking at that gate was postponed to a later Oxonian visit.

Fate played another curious trick on Rebekah Owen at this time. Just as she had been absent in South Carolina, at a time when New York printers and publishers were vying one with another in making the name Thomas Hardy known to American readers, so now, while she was in Oxford, Rebekah missed a chance which would have been hers if she had stayed in New York, or would still have been hers if she had gone to England earlier in the year and had settled in London instead of in Oxford. But by the time she and Catharine had taken up residence in the university city, the London *Graphic* had ended its serialization of a new novel by Thomas Hardy, and its large-scale pictures were no longer being displayed in the book shops. This was the first novel Hardy had published since moving into his new home. He had completed building himself a house on the outskirts of Dorchester, and had moved into it less than a year before the Owens arrived in England. Six more years were to pass, before Rebekah Owen was destined to turn up at the door of this house. But just about the time when Catharine and Rebekah were settling down at Oxford, ready to enjoy the boat races, there arrived at the door of Max Gate another writer who came to pay

his respects to the great novelist. Robert Louis Stevenson came
from Bournemouth, where he had just finished writing *The
Strange Case of Dr. Jekyll and Mr. Hyde*. Stevenson had not been
too busy with his own work to miss Hardy's latest product, and
Stevenson's reaction to it was as immediate as it was enthusiastic:
"I have read *The Mayor of Casterbridge* with sincere admiration,"
he declared. "Henchard is a great fellow, and Dorchester is
touched in with the hand of a master."

It is indeed ironical that Rebekah Owen, now only a hundred
miles or so away from Max Gate, should have missed *The Mayor*
completely. She and Catharine were too busy getting acquainted
with Carfax, the Isis, and the Cherwell. Partly as a result of their
un-bookish activities during this initiation into the varied life of
Oxford, and partly because of the fact that a number of the contacts they made there (both in and outside of university circles)
have nothing to do with the main theme of this book, there is little to be said here about these crowded months of 1886. The date
for the return to America came all too soon: when Rebekah had
made her plans in New York, she had not realized how very
short a short stay in England would seem. But the sailing-date
put in its inexorable appearance, and in November the Owen sisters "and maid" sailed for New York on the S.S. "City of Chicago." As the ship plowed its way westward across the ocean, Rebekah had a chance to think of things she had planned to do and
had not done. She got out her copy of *A Pair of Blue Eyes* and
completed her third reading of this novel before the steamship
reached New York.

As soon as the Owens were once again settled in their Madison
Square home, the friendly relations with Mary Drisler, Susan
Butler, and others were resumed. Rebekah then learned that,
during her absence abroad, her favorite author had been enjoying "quite a run" in New York. Henry Holt had published the
new novel by Hardy entitled *The Mayor of Casterbridge:* it had
come out on May 22, 1886, while Rebekah was basking in the

glories of Oxford. In addition to the one-dollar book edition, Henry Holt had issued *The Mayor* in the cheap Leisure Moment Series of paper-bound novels at thirty cents with which Rebekah was already acquainted. What Holt was obviously trying to do was to put Hardy's novel on the market at a price so low that the piratical publishers, who were then swarming in New York like locusts, would not be encouraged to compete with him. But in this attempt Holt did not succeed. George Munro almost immediately offered *The Mayor of Casterbridge* for twenty cents. His brother Norman L. Munro published yet another twenty-cent edition, and long before the Owen sisters returned from England, the J. W. Lovell Company had a fifth *Mayor* ready. As if this were not enough to supply the American demand for Thomas Hardy's wares, Rand McNally in Chicago and A. L. Burt in New York both offered their own additional printings of this same novel. It is easy to understand why, after this discouraging experience with Hardy throughout the year 1886, Henry Holt ceased to publish him. Hardy's immense popularity with American readers made him immensely *un*profitable to publish.

Rebekah Owen now, somewhat belatedly, equipped herself with one of the cheap editions; it was later worn out with frequent readings and had to be replaced later on. At the end of the story, she came in her reading to what she decided was the "saddest incident in fiction, the slow starvation of the little bird" which Henchard brought to give to Elizabeth-Jane on her wedding-day. We are to hear more about that incident later on.

Early in the year 1887 Miss Owen made the acquaintance of still another Hardy novel. It would, in fact, have been difficult for any book-lover living in New York in the spring of this year to have remained long in ignorance of the fact that Thomas Hardy had written a new novel. *The Woodlanders* was published on March 25 by Harpers, as No. 572 in their Franklin Square Library—one of the paper-bound series that sold for twenty cents. By the middle of April George Munro, chief of the pirates, had an unauthorized edition ready; two weeks later, Norman Munro repeated this act of piracy; and on May 7 *The Woodlanders* appeared as No. 956 in the "Library" published by the J. W. Lovell Company. Which of these four printings Miss Owen used, in making her first acquaintance with *The Woodlanders*, I do not know; but by June 4 she had finished reading it, and had thus learned that Thomas Hardy possessed a side he had not shown in previous publications of his.

If Hardy could undertake something new, so could Rebekah Owen. She had by now become so addicted to reading Hardy's books that, like William Dean Howells, she "wished to read the books of no other author and to read his books over and over." But the real innovation was not this habit of reading Hardy over and over; it was the habit of reading him *aloud*. In this practice Rebekah was unconsciously imitating Coventry Patmore. After reading *A Pair of Blue Eyes* for the first time in 1875, Patmore is said to have continued having his wife read it *aloud* to him over and over again throughout the next twenty-one years. Was there ever anything like it? Rebekah Owen began this same practice in 1887 and continued it for thirty years or more. At home or abroad, in the family circle or in the group of members of the book-league that Rebekah was eventually to organize, Rebekah Owen read Hardy. Novel after novel, story after story: the reading was never ended. With each new reading came renewed delight and increased keenness of desire to begin all over again.

To some readers Rebekah Owen will seem a very silly female. They will, however, learn of her reading the same work aloud a dozen times with very false conclusions, unless they pause long enough to recognize that repetition is not necessarily monotony, and that not all repetition is alike. When Joseph Jefferson reached Rebekah Owen's age at this point in her life, he dramatized *Rip Van Winkle;* and after his London performance in 1865, when he played the part of Rip, he never created another new character. For the next twenty years he went on repeating the same play over and over again, and no man in his profession was more honored than Joseph Jefferson. In Philadelphia Thackeray once met a girl who had read *Vanity Fair* twelve times. Only a few months ago, readers of the New York *Times* were told that General Omar Bradley's favorite book is *Ivanhoe* and that he reads it over and over again, once a year.

An apt comment on this subject comes from another great admirer of Thomas Hardy. The late William Lyon Phelps once remarked (in *Teaching in School and College*) that "no one believes that an actor who acts Hamlet finds it monotonous, although he repeats not only the same words, but the same gestures, the same attitudes, the same intonations. There is no monotony in teaching the same lesson to different pupils, not if the teacher is a good actor. In my first year at Yale, I taught short lessons in *King Henry IV, Part I* to twelve different divisions: it was just as interesting the twelfth time as the first. In fact, the first time was a kind of dress rehearsal, and I think I did better the longer I kept at it."

From the enthusiastic response shown by Rebekah Owen's listeners, one is safe in believing that she too did better the longer she kept at it. After she had read *Under the Greenwood Tree* twelve times, she was all the better trained for the next reading. And as for wearing out her own inexhaustible enthusiasm for Hardy, there was no more danger of that result, after a dozen readings, than there would be for those devotees of Tschaikowsky who do not exhaust their enthusiasm for his music after playing their recordings of the Nutcracker Suite a hundred times.

The act of repetition can, in fact, be pleasurably confined within an even narrower boundary than that which Rebekah Owen set for herself. She had at least a dozen full-length novels to work with, but there have been readers content with just a single title. William Makepeace Thackeray once declared:

There are creations of Mr. Dickens which seem to me to rank as personal benefits, figures so delightful that one feels happier and better for knowing them, as one does for being brought into the society of very good men

and women. . . . As for this man's love of children, that amiable organ at
the back of his honest head must be perfectly monstrous. All children ought
to love him. I know two that do, and read his books ten times for once that
they peruse the dismal preachments of their father. I know one who, when
she is happy, reads *Nicholas Nickleby;* when she is unhappy, reads *Nicholas
Nickleby;* when she is tired, reads *Nicholas Nickleby;* when she is in bed,
reads *Nicholas Nickleby;* when she has nothing to do, reads *Nicholas Nickleby;* and when she has finished the book, reads *Nicholas Nickleby* over again.

There you have precisely the formula which Rebekah Owen
followed. In her first record of reading Hardy aloud, she names
Under the Greenwood Tree as read to Mary Drisler in 1887, "the
first of many Hardy readings." Thereafter "dear Tat," "Ashy,"
Mrs. Nicholas Murray Butler, Mrs. Edmund S. Hamilton, Mrs.
Scott, Mrs. Gangewer, Miss Grace Alexander McElroy—I don't
know how many others—were invited to join Miss Drisler in
listening to Rebekah read the magic tales out of Wessex, one after another; and after the entire canon had been presented, a
prompt return to the beginning was made, and the stage set for
doing it all over again.

The Hardy readings did, however, suffer eventual interrup-
tion, for there was one thing that provided a diversification of
Rebekah's intellectual diet. This was the fact that her 1886 introduction to Oxford had left her eager for more, and there was
no way of satisfying her hunger other than by making another
trip to England—this time with preparations for a longer stay
at Oxford. She wanted to be there, not during the summer when
the students were all away, but during term time. So in April,
1888, the Owens sailed again. On April 30 they were in Worcester, with the Reverend George Oliver and his wife, and in May
they were again settled at Oxford.

Rebekah not only learned to know the colleges well, but also
found renewed delight in walking out to the neighboring villages
that cluster around Oxford. Woodeton, Sandford, Nuneham,
Beckley, Wolvercote, Kidlington, and Bagley Wood, all turn up
in her notes. Then came a fresh step of exploration.

During the summer the Owens visited the Lake District, and in July they were in Grasmere, not far from Wordsworth's one-time abode at Dove Cottage. But instead of reading Wordsworth in that lovely spot, Rebekah Owen read Thomas Hardy's latest volume—for *Wessex Tales* had appeared early in May. Rebekah promptly obtained a copy and was delighted to find her old friend "The Three Strangers" in this book; and in Grasmere she read it aloud to Catharine and Miss Ash. She read "The Withered Arm" too, but rated it below "The Three Strangers." The Owens liked the Lake District but Wordsworth had surprisingly little to do with that delight.

At the end of the summer, Rebekah marched her two companions back to Oxford for another sojourn there. They remained in the university city over Christmas. When it became too cold to take walks, they hired a conveyance and drove, and thus extended their knowledge of the Thames valley. On the day after Christmas they enjoyed a drive out to Godstow, Portmeadow, and Wytham. Rebekah did not know it, but she was carefully laying the foundations for her future knowledge of the country of the as-yet-unwritten *Jude the Obscure*.

When Spring tripped north again next year (1889), Rebekah and Catharine set forth with it. Leaving Oxford early in June, they stopped at Bakewell in Derbyshire, in order to visit Chatsworth, the famous country mansion built by the first Duke of Devonshire shortly before 1700, and the nearby mediaeval house known as Haddon Hall, and by June 23 they reached Coniston in the Lake District. Here they spent the summer, using a Mrs. Raven's home, "Mountain View," for their headquarters. Their choice of Coniston instead of Grasmere doubtless had a direct connection with the fact that five volumes of Ruskin had been present in the Owen library in New York during Rebekah's girlhood. She had carefully studied *Modern Painters*. Wordsworth's poems, however, were *not* in the Madison Square home; and we have noticed that in 1888 Rebekah had read "The Three Stran-

gers" at Grasmere, and not "Peter Bell" or "The Leech Gather-
er." One can be certain that Ruskin's home at Coniston meant
more to the Owens—at least to one of them—than Wordsworth's home at Grasmere. Fate eventually ordained a highly
appropriate destiny for two members of the Owen party, in de-
creeing (as we shall see) that they should become eternal neighbors of John Ruskin.

The Owens remained at Coniston until the end of August. In
September they were back at Bakewell—perhaps for another
look at Haddon Hall—and on September 22 George Oliver
wrote that he could tell from her letters that Rebekah was "still
hankering after Oxford for five or six weeks. Well, it is very ex-
cusable," said he, "with so many attractions and the certainty of
being made welcome."

The Owens shortly established themselves at 34 Wellington
Square, in a section of Oxford which has become well known to
thousands of American Rhodes Scholars since Rebekah Owen's
day. But she wasn't satisfied with five or six weeks. She eventually got four months more of Oxford. The walks among the colleges were resumed, and throughout November there were tours
of the countryside. On December 2, 1889, there was a stroll out
to Headington, east of Oxford, and on the eighteenth, just a
week before Christmas, a visit to Woodstock to the north. Even
the month of January (1890) proved attractive enough, damp
and gray and cold though January is at Oxford; and not until
the first week in February could Rebekah tear herself away. At
last—in midwinter—she and Catharine and "Ashy" sailed for
home. They had been away from Madison Square for twenty-
two months. On February 10, 1890, George Oliver wrote the sisters a "welcome home" letter, saying: "Tomorrow you will be so
near home that you may count the hours. We have been with you
in spirit every day."

The return to the neglected house at 26 West Twenty-fifth
Street doubtless had its attendant shocks. Throughout 1890 there

is a noticeable absence of records of further readings. The Hardy
"fans" were *not* immediately summoned into session; instead,
there was talk of painters and plumbers. In October the Olivers
in England were responding to the news that the Owen house in
New York was in the hands of the painters. But once Christmas
was out of the way, the New Year (1891) permitted the happy
resumption of the old routine. During Rebekah's absence, Miss
Drisler had discovered *Two on a Tower*, and the reading of this
novel aloud was shortly added to the Owen repertoire. Even the
heat of a New York summer did not interrupt the readings: on
August 13 Rebekah finished the oral delivery of *Far from the
Madding Crowd*, and eight days later she had completed the fifth
reading of *Under the Greenwood Tree*. Then she promptly turned
back to her old favorite, *A Pair of Blue Eyes*, and the fourth reading of this novel was completed on September 16. By October 1
The Mayor of Casterbridge had been read aloud; *The Hand of
Ethelberta* was completed by October 17; *The Trumpet-Major* by
October 29, *The Return of the Native* by November 12, *A Group
of Noble Dames* by November 28, and *The Woodlanders* by December 14. Thus at least ten of Hardy's books were read aloud
by Rebekah Owen in the latter half of the year 1891.

There was now a brief interlude for Christmas. But in January the readings were resumed. By January 26, 1892, Rebekah
had plowed her way through all the tedium of *The Romantic Adventures of a Milkmaid*; and then, when Harpers published the
new novel, the notorious *Tess of the D'Urbervilles*, Rebekah went
to work at once with the adventures of this very very different
milkmaid. Miss Owen's critical discernment was keen enough to
leave her with no doubt about what Hardy had produced in *this*
novel. She carried on two readings of *Tess* simultaneously. She
read it to "Tat and Ash" in the home, and to Miss Drisler's circle
of friends; and these friends were eager enough to hear about
Tess, so that they met often enough to permit Rebekah to read
the novel to them almost as rapidly as she read it at home. Sister

Catharine heard the sad end of the story on February 12, and the Drisler circle learned of Tess's tragic fate on February 13.

The reader of this present record might easily imagine that Rebekah Owen, having now read a good round dozen of Hardy's works aloud, would pause and take a breath. Not so! Like Billy Phelps, she did it better the longer she kept at it. *Far from the Madding Crowd* was read again immediately, and *Two on a Tower* was completed by February 27. Only two days remained in February, but this was time enough for Rebekah: she galloped through all five of the *Wessex Tales* aloud before March blew in from the South.

Even though some readers may find this list of dates and titles tedious, I have given it because, without it, no one can have a clear understanding of the persistence, the thoroughness, and the enthusiasm of Rebekah Owen's interest in Thomas Hardy. Her infectious delight swept her friends along with her, and one can well believe that, among those friends, Mary Drisler and Susan Butler were more stirred by Rebekah's glowing mental pictures of Wessex folk than they were by the actual pictures of Professor Henry Drisler, now Dean of the School of Arts in Columbia University, and of Professor Nicholas Murray Butler, now Dean of the School of Philosophy—pictures which appeared on one page of *Harper's Weekly* (February 6, 1892) while the rendering of *Tess* aloud was under way.

In spite of all this activity, Rebekah Owen still had surplus energy. Even while the readings were going on, she was already making plans to return to England. She was fully convinced that the Hardy books demanded an exploration of the Hardy country. Ruskin had taken her to Coniston; why shouldn't Hardy take her to "Casterbridge"? The thought of this as a possibility doubtless had something to do with the concentrated attack that Rebekah made on the Wessex Novels in 1891 and 1892: sixteen readings aloud in eight months. By November 20, 1891, Mrs. Oliver had already received word in Worcester that Rebekah was "really thinking of setting out." But something or other interfered. We may wonder what Catharine was "really thinking." Could it be that she objected to another winter voyage? We learn later that she was not a good sailor. In any case, plans had to be changed, and in December the trip to England was postponed. But when Spring rolled 'round once more, "Tat" and "Ashy" were again ready to obey orders, and Rebekah walked on clouds. And well she might, for the year 1892 was to be her Annus Mirabilis: in this year she was at last to meet face to face the Master of Max Gate. The date is an easy one to remember:

> In eighteen hundred ninety-two
> Rebekah crossed the ocean blue.

At a later date Hardy himself was to write a poem entitled "A Man Was Drawing Near to me" (it was published in *Late Lyrics*, 1922), some words of which are quite applicable to the approaching meeting:

> On that gray night of mournful drone
>   Apart from aught to hear, to see,
> I dreamt not that from shires unknown. . . .
>   A man was drawing near to me.

Catharine and Rebekah and their maid "Ash" (now seventy-two years old) sailed from New York on April 6, 1892, on the steamship "City of Paris." Mrs. Edmund S. Hamilton sent flowers to wish them *bon voyage*, and Mrs. Nicholas Murray Butler sent Rebekah a card of "best wishes," signed by "the most dismal and doleful girl you leave behind you." A week later, the Owens landed at Liverpool—a seven-day crossing in 1892—and went immediately to Oxford, where they were soon installed at 23 Museum Road.

With characteristic energy, Rebekah threw herself at once into the madding crowd. She lost no time in notifying the friends she had made on previous visits that she was back again in England. She sent a "basket of beautiful sweets" to a Mrs. A. Powell in London, and wrote a letter to the Reverend Canon C. Baldwin, Rural Dean of Northumberland at Berwick-on-Tweed, to give him her Oxford address. She purchased a copy of A. T. Shrimpton's *Rambles and Rides Around Oxford* and clipped a list of the April services to be held in Oxford Cathedral. On Sunday, April 17, Rebekah attended the Easter service in St. Giles's Church, though the weather was very cold—more like Christmas than Easter.

The next Saturday—April 23, 1892—was Shakespeare's birthday. Rebekah Owen observed the anniversary by dashing up to Stratford-on-Avon and attending a performance of *Timon of Athens* at the Memorial Theatre. The next day, she and Catharine hurried on to Worcester for another visit with the Olivers. They heard a choir of eighty voices sing in Worcester Cathedral; but after four days with the Olivers, the Owens were back in Oxford. One reason for the prompt return to the university was an invitation which Rebekah had received from the Chichele Professor of Modern History, S. M. Burrows. Professor Burrows had invited her to join his son and his daughter-in-law in "worshiping the rising sun" in traditional Oxonian fashion on May Day. This meant getting up at half-past four on Sunday morning, walking to Magdalen Tower, and there climbing to the belfry where the choir-boys annually welcomed in May by singing a Latin hymn and by jangling all the bells in the tower. Rebekah had accepted the invitation and when May Day arrived, she was on hand at Magdalen College to be initiated into the ancient custom.

On the next day, having met the university librarian, Miss Owen further cemented her connection with Oxford by presenting to the Bodleian Library a copy of R. H. Lamborn's *Mexican Painting and Painters*, and later followed this up with the gift of three or four other volumes. She had already learned that the giving of presents has certain advantages when one is about to ask for favors.

Then came "Eights Week," when sounds from the river "revealed that the town was in festivity. . . . The grand procession of boats began, the oars smacking with a loud kiss on the face of the stream. . . . O, . . . how jolly!" These words are quoted, not from Rebekah Owen's journal, but from Thomas Hardy's as-yet-unwritten *Jude the Obscure*. Like Hardy's Arabella, Rebekah was on hand to see and hear it all. O how jolly! Moreover, she had, as it were, an inside position for witnessing the annual boat races, for she had made the acquaintance of the coxswain of one of the college boats. Canon Baldwin had written Rebekah from Berwick to tell her that he had asked an Oxford student named Clay to call on her. Patrick A. Clay was then in his last year at Keble College. He was to cox the Keble eight, and (as Canon Baldwin put it) "you will know from this that he is not a giant, but he is one of the nicest young fellows I know."

Patrick Clay did call and promptly proved himself to be "one of the nicest." On May 19 he escorted the Owen sisters to the Oxford Union, where they heard a student-debate on the subject: Resolved, that the present is the Truest Age of Chivalry. After the boat races were over, Clay confessed that he was "beginning to get frightened" about his final examinations, but he was still thoughtful enough of the American visitors to offer them tickets for a concert at Keble College scheduled for June 16.

While the final examinations were going on, Rebekah hurried up to London to see Oscar Wilde's new play, *Lady Windermere's Fan*, when it was given at St. James's Theatre on May 28. She returned at once to Oxford and was there on June 6, when she walked up Headington Hill and out to Shotover with her sister. On the fourteenth the Owens again visited Blenheim Palace at Woodstock. Before the Keble concert on the sixteenth, there was a garden party at Wadham College, and on the twenty-first of June a band concert at St. John's. A day later, the Owens went to "Commem"—the Commemoration exercises of the University—at which honorary degrees were awarded. After these exercises, which were held in the Sheldonian Theatre, the Owen sisters were invited to luncheon at All Souls' College. Here they found themselves so surrounded by dignitaries and big-wigs that Rebekah could not afterwards refrain from boasting of her presence there. In writing to Mary Drisler back in New York, Rebekah called this "the proudest hour of our lives." Miss Drisler was not surprised; she knew Rebekah Owen of old. "You know," she wrote back, "you get in more than any other woman would."

And at this point we must bring this amphibious chapter to an end. Rebekah's luncheon at All Souls' was a proud honor, but she was shortly to enjoy an ever prouder one, and we must pause long enough to set the stage for it. This Great Event indeed calls for a chapter by itself.

Chapter IV

"Now!"

REBEKAH Owen's last Oxford note for the Spring of 1892 records a visit to Iffley on June 26. With the closing of the university for the summer, she was ready to carry out the idea she had had, even before leaving New York. Although she had been extremely busy at Oxford—for two months she had gone everywhere, had seen everyone, had done everything—this intense activity had not driven Thomas Hardy from her mind. Cathedral choirs, boat races, carriage drives, garden parties, student debates, May Day festivals, trips to the theatre—all these were interesting enough as diversions, but they did not distract her attention from the main project for 1892: the Hardy Country and, if possible, the man who had restored "Wessex" to the map.

Even when Canon Baldwin provided Rebekah with the "nicest" escort he knew, in the person of Patrick Clay, Rebekah was, even at the very moment of saying thank you, frank enough to admit that there was one introduction she would *much* rather have than a presentation to the nicest coxswain in Oxford. Mr. Thomas Hardy, of Max Gate, Dorchester, was the goal of her desire. She explained to Mr. Baldwin that she "did not as a rule like authors," but Hardy was different. If Mr. Baldwin could only manage an introduction to *him*—a "legitimate introduction"—that would provide an incident prouder than any All Souls' luncheon! Canon Baldwin promised to see what he could do.

Just how could a decorous American lady manage to secure a "legitimate introduction" to a total stranger in a foreign land? Rebekah Owen was equal to many things, but the answer to this question stumped her. She was very much the Victorian "lady," and anything that called for conduct that was at all or in any way "improper" was not to be thought of. She had once written to Longfellow and had received a polite reply from him. But at that date she was only a twenty-one-year-old girl, and her letter had contained no request for personal admittance to the drawing-room of the Longfellow house. Now, however, that was exactly what Rebekah wanted to achieve. She had already done what could be done by a mere reading of Hardy's books; the next thing was to meet their author face to face, and in his own home. But how?

If Rebekah had been able to put her question to Hardy's old "chief" at the office of *The Cornhill Magazine*, Leslie Stephen, she might have received a challenging answer. Stephen had become editor of *The Cornhill* in 1871, just at the time when Hardy published his first novel, and three years later it was Stephen who invited Hardy to contribute *Far from the Madding Crowd* to the pages of the *Cornhill*. But in 1882 Leslie Stephen relinquished this editorship and shifted to another: he became the first editor of the *Dictionary of National Biography*. In 1887 he issued a volume in this series—it was Volume IX—in which he would have found an answer to Rebekah Owen's question. If anyone ever wonders how a woman can solve a hard practical problem, he should think of Margaret Catchpole. Leslie Stephen liked to call attention to her notorious abilities. "Her command of expedients to gain her own ends was," says *DNB*, "conspicuous." She was a farmer's daughter, the youngest of six children. When her mother was suddenly taken sick, Margaret, at the age of thirteen, mounted a horse and galloped, with only a halter around its neck, to Ipswich to summon a doctor. After this she became a household servant and saved one of the children of her employer from drowning. Then she fell in love with a worthless sailor, and in order to meet him, she stole her master's horse and rode it the seventy miles to London in eight and a half hours. For this theft she was tried and sentenced to death. She broke out of the Ipswich jail and let herself down, uninjured, from the spikes on the top of the wall around the jail. She was again arrested and again sentenced to death. But her undaunted speech and her demeanor at her trial gained her many friends. Her sentence was commuted, she was "transported" in 1801 to Australia, and there she lived—surprise!—a quiet and sober life, and died there just a short time before Henry Owen set out from Yorkshire for New York.

If only Rebekah Owen had had the spirit of Margaret Catchpole, the storming of Max Gate would have been an easy matter. It would also have been an exciting matter, for—as Rebekah was later to discover—there was something of the dauntless spirit of Margaret Catchpole about the first Mrs. Hardy. But *DNB* calls Margaret an "adventuress," and while a former editor of the *Cornhill* had made a certain Becky famous as an adventuress, her last name was not Owen. And of course our New York lady could not do what a fellow-countryman of hers did just eight years later. When William Lyon Phelps was enjoying a bicycle trip in England, in September, 1900, he turned up one day at the door of Max Gate, all unannounced and unexpected, unwanted and unknown; and when the maid answered his resolute American knock, he startled her by proclaiming that he "adored her master" and would like to see him. The maid fled, but Phelps stood his ground and eventually had his wish. Hardy was then a frail, depressed man of sixty, and during this interview with William Lyon Phelps he "neither laughed nor smiled"; but, as the Yale professor later reported in his *Autobiography*, Hardy "was, after the first moments, exceedingly gracious, kindly, and sympathetic."

Other Americans have been known to write letters announcing their approach to Max Gate, sometimes with "leading questions" that were successful in producing replies, sometimes with a frank and unabashed request for permission to call. Miss Owen could not bring herself to try any such unsolicited and uninvited approach. One thing, however, she could do. If she couldn't march up to the door of Max Gate and knock, she could at least investigate the Hardy Country. No permissions were needed for that. And it was to just this inviting task that Rebekah addressed herself when, at the end of June, 1892, she and Catharine left Oxford.

There is a great difference between exploring the Hardy Country in 1952 and attempting the same thing in 1892. Sixty years ago the literary tourist had none of the aids that make the Wessex Tour a simple thing today. Not until 1895 did Hardy begin the practice of including a map in all the Wessex novels. Not until the turn of the century did the New York *Bookman* run a series of articles on Hardy's Wessex, for the enlightenment of American readers. Not until 1913 did Hermann Lea provide the tourist with expert assistance in exploring the highways and byways of Dorset, "with a view to discovering the real places which served as bases for the descriptions of scenery and backgrounds given us in the novels and poems." And not until still more recently was it possible to buy a Guide Book to the Hardy Country in almost every bookshop in England. Rebekah Owen went as a pioneer. That means that she had to work "on her own," slowly. She had to explore thoroughly, to notice every detail. But that is the way to learn. Moreover, although she carried no guide book to Wessex, she had something a great deal better than a guide book. In her head Rebekah Owen carried the Works of Thomas Hardy. He knew more about Wessex than Baedeker or Muirhead. Barrie had called him "the Historian of Wessex" (in the *Contemporary Review*, July, 1889), and Kipling had recently dubbed him "Lord of the Wessex Coast and of the lands thereby" (in the *Athenaeum*, December 6, 1890). Rebekah's frequent reading and re-reading of the Wessex Novels was now to begin to pay dividends; she found herself equipped with the most expert help then available. She was later on to meet Hermann Lea, but when she did meet him she could tell *him* things instead of his telling her.

Although the names of many of the places described by Thomas Hardy appeared on no map of England then available to Rebekah Owen, her repeated readings of the novels had made her aware of at least one thing—the fact that the Cathedral City of the Hardy country was Salisbury. His frequent references to it in *Ethelberta,* in *Two on a Tower,* in *Tess,* and in other works, had made her perfectly familiar with "Melchester," as Hardy called it; and it was towards Salisbury, therefore, that the Owens directed their steps on leaving the University of Oxford.

Whether they knew that Hardy's "Melchester" and Trollope's "Barchester" were one and the same, I do not know. I have not found any statement among Miss Owen's notes to show that Hardy ever repeated to her the admission he later made to Vere Collins, that he "liked Trollope." Nor is there any note to show whether she had read Trollope's own recently published statement in his *Autobiography.* Said he: "I visited Salisbury, and whilst wandering there . . . I conceived the story of *The Warden,* —from whence came that series of novels of which Barchester . . . was the central site. I . . . stood for an hour on the little bridge in Salisbury, and . . . made out to my own satisfaction the spot on which Hiram's hospital should stand." If Miss Owen did know any of this—as a reason for going to Salisbury—she was tactful enough not to disclose the fact to Hardy when (later on) she had a chance to talk with him about Salisbury.

At the end of June, then, the Owens headed for "Melchester." On Sunday, July 3, they were in Amesbury and attended divine service in St. Mary's Church there. The next day they moved on to Salisbury and established themselves at 86 Exeter Street for the rest of the month. Rebekah was not a hasty or superficial explorer, and if "Melchester" was worth doing, it was worth doing well.

She remembered Hardy's reference to a jeweler's shop in Melchester, which (according to *The Hand of Ethelberta*) "completely outshone every other shop" in the city. Rebekah tried to identify it but couldn't be sure. Instead of jewelry she bought some silk in Salisbury. On the twentieth she attended Wednesday service in the beautiful Cathedral and thought of Hardy's bishop in *Two on a Tower*. She shortly managed to make the acquaintance of the real Bishop of Salisbury, who at this time happened to be the grand-nephew of the poet Wordsworth. Mrs. Wordsworth was not well—in fact, her death seemed quite imminent—but even this sad prospect suggested Thomas Hardy to the retentive mind of the American visitor who had so often read aloud about Lady Constantine's death in *Two on a Tower*. On July 26, Rebekah was invited to Mrs. Wordsworth's garden-party, and from reading *about* the bishop's palace in *Two on a Tower* Rebekah suddenly found herself *at* that palace and promoted to acting a part, as it were, in an actual Wessex novel.

She was still in Salisbury on July 30 when a letter came from the vicarage at Berwick, saying that Mr. Baldwin had made some progress in his attempt to arrange a "legitimate introduction" to Hardy. Canon Baldwin had thought of approaching the author through his publishers. That sounds simple enough but actually it was no easy matter. For the house that had issued Hardy's books all through the eighteen-eighties had just been going through a re-organization that changed the name of the firm, and at this same time they ceased to be the authorized publishers of the novelist. Hardy had, it so happened, recently transferred all his publishing arrangements into the hands of an enterprising firm of Americans in London, James R. Osgood, McIlvaine & Co. They had acted promptly when the international copyright law of 1891 went into effect and gave them a chance to offer Hardy, for the first time, protection in America as well as in England. Hardy had accepted their offer, and as a result it was this new firm that had published *Tess of the D'Urbervilles* in Novem-

ber, 1891—the novel that was now piling up sales in 1892 beyond anything that Hardy had previously experienced. Unfortunately, just then Osgood suddenly died, and Hardy's business
arrangements became still more complicated. The sales of *Tess*,
however, kept on mounting, and during the month of July, while
the Owen sisters were in Salisbury, Hardy was busy writing a
new "Preface to the Fifth Edition" of *Tess*.

Canon Baldwin was of course not aware of all these changes in
Hardy's publishing arrangements. All through the preceding
decade, the Wessex novels had been published by a well-known
London house that issued cheap reprints, and the name of Sampson Low, Marston, Searle, and Rivington was thus known to most
of Hardy's British readers. Mr. Baldwin's investigations led him
first of all to this publishing house; but by the time his letter of
inquiry reached the right office in London, Messrs. Searle and
Rivington had both withdrawn from the firm and had been replaced by a mere "and Company." It was accordingly into the
hands of Sampson Low, Marston & Co. that Canon Baldwin's
application eventually came. Stuart J. Reid, one of the directors
of the new company, replied that they no longer published Hardy, but that he would be willing to communicate with the author
and ask him whether he would care to permit an American lady
to call on him.

As soon as Rebekah received this information from Mr. Baldwin, she hurriedly wrote him that she would take steps to proceed at once to Dorchester. She did not know where she would
stay when she got there, but he could address her at General Delivery or could wire her at the post office. Neither Miss Owen
nor her clerical friend in Berwick could have any idea that their
application had reached Hardy at a particularly inauspicious time.
It came, as Mercutio might have said, at a grave time. I think it
has not been previously known that earlier this year Hardy had
attended the funeral of his American publisher, James R. Osgood, in London. His death was announced in the *Times* on May

20. Hardy and William Black, another English novelist, had walked just behind the Chief Mourners, Clarence McIlvaine and another American friend. Hardy afterwards reported: "The grave was in wet clay. . . . Very sad." And now, two months later, he had just come from another open grave—one calculated to make him more than "very sad." The novelist's father had just died, and on July 31 Hardy attended a service for him in Stinsford Church near Dorchester. If Rebekah Owen had known all this, she might well have thought that her chances of being welcomed at Max Gate were pretty slim.

On the very next day, however, Hardy wrote to his former publisher in London, and the latter promptly relayed the message to Berwick. Here it is:

St. Dunstan's House, Fetter Lane,
London, E. C.

August 2nd, 1892

Rev'd C. Baldwin.

Dear Sir:

I have been in communication with Mr. Hardy and am pleased to tell you that I have heard from him to-day. He says that he will be glad to make Miss Owen's acquaintance if she will call upon him at Max Gate, Dorchester, any afternoon between 4 and 5. He asks that she should send a line to say when he may expect her. I enclose a card which the lady may care to have.

Yours faithfully,

SAMPSON LOW, MARSTON AND COMPANY, LIMITED
Stuart J. Reid, *Director*.

The card enclosed by Mr. Reid read:

To introduce Miss R. Owen
To Thomas Hardy, Esq.
SAMPSON LOW, MARSTON AND COMPANY,
Publishers
Stuart J. Reid.

Having been infected by Rebekah's excitement and impatience, Mr. Baldwin telegraphed her the good news as soon as he received Stuart Reid's letter. From Berwick he wired: "Miss Owen, Postoffice, Dorchester. Have succeeded. Will send introduction today. Baldwin."

The telegram arrived in Dorchester Wednesday morning, August 3, but the Owens had not come yet. They arrived at noon on the fourth, and no reader of these pages will have to be told that Rebekah went at once to the post office. There she found, not only Mr. Baldwin's telegram, but the following letter as well:

August 3rd [1892].

My dear Rebekah

I am very glad indeed to have obtained for you the introduction which you desire.

I telegraphed to you as soon as I received Mr. Stuart Reid's note that you might know as soon as possible. I now send the card of introduction by the first post, and I shall be most interested to hear of your interview. I hope it may not result in a dis-illusion. Mr. Stuart Reid is a director of Sampson Low, Marston & Co. The old firm has been formed into a [new] company. I dare say you will write a few lines of thanks to Mr. Reid directly to him at St. Dunstan's House, the office of the publishing company.

In haste, with very kind regards,

Truly yours

CHARLES BALDWIN.

The reader will use his own imagination for sensing the excitement with which Rebekah Owen read the words: "Mr. Hardy . . . glad to make Miss Owen's acquaintance . . . send a line to say when. . . ." She promptly sent her "line": Tomorrow!

It would be some years yet, before Hardy would write his poem on "The Convergence of the Twain" (published in *Satires of Circumstance*, 1915), but there are lines in it which inevitably offer themselves as a fitting comment on Rebekah Owen's note of August 4. When she named the fifth as the date for her long-wished-for call, it was as if "the Spinner of the Years" had said "Now!" right out of Hardy's poem:

> The Immanent Will that stirs and urges everything
>   Prepared a . . . mate
>   For her—so . . . great. . . .
>   Alien they seemed to be:
>   No mortal eye could see
> The intimate welding of their later history,
>   Or sign that they were bent
>   By paths co-incident. . . .
>   Till the Spinner of the Years
>   Said "Now!" and each one hears. . . .

And "now" it was to be.

Rebekah of course had no way of knowing that her arrival in Dorchester followed with almost magic immediacy Hardy's recent expression of regret that he lived "in a world where one so often hungers in vain for friendship." While the Owens were getting acquainted with Salisbury, Hardy had been busy preparing the preface (already referred to) for the new edition of *Tess*. After acknowledging "the responsive spirit" in which his novel had been received "by the readers of England and America," Hardy had remarked: "For this responsiveness I cannot refrain from expressing my thanks; and my regret is that, in a world where one so often hungers in vain for friendship, where even not to be wilfully misunderstood is felt as a kindness, I shall never meet in person these appreciative readers, male and female, and shake them by the hand." A few days after Hardy's regretting that he would never meet in person these appreciative readers, Catharine and Rebekah Owen arrived at Max Gate. Fate was doing its best to teach him a lesson.

The perspicacious reader will at once grasp one aspect of Thomas Hardy which it took Rebekah Owen many years to come to recognize, or at least to be willing to admit. Only three years after she had turned up at Max Gate to shake its owner by the hand and to satisfy (in so far as he was willing for her to satisfy) his avowed hunger for friendship, he wrote (in *Jude the Obscure*) about Jude's looking in vain for some one to come along who would help him in his distress. "Somebody might have come along that way who might have cheered him. . . . But nobody did come, because nobody does." Hardy's conviction that "nobody does come"—a conviction expressed so dogmatically and so soon after some one *had* come—marks one of his blind spots. Eighteen months before Rebekah's arrival in Dorchester, James R. Osgood had also come, to bring Hardy the good news about the international copyright-protection that would henceforth be his. Hardy was almost alone among Victorian novelists in living long enough to enjoy this protection, for Thackeray, Dickens, Kingsley, George Eliot, Trollope, Reade, and Wilkie Collins had all died. Thirty-six years later, Hardy died, leaving a fortune of nearly $450,000; but he still believed that "nobody did come, because nobody does." He had lived so long with a belief in his being the chief butt of Crass Casualty that he was unable to respond fully and generously to the arrival of "appreciative readers" like Rebekah Owen. She came not only to offer him her exuberant friendship, but also to flatter him with a detailed and almost scholarly acquaintance with his writings that was quite without parallel. Where else could he have found a person who had read his works aloud, over and over and over again, in family circles and in larger groups, until she knew them almost by heart? Fortunately each of "the twain" was to find pleasure enough in the meeting of August 1892 to be unaware, at first sight, of the defects that were eventually to appear on both sides, both in the author and in his reader.

Upon their arrival in Dorchester, the Owens looked about for a place of residence, and they shortly decided on a four-months' tenancy of a dwelling at No. 2 Temple Terrace. Here they were near the Top o' Town, and could look out on the old Roman wall —already familiar to them from their frequent reading of *The Mayor of Casterbridge*—and across the river valley towards Egdon Heath—familiar to them from their acquaintance with *The Return of the Native*. On the fifth of August, Rebekah prepared for her call at Max Gate by purchasing a copy of *The Mayor of Casterbridge* at the Dorchester booksellers, M. & E. Case. At tea-time she carried the book with her.

One of the most regrettable gaps in the Owen notes on this occasion is the absence of any description of Rebekah's feelings as she approached the door of Max Gate for the first time. She really had no need of Mr. Reid's card or of her copy of *The Mayor* to insure the success of the occasion, for certainly Hardy had never had a caller more genuinely interested in his work or more intimately acquainted with it.

On an earlier page of this book the statement has been made that "the similarity between Rebekah Owen and James Boswell is, in many ways, a striking one." That is true. But the events at Max Gate on August 5, 1892, show how very different Miss Owen and Boswell were. On that day she accomplished her great purpose, and if she had ever played Boswell to Hardy's Johnson, to the extent of writing a biography of the great man, we might then have had something from her pen to compare with the famous and well-known passage written by James Boswell:

This is to me a memorable year [1763]; for in it I had the happiness to obtain the acquaintance of that extraordinary man whose memoirs I am now writing; an acquaintance I shall ever esteem as one of the most fortunate circumstances in my life. . . . I had for several years read his works with delight and instruction. . . . At last, on Monday the 16th of May, when I was sitting in Mr. Davies's back-parlor, . . . Johnson unexpectedly came into the shop; and Mr. Davies having perceived him . . . advancing towards us, he announced his awful approach. . . . Mr. Davies . . . introduced me to him.

With a change of names and date, Miss Owen might have written much the same sort of description; for the year 1892 was to her a memorable year, since in it she had the happiness to obtain the acquaintance of *her* extraordinary man. The recent publication of Boswell's *London Journal* of 1763 shows us, however, that the two meetings were really very, very different. Rebekah's meeting with Hardy was the result of her own plan, her desire, and her persistence. When it had been achieved, she knew exactly what had been accomplished. Boswell's meeting with Johnson was an unforeseen accident. On May 16, 1763, Boswell had jotted down, among his memoranda for the day: "Send breeches by barber's boy," and "At night see Pringle. Go to Piazza." He had, of course, no way of knowing in advance that this day was to provide him with the most important event of his entire life; but even *after* it had happened, the *Journal* shows little recognition by Boswell that anything had taken place out of the ordinary. The meeting with Johnson was recorded in the journal, but it was merely one more in a series of exciting adventures of a young man of twenty-two on the loose in London. Boswell wrote: "Mr. Johnson is a man of a most dreadful appearance . . . , very slovenly in his dress and . . . with a most uncouth voice." Rebekah Owen paid no attention to Hardy's dress, though he too could be slovenly, and she recorded not a word about his voice. Whether she noticed his Dorset accent or not we do not know, for she never said. Did he say "Darset" to rhyme with Trollope's "Barset"? She left no doubt, however, about her realization that a memorable meeting had taken place.

Unfortunately, a detailed account of her conversation with Hardy on that day is missing. But if her report of the interview should ever come to light, we can be sure that it will show her to be in agreement with Professor Phelps about Hardy's graciousness and kindness, and that she will be found to support the judgment of other callers who found Hardy "so modest, so unaware of his own great fame, so kind, natural, and unaffected, so free from jealousy and envy that to listen to him, and to talk to him, was an inspiration." The records which *have* survived show that Rebekah Owen found Hardy natural and unaffected, and her own response to him was easy and captivating. Subsequent events proved that Mr. and Mrs. Hardy were both as much taken with the American ladies as the Owens were with the Hardys. Rebekah's vivacity stimulated the novelist to unwonted zest.

After tea, Rebekah produced her newly-purchased copy of *The Mayor*, in which Hardy not only signed his name at her request but also volunteered to add some notes—identifications of Dorchester spots described on half a dozen pages or so—notes which would, he said, help her in her exploration of the town. When Rebekah departed, she glowed with the knowledge that the meeting had been as pleasant in Hardy's eyes as in her own.

Remembering the Rev. Mr. Baldwin's words, "I hope it may not result in a dis-illusion," Rebekah wrote him exultantly: "Interview by legitimate introduction successfully consummated. Great and immediate success! ... No Dis-Illusion!!" And to the Olivers at Worcester, who had also been apprised of the arrangements for Rebekah's meeting with Hardy, she announced her success with even greater pride. Mr. Oliver had written: "We expect you will write a book some day." Rebekah accordingly sent him the following imaginary sampling of her report of her interview—an unwritten chapter from her never-to-be-written biography. Imitating the sort of "poster" or bulletin which she had seen in the hands of newspaper vendors in London, she wrote:

Interview effected by legitimate Introduction.
VENI. VIDI. VICI.
Afternoon Tea at Max Gate.
The Great Novelist unbends to American.
Interesting particulars of Mr. Hardy's appearance and conversation.
Title of the forthcoming Novel, etc.
Latest edition.

One of the reasons for the staccato nature of Rebekah's reports to Mr. Oliver and Canon Baldwin was the irresistible urge to begin a new reading of *The Mayor*. The newly purchased and now-autographed copy of the novel was put to immediate use, and in spite of all the other activities that were crowded into these first days in Dorchester, Rebekah pursued the reading to Catharine and Miss Ash with such energy that she was able to record, on

August 12, that the first performance of *The Mayor of Caster-bridge* "on the spot" had been completed. It had taken her just one week.

This new reading had at once presented her with a puzzling question. The copy of *The Mayor* she had bought at Case's bookstore was of the second English edition, published in London in 1887. But as Rebekah approached the conclusion of the novel, she discovered that the text of this English copy differed from the text of the American copy which she had used in her readings back in New York. Almost an entire chapter was missing at the end—a chapter which Rebekah Owen thought was beautiful and touching. It was the chapter that told of Henchard's return to Elizabeth-Jane's marriage and included what Rebekah had called "that saddest incident in fiction, the slow starvation of the little bird." All this was left out in the Dorchester copy of *The Mayor*, and Rebekah found it so impossible to explain the omission that she determined to ask Hardy about it as soon as she had a chance.

Meanwhile, in preparation for further literary activity, Miss Owen returned to Case's bookshop on August 6 and bought copies of five more of the Wessex novels: *A Pair of Blue Eyes, Far from the Madding Crowd, The Hand of Ethelberta, The Return of the Native,* and *The Trumpet-Major.* They were all Sampson Low editions, in cheap red cloth, published 1888 to 1890. Rebekah Owen had no interest in First Editions and was satisfied with these three-and-sixpenny copies, in bindings uniform with her new copy of *The Mayor.* Hardy eventually autographed all of these books for Rebekah.

On Wednesday afternoon, August 10, the Owens were out exploring the town. When they got back to No. 2 Temple Terrace, they found that Mrs. Hardy had called and had left them this message, written "in haste":

Dear Miss Owen,

Fearing you may be out this afternoon I write this little note to leave at your house as I want to ask you and your sister to come to tea with us on

Friday afternoon about 4 o'clock to meet some friends (two ladies). I hope that you will be able to come.

Yours sincerely,

E[MMA] L[AVINIA] HARDY

The Owens were of course glad to accept this invitation. On Friday, when they arrived at Max Gate, they found the novelist talking with another lady whom he introduced merely as Tess. This lady was telling Hardy about an event during the recent London "season." Hardy, while in London, had given her his ticket to the Private View at the Royal Academy, and she had laughingly suggested to her father that she write "Tess" under Hardy's name and that they thus represent to the public the much-talked-of author and his notorious book. (*Tess* at that time was being wrangled over at every London dinner-party, and everyone had his own idea as to what Hardy had meant by "a pure woman.") The lady had repeated her suggestion later to Lord Portman, so she told Hardy, and he went about declaring that she *had* carried out her idea.

As all Americans in England learn, sooner or later, the English are not very good at introductions, and Thomas Hardy and his wife were no exceptions. Rebekah eventually learned, however, that the lady introduced merely as Tess was Miss Teresa Charlotte Fetherstonhaugh-Frampton, of Moreton, Dorset, and that she was a direct descendant (great-great-great-granddaughter) of Betty, First Countess of Wessex (the first of the *Noble Dames*). Her family—the Framptons—had owned a great part of Egdon Heath for seven centuries. Miss Fetherstonhaugh invited the Owens to visit parts of the estate, of which Hardy had made fictional use not only in *Tess* but in others of his writings; and before the tea-party was over, it had been arranged that the novelist and Mrs. Hardy would escort the Owens on such a visit the following week.

That evening Rebekah finished reading *The Trumpet-Major* aloud to her sister. She had also succeeded in adding another book to her growing collection: a brand new edition of *Under the Greenwood Tree*, just issued by Chatto and Windus in London.

The very next day the following letter reached her hands:

Moreton, Dorchester

Sat. August 13th [1892].

Dear Miss Owen

I have been thinking that it would be nice if your party could join mine at Bindon Abbey on Monday.

If [the weather is] fine, I shall be there with a class of girls in the afternoon and we should be happy to entertain you at our pic-nic tea if you would partake with us?

The trains are very convenient from Dorchester—one which arrives at Wool (the station for Bindon) at about 3 o'clock. We could then arrange a further meeting on Egdon Heath perhaps!

Believe me

Yours truly

TERESA FETHERSTONHAUGH

This letter called for a consultation with Mr. and Mrs. Hardy, and Rebekah used the opportunity provided by a Sunday afternoon call at Max Gate to get the novelist to autograph her new copy of *Under the Greenwood Tree*.

The next day, Monday the fifteenth, the Hardys and the Owens set out togehter. At Wool, where they left the train, Hardy pointed out the old manor-house to which Tess (in the novel) went on her wedding-day. Mrs. Hardy told of the ruse, some years before, by which she had managed to obtain admittance to the house, so that her husband might see the two horrible "life-size portraits" which are described in the novel. Now, with the novelist's help, they were all again admitted to the house and Rebekah climbed the stairs, just as Hardy himself had done before he wrote his famous description. That night Rebekah wrote her own account of the sight: "The portraits are of most brutalized women of a fleshly type, with enormous noses and supercilious mouths, revealing great fangs; they are very indistinct and dark and disfigured."

From Wool, the Hardys and the Owens proceeded to Bindon

Abbey, not far away, where Miss Fetherstonhaugh and her girls met them. Here Hardy pointed out the old stone coffin which he had used as the place where Angel Clare, in the sleep-walking episode, had deposited Tess. This statement puzzled Rebekah Owen, for she recalled from her New York reading of *Tess of the D'Urbervilles* that Angel Clare was said to have reached "the graves of the monks" and that "upon one of these graves he carefully laid her down." Hardy explained that he had, as an afterthought, substituted the abbot's stone coffin for the monk's grave, and that all later editions of the novel would contain the coffin instead of the grave. Miss Fetherstonhaugh remarked that it was a common practice for tourists to stretch themselves out at full length in the abbot's old coffin; whereupon, as the reader will have already guessed, Rebekah Owen proceeded to do likewise.

This discovery that *Tess*, like *The Mayor*, was published with variant texts led of course to Rebekah's decision to acquire a fresh copy of *Tess of the D'Urbervilles* just as soon as the new edition was available.

Upon their return from Wool and Bindon Abbey, the Owens continued with their exploration of Dorchester. They took photographs of its houses and streets, its bridges and Walks, and thus constantly improved their acquaintance with the background of *The Mayor of Casterbridge*. When several days of stormy weather set in, they went on with their readings. How different the novels seemed, here "on the spot," from the way they had seemed during the New York readings!

On Tuesday morning, August 23, a maid from Max Gate brought the following letter from Mrs. Hardy:

Dear Miss Rebecca Owen,

I returned from Bournemouth on Saturday, as the place was in a congested state with tourists and excursionists. I hope to drive out this afternoon, and wonder whether you would care to join me. I have to make one or two calls at houses and shops, and then I thought of going to Upwey, if you have not already been there. What delightful weather we are having after the late storms. I shall be so glad to see you and your sister again. I also want to know if you will both give us the pleasure of your company to dinner at 7 o'clock Monday evening [August 29]? I hope to have one or two friends to meet you. Please give verbal reply to the maid who brings this as to the driving question. I will call for you about 4 o'clock if you say "yes." Believe me

Yours very sincerely
EMMA L. HARDY.

Rebekah gave her "verbal" reply and said "yes." She had read *Under the Greenwood Tree* so often in New York that no one had to tell her now that Upwey was a tiny hamlet on the road to Weymouth and that "things happened" there in Hardy's *Greenwood* idyll. The sisters accordingly took the drive with Mrs. Hardy, and as soon as they had returned, they began their sixth attack on *Under the Greenwood Tree*. The reading was completed on the twenty-seventh.

Two days later the Owens dined at Max Gate, but the expected "two friends" did not arrive. Mrs. Hardy explained that she had invited the Rev. Mr. William Barnes, the Dorset poet, and his wife; but torrents of rain fell that evening and kept the elderly poet at home. This gave Rebekah all the better opportunity to talk with the novelist, chiefly about Weymouth, and she also had a chance to explain to Mrs. Hardy that she spelled her name "the Hebrew way."

Their cordial reception at Max Gate encouraged the Owens to send a thank-you note on the next day, and at the same time to mark their progress in intimacy by inviting Mr. and Mrs. Hardy to come and have tea with them at Temple Terrace two days later. The following reply came:

Max Gate, Aug. 31, 1892.

My dear Miss Rebekah,

We will come to tea with you with pleasure on Thursday, if [the weather is] fine, and then we can talk over the enterprise about Winterbourne [*sic*]. It is one I feel very eager for, and hope nothing will set [it] aside. I am expecting to go to a garden party on Saturday, but the weather may

still be in a boisterous mood and prevent my going. Last Monday evening
Mr. Barnes had donned his evening suit, and half-ascended his bycicle
[*sic*], with misgivings in his mind about his *sails* behind interfering with
his locomotion, when the rain fell suddenly again in torrents, and ended
his difficulties and our chance of seeing him that evening. He and his wife
will come one afternoon to tea and then you must meet them.

With kind regards to Miss Owen and yourself, dear Rebekah, in haste,

Yours very sincerely,

E. L. HARDY.

Rebekah prized this letter, for it told her that the Hardys would
come "with pleasure." And she had now become "dear Rebekah." No wonder she felt moved to report to Mr. Oliver in
Worcester: "The intimacy thickens!" The absence of any record
among her notes—and Rebekah knew how to make and keep
records—of her entertaining Thomas Hardy at tea on September first makes it seem likely that the weather was again stormy
and that the novelist and his wife did not come. But there is no
doubt that the couple at Max Gate felt that *they* had thereby suffered a loss just as truly as the Owen sisters felt disappointed at
having been deprived of the company of their great writer.

Two days later Rebekah received a Max Gate postcard:

I am going to Stafford Rectory this afternoon [Saturday, September 3,
1892] (unless very dreadful weather: showery will not matter) and
should like to take a friend. If you have nothing better to do, will you go
with me? I start at 4.30.   E. L. H.

It was this drive that acquainted Rebekah for the first time with
some of the western fringe of the country of *The Return of the
Native*.

On the sixth the Owens again took tea at Max Gate, and Rebekah now had a good chance to ask Hardy about the missing
chapter in *The Mayor of Casterbridge*. He had had an idea—so he
explained—that it weakened the story to have Henchard go
away twice, and so, after the serial version (on which all the
American editions were based) had finished its run in the maga-

zine, he revised the text for the first English edition in book form. In this edition Henchard, instead of finding employment away from Dorchester and later purchasing the caged goldfinch and carrying it back to Elizabeth-Jane, was merely to "wander on." He never again saw Elizabeth-Jane. What Rebekah Owen had missed, when she came to read the story in the copy she had bought in Dorchester, was the passage in which Elizabeth-Jane's accusing words, "You have bitterly deceived me," are followed by Henchard's tragic reply: "I'll never trouble 'ee again." Not only had all this disappeared in the English edition, but there was of course no "dead body of a goldfinch . . . starved to death."

If Rebekah Owen had not obtained from Hardy an explanation of his revision of his novel, and if she had not bothered to write the explanation down, and if her written record had not survived, we would never have had the answer to the question that had puzzled other readers besides Rebekah Owen. When Mary Ellen Chase was engaged in her study of *Thomas Hardy from Serial to Novel* (Minneapolis, University of Minnesota Press, 1927), she made the same discovery that Miss Owen had made before her; and "after noting carefully the differing conclusion of the story in the early English editions" as compared with the early American editions, Miss Chase declared: "It is difficult, indeed, to understand what line of reasoning could have decided the author to take this incident [of Henchard's return to the wedding and his pathetic departure] from the . . . book. . . . It must have been that, in his effort to avoid the sensational and the melodramatic . . . , he so far misinterpreted the effect of Henchard's return upon his readers as to sacrifice . . . the culminating episode which so fittingly brings his great tragedy to a close." Well, thanks to the lady from Madison Square, we now know exactly "what line of reasoning" led Hardy to his decision.

Nor is that the limit of our obligation to her, for Rebekah Owen was not satisfied with Hardy's explanation. She argued with him that Henchard's going away twice does *not* weaken the story, and that Elizabeth-Jane's repulse of him is entirely reasonable and in character. She said that her sister Catharine agreed with her conviction that the earlier form of the story was better than the revised version. Hardy was impressed with the force and sincerity with which Miss Owen urged her point, and this is not the last time we shall hear about it.

The tea-time call was stretched out until the sun began to sink. Then Hardy offered to walk home with the American ladies, but he was obviously in no hurry to get them back to Temple Terrace. They went "by devious ways," as Rebekah put it, following the river through the fields to Grey's Bridge, which Rebekah knew well from its description in *The Mayor*. As they walked, Hardy told the ladies about the original events which he had reported in "The Withered Arm." He learned the actual details, he said, only after he had published the story.

At the bridge, instead of turning towards Dorchester, they turned away from the town and proceeded to the first mile-stone, "the last one which poor Fanny Robin passed on her toilsome journey to Casterbridge, just before she met the dog." Rebekah wanted to take a picture of this mile-stone and Hardy obligingly chalked the words DORCHESTER I MILE for her, but it was too late in the day. "The shadows were too heavy for an instantaneous picture. Mr. Hardy was much interested and wanted one, if good."

As they retraced their steps towards Dorchester, they paused again at Grey's Bridge. The sun had now set, but Hardy wanted the ladies to see Ten Hatches Weir, where Henchard debated suicide. "Only last week an old man attempted suicide there," so the novelist informed Rebekah. She later recorded that "Mr. Hardy showed us another deep place further on, where he used to swim when a boy. It and the Ten Hatches were always favorite spots for suicides."

When Hardy finally left the ladies after dark at their own residence in Temple Terrace, it was with the understanding that he would see them again the very next day. On September 7 the Dorset Field Club held its annual "Expedition"; the goal in 1892 was Swanage, and the Owen sisters were invited to accompany the Hardys. Rebekah was at once interested in Swanage when she learned that it was the "Knollsea" of *The Hand of Ethelberta*, so off to Swanage they all went.

Hardy was engaged much of the time with other members of the Field Club, and Rebekah heard him use the word "scammish," which she recognized as one she had come upon in her readings of *The Return of the Native*. When the party got to Swanage, the Owens were left in Mrs. Hardy's company. Rebekah now learned that Mrs. Hardy did not care to talk much about *The Hand of Ethelberta*. She had never liked that novel: "too much about servants in it." But she was very willing to talk about her own experiences in Swanage. She and the novelist had spent an autumn and a winter there, a year or so after their marriage, and the cottage where they had lived was still standing. Would Miss Owen like to see it? She would; and seeing it gave her a chance to perform one of her useful Boswellian services as Hardy's biographer—or as note-taker for some future biographer:

Mrs. Hardy took me to the sailor's cottage where they lived in those days. They were very poor then [1875]. We saw his [the sailor's] widow. While they lodged there, he broke his leg, in a life-boat, I think, and died suddenly a few months later. He was very nice, Mrs. Hardy said, and taught Mr. Hardy all that he knows of the sea and sailing, or the Weal charts and roads and currents. The wife stole, but on the whole was fairly pleasant. She seemed pleased to see Mrs. Hardy and wanted her to go in, but she would not. I don't think the woman had any idea of Mr. Hardy's fame, though she knew of his writing books.

During this visit to Swanage, Rebekah Owen elicited from Mrs. Hardy an explanation of one aspect of *The Hand of Ethelberta* which has often puzzled readers of the Wessex Novels. They have found it hard to understand why, in this novel, Hardy so obviously and apparently so deliberately turned his back upon that kind of fiction which he had till then been writing so successfully. The pictures of country life and character which he had given in *Under the Greenwood Tree,* in *A Pair of Blue Eyes,* and in *Far from the Madding Crowd* were all so distinguished, so inimitable, that one inevitably wonders why he turned his back on a kind of writing which he could do so well, in favor of a kind for which his fitness is not so obvious—is, indeed, quite questionable. For in *The Hand of Ethelberta* he forsakes the farm for the drawing-room. In place of talk about sheep and the seasons, there are stilted dialogues of literary criticism. I think no one has ever given any satisfactory explanation of this curious shift; critics have talked about Hardy's unevenness as a writer—about the ups and downs in his work—but they have not arrived at any wholly satisfactory explanation as to why Hardy dropped what he could do well and attempted something quite different. Rebekah Owen provides the answer. She learned from Mrs. Hardy that adverse criticism of *Far from the Madding Crowd,* Hardy's last-published book before *Ethelberta,* had discouraged him greatly. When its first chapters were appearing anonymously in the *Cornhill,* some readers guessed that it was the work of George Eliot. Other critics called it an imitation of George Eliot, and not a very good imitation. This kind of criticism, blind though we now see it to be, disturbed Hardy greatly. So, according to Mrs. Hardy, he "went off at a tangent and wrote *The Hand of Ethelberta* by way of contrast."

Talking of writing books, Mrs. Hardy asked whether Rebekah had ever thought of writing. Travel is such a fertile source of ideas for books. Mrs. Hardy remarked that she had often had an impulse to record her own impressions of places: she felt a crowd of fancies thronging in her brain, but she couldn't find the energy to put these impressions systematically down on paper. She sometimes thought that dictation might be a possible way out of this difficulty. Rebekah kept her thoughts to herself, but she was under no illusion as to Mrs. Hardy's qualifications as an author.

Emma's request for a "verbal reply" and her spelling of "by-cicle" were not lost on Rebekah.

After their return from the outing to Swanage, the Owens went on with their readings, and on September 9 Rebekah once again finished reading *Far from the Madding Crowd* aloud. With-in a few days of that achievement, she was invited to accompany the novelist and his wife to the "hoary building" occupied by Bathsheba in the novel Rebekah had just been reading. They ac-cordingly visited Puddletown, and found Waterston House not far off. Mrs. Hardy drew a sketch of the house and talked, while Rebekah photographed and listened. "Walterstone House was built in 1586," so she afterwards recorded, "by the second son of the first Viscount Bindon. It belonged to Sir John Strangways, and so passed to the Earls of Ilchester, who rent it as a farm house. Farmer Paul's daughter was so like Bathsheba that Mrs. Hardy made her husband present a copy of the novel to her."

A few days later the Hardys proposed another ride to the sea-coast, and the Owens were again glad to accept. On Wednesday, September 14, just a week after the trip to Swanage, they pro-ceeded first to Weymouth, center of the action in *The Trumpet-Major*. There Hardy and Rebekah strolled about, while he iden-tified spots that figure in the action of the novel. Catharine ap-parently stayed with Mrs. Hardy. The novelist pointed out "the old-fashioned house" in Portisham, but Rebekah confessed that she found it a little difficult to take as much delight in the back-ground of this novel as she did in others—in *Tess*, for example. Upon her saying this, Hardy pulled a letter from his pocket, ex-plaining that he had received it only that morning. He held it out for Rebekah Owen to read. The letter was from Sir Freder-ick Pollock; it dealt with *Tess*, and Rebekah's record of it goes thus:

It began "My dear Hardy," and went on to say that Pollock was almost the last of his race to read *Tess*, but he had left it for holiday perusal. It seemed to him the finest, most serious piece of work of modern fiction, approaching the grandeur of Greek Tragedy. He doubted if any judge and jury would have convicted Tess without a recommendation to mercy, and thought that the landlady's evidence of hearing a scuffle up-stairs might have been brought forward.

"Perhaps it was," remarked Miss Owen. "The jury might have recommended to mercy but all in vain. You don't give the trial." Hardy must have been constantly impressed by the immediate and ready knowledge which Rebekah always showed as to just what Hardy had or had not given in his fiction. She knew the books.

From Weymouth the party proceeded to the suburban village called Wyke Regis, where Rebekah and Hardy stood by the old tower and talked a while about *A Pair of Blue Eyes*. Then, returning to Weymouth, they continued along the coast road, past Osmington and Poxwell Hall (of *The Trumpet-Major*)—Hardy pointing out the chalk White Horse on the steep hillside—and so, on to Wareham. By the time this town was reached, it was evident that they would all be late in getting back to Dorchester. Rebekah therefore went to the Wareham postoffice to send a telegram—doubtless to "Ashy," so that she would not expect them to dinner. Perhaps Hardy telegraphed too; at any rate the postmistress learned his name and at once connected him with *Tess*. She then called Rebekah's attention to a telegraph clerk, a very swarthy youth of nineteen or twenty. He happened to be a Thomas George Tollerfield—"really one of the last of the ancient Turberville family"—who was extremely sensitive on the subject of his descent, "for he is teasingly called Tess by his mates. He has never read the book. Mr. Hardy wondered whether he ought not to send him a copy. I suggested, ironically, inviting him to a garden party at Max Gate. 'And Bathsheba,' said Mrs. Hardy, meaning the lovely farmer's daughter at Walterstone House."

Hardy informed Rebekah that Wareham was the "Anglebury" of *The Withered Arm*, and pointed out that the names of two villages nearby, East Stoke and East Holme, are combined in the "Holmstoke" of this same story. When Rebekah got back to her books, she opened to *The Withered Arm* and wrote: "I was in Anglebury with Mr. Hardy." Some time later, when her eye happened to fall upon this note, she took a circumspect and cautious Victorian pen, dipped it in another kind of ink, and added to her note the words: "and Mrs. Hardy"!

After their return from their pleasant excursion to Weymouth and Wareham, the Owens continued with unabated zeal their reading and exploring and photographing. Rebekah went one day to take pictures of Lucetta's old home (in *The Mayor*) and "of the barn hard by." Some cattle frightened her, and she ran into the old barn for refuge. On the seventeenth, she went to photograph the old Roman Ring and again had to run. The Ring proved a convenient haven. "There I took refuge from a bull that was staked close by. When he got free, he became very dangerous." But eventually Rebekah got her picture of the Roman amphitheatre.

The next day, September 18, the Owens and the Hardys were again together, visiting old churches and churchyards in the neighborhood of Dorchester. In one of them, probably Stinsford, Rebekah snapped a picture of Mrs. Hardy, but she never risked pointing her camera at the novelist. On the next day the Owens received a note from Mrs. Hardy, asking whether they would like to accompany her on a short drive to another house that figures in one of Mr. Hardy's stories—probably Wolfeton House of "The Lady Penelope" in *A Group of Noble Dames*, a house that stands a mile or so north of Dorchester. The Owens were of course delighted. On the twentieth there came a characteristic card from Mrs. Hardy: "Thanks. May I call for you both? Shall hire from the Antelope.—E. L. Hardy." Rebekah at once recalled that the Antelope was the Dorchester inn where Lucetta (in *The Mayor of Casterbridge*) planned to stop.

Miss Owen's reading of the novels sometimes had surprising

results. She was one day passing Wareham House, next door to Max Gate, and there saw several Roman skeletons lying in the garden, exactly as Hardy had described some in *The Mayor*. The sight aroused in her an intense desire to have some "Roman remains" of her own; and when, subsequently, she learned that a Roman skull had been dug up in that part of Dorchester known as Fordington, her desire was magnified into a craze. When Rebekah Owen very much wanted a thing, she usually got it. Eventually she got her Roman skull. She promptly reported to Hardy this unexpected result of his vivid descriptions of Roman relics in *the Native* and *The Mayor*. The novelist's response can be given in Rebekah's own words:

Mr. Hardy was rather taken with the idea of my buying a Romano-British skull, and having had a craze to possess it. Said he must see it. Anent its name (given by me) Metellus, he recalled at once the conspirator and Cecilia Metella. I said perhaps I ought not to take it to America, but I fancied I should like to give Metellus a turn in the States and then, if I tired of him, could bring him back to Wessex for re-interment. He said: "I should think he would much rather go to New York with you than to stay in Fordington. I am sure I should."

Now just what did Hardy mean by that? Perhaps Rebekah wondered.

At the end of September Hardy had business that took him up to London. Mrs. Hardy did not go with him, but Max Gate at once lost its interest for Rebekah, once the novelist had gone away. That obvious fact was probably not lost on the novelist's wife. Upon Hardy's departure from Dorchester, Rebekah Owen closed the chapter on the most wonderful two months she had ever lived.

Chapter V

"Those Two Seasons"

AS soon as the master of Max Gate had left their neighborhood, the Owen sisters were able to do some of the things they had not found time for during recent weeks. The Hardys had kept them so busy that there had been less opportunity for making friends with other people and for writing letters to old friends. The Owens liked to do both.

There can be little doubt that during the rush of events in 1892 Rebekah had had little time to write to the New York ladies who had listened to the reading of the Hardy novels. During her absence, there can also be little doubt that the temperature of Hardy enthusiasm in New York had dropped. Rebekah now set about watering the seeds she had planted. She wrote to Mary Drisler, telling her about the discovery that in England *The Mayor of Casterbridge* had a defective text, and soliciting her support of the position Catharine and Rebekah had taken, that the American version provided a much more powerful and artistic ending than did the British version of the novel. Miss Drisler replied that she did indeed support Rebekah's contention that it would weaken the conclusion of *The Mayor of Casterbridge* not to have Henchard return to Elizabeth-Jane's wedding. Rebekah felt that she had thus acquired fresh ammunition for renewing her attack on Hardy, and she decided that she would renew it the next time she had a chance to talk with him about *The Mayor*.

Rebekah wrote also to some Americans who had *not* been present at the New York readings of Hardy's novels, and in such virgin soil she tried to plant new seeds. To Fanny Patteson, for example, she wrote, singing Hardy's praises and urging Fanny to read his books—that is, if she ever found time to read novels.

Miss Patteson replied: "Very many and warm thanks for your letter. . . . I will certainly try something of Mr. Hardy's as I often read novels. . . . I don't deny him the palm of fame, only as . . . I never had heard of him, I thought perhaps you exaggerated his fame in England, but I cry 'peccavi'!"

Among the new friends with whom Catharine and Rebekah became acquainted in and near Dorchester were Mr. and Mrs. Albert Bankes, who lived in the "ivied manor-house" described by Hardy in "The Lady Penelope"; and Mrs. Sara Clapcott, who lived in South Walk, Dorchester, where Donald Farfrae (in *The Mayor*) erected his pavilion for dancing; and above all, they came to know the Moule family. Since the Owens were entertained "repeatedly" by the Moules, and since Rebekah and Catharine came to have contacts with so many members of this friendly and hospitable family, the reader will find it helpful if a few words about the Moules are inserted here, before we proceed further with Rebekah Owen's story.

It will be remembered from the last chapter that the Roman skull bought by Miss Owen was dug up at Fordington. For over fifty years the vicar at Fordington was the Rev. Henry Moule (1801-1880). Hardy, during his boyhood, often attended services in Mr. Moule's church, and his poem "Waiting Both" (published in *Human Shows*, 1925) recalls a sermon Hardy had heard Mr. Moule preach "one Sunday evening about 1860." The Rev. Mr. Moule had died before Rebekah Owen's arrival in Dorchester, but she came to know several of his sons and grandchildren. The vicar had eight sons:

1. Henry J. Moule (1825-1904), who was the curator of the Dorset County Museum in Dorchester at the time of Rebekah Owen's sojourn there. It was probably at the Museum that she met him. She was later invited to his home, where she met Mrs. Moule and their daughter "Margie." Rebekah was interested to discuss Dorchester antiquities with Curator Moule, particularly those that figured in any way in Thomas Hardy's writings. The earlier Wessex novels—those that Rebekah knew best—

were richer in this respect than Hardy's more recent publications. "Margie" Moule was shortly to marry the Rev. Edward C. Leslie, rector of Came Church, near Dorchester.

2. George E. Moule (1828-1912), who became a missionary in China.

3. Frederick Moule (1830-1900).

4. Horace Moule (1832-1873), who was Hardy's closest friend among the Moules. He went to Queens' College, Cambridge, and shocked the novelist by his suicide in 1873.

5. Arthur E. Moule (1834?- ?), who became rector of Burwarton in Shropshire.

6. Charles Moule (1836?- ?), Senior Fellow and, later, President of Corpus Christi College, Cambridge. He served Hardy as a model for Angel Clare in *Tess of the D'Urbervilles*.

7. Christopher Moule (1838-1839).

8. Handley C. G. Moule (1841-19 ?), who became Bishop of Durham in Rebekah Owen's time. Through the Dorchester curator, she came to know the Durham bishop and, eventually, his two daughters Isabel and Mary.

Rebekah established particularly friendly relations with Margie Moule, who was about Rebekah's age and who equalled Rebekah in vivacity and good humor, if not in her devotion to the writings of Mr. Thomas Hardy. The Owen sisters were of course as devoted as ever. Ever since their return from Swanage, they had been studying *The Hand of Ethelberta* and on October 4 Rebekah finished reading it aloud. Next they turned to the study of *The Return of the Native*, and to further exploration of the country of *Tess of the D'Urbervilles*. On the tenth they went to Bere Regis, where Rebekah photographed the church, inside and out. She took pictures of the Turberville Chapel, of the memorial window and the tomb beneath it. Then, with Catharine, she ventured out into the cow-pasture to get a picture of the south wall of the church, against which Tess (in the novel) set up the beds for the Durbeyfield children. But again the ire of a Dorset bull was aroused and the Owens had to flee. They took refuge in the cottage of a "hurdler"—a maker of hurdles, or movable sheep-fences—and were surprised to learn that his name was Toller-field, a corruption of Turberville, and that he had a daughter. (Hardy had originally proposed to call his novel *A Daughter of the D'Urbervilles,* and he had taken the daughter's name from the Turberville tomb at Bere Regis.)

The reading of *the Native* aloud was completed on October 19, and on the next day Rebekah was at last able to get her copy of the new edition of *Tess*—the Fifth Edition, in which the novel was, for the first time in England, made available in one volume. Previous English editions had been in three volumes. The Owens promptly went to work with it, and by November 4 they finished reading *Tess* aloud in the new and revised text.

Meanwhile Rebekah's Hardy Collection continued to grow. On the twenty-fourth of October she went again to Case's book-shop and bought new copies of *The Woodlanders* and *Wessex Tales.* She read *The Woodlanders* aloud within twelve days of finishing *Tess,* and then turned to the *Tales.* On the eighteenth she read "The Three Strangers"—Rebekah's favorite—and on the nine-teenth "The Withered Arm"—a favorite with Hardy—and "Fellow-Townsmen."

On October 25 there came a friendly letter from Teresa Fetherstonhaugh of Moreton. On November 7 they called on Mr. and Mrs. Bankes at Wolfeton House. While Rebekah was strolling with Mr. Bankes on the bowling-green he said: "I be-lieve Mr. Hardy has written a story about this house." But Mr. Bankes had not read it. The story was "The Lady Penelope," the eighth in *A Group of Noble Dames.* Mr. Bankes said his ac-quaintance with Mr. Hardy was very slight; he liked him per-sonally but disliked his books! Catharine, meanwhile, had been talking with Mrs. Bankes and had apparently made herself most agreeable, for hardly had the Owens departed when their hostess sat down and wrote Catharine the following note:

Wolfeton House, Dorchester

[Postmark: "Charminster, Nov. 7, 1892"]

Dear Miss Owen,

Will you and your sister come to Charminster Church on Sunday morning at 11 o'clock and then come back here and have luncheon with us at 1 o'clock? We shall be so glad if you will do this and it would not bore you. We *so* enjoyed seeing you today and your visit was too short.

Yours very sincerely,

FLOSSIE BANKES

If, however, the luncheon on the thirteenth (Sunday) took place, it has left no trace in Rebekah Owen's notes.

During the three weeks that remained of November, the Owens had at least one more opportunity to talk with Thomas Hardy before the termination of their four months' residence in Dorchester. Rebekah announced their intention of returning to Oxford for the winter, and this led Hardy to say that he had been in the neighborhood of Oxford only a month before, for he had gone into Berkshire to inspect the country he was planning to use in his next novel. He had never been in Oxford, but at Great Fawley you could see the university city in the distance—at least on a clear day. And when the sun went down in a blaze of golden light, the distant gleaming spires of Oxford looked like— like— like he didn't know just what.

"Like the heavenly Jerusalem," Rebekah suggested, little thinking that she would at some future date see her words in print.

When the day of departure arrived, Rebekah had to leave her prized Roman skull behind after all. By Thanksgiving Day the Owens were once again settled in Oxford, but it was a very changed Rebekah that returned thither. True, she was loyal enough to old friends and grateful enough for former kindnesses, not to cut herself off from her previous contacts in Oxford; but with almost every act of picking up the threads she had dropped in June, she now involved Thomas Hardy in the tapestry she was weaving. She learned that little Patrick Clay of Keble

College had passed his final examinations successfully, and on December 17 she went to see him receive his B.A. degree. But that was the end of *him*. She resumed her old habit of going to church on Sunday—a habit she had had too little time for in Dorchester. She communicated with the dons she had previously met, and invited Professor Holland and Professor Burrows to call and see the photographs she had taken in the Hardy country. On Christmas Eve, Rebekah went to hear the carols sung at Magdalen College, and on Christmas Day (1892) she saw the boar's head brought in, according to the old custom, at Queen's College. Doubtless her interest in the ceremony would have been increased, if she could have foreseen the day when Thomas Hardy would be made an Honorary Fellow of that same Queen's College.

News of him came to her from various sources in Dorchester. On Christmas Eve Margie Moule wrote as follows:

My dear Rebekah,

... I am sincerely delighted to hear of the excellent effect of Oxford upon your church-going!! I don't see why poor Dorchester should have had such a distressing effect on your morals—unless it is that the atmosphere is permeated by Mr. T. Hardy's influence!

I had a most pleasing encounter with that author the other day—he gallanted me half [way] down South Street, and told me of his having been in Mr. Barrie's company and how delightful he was.

They asked us to a party lately. . . .

And from Mrs. Sara Clapcott Rebekah received a brief but expressive note dated December 31, 1892, in which she read: "Thanks for your letter. . . . I expect you will be as happy without the Roman skull after all. . . . [I have] heard nothing about the Hardys—never do. His last story ends pitifully. It reads to me like a disappointed home life, very thinly veiled, in the author's experience." Rebekah could make out of that whatever she wished; she of course had had her own opportunities for observing Mrs. Emma Lavinia Hardy at first hand.

From Teresa Fetherstonhaugh, Rebekah received this pointed note, dated Moreton, January 5, 1893:

I spent the afternoon with the Hardys a day or two ago. She seemed poorly and out of spirits, I thought. He had just returned from a visit to Lady Jeune in London, where he had been seeing something of Irving and Ellen Terry. He told me Austin's "Pessimist" was not thought much of by the literary world. However, I wish you would read it and judge for yourself.

The chief mark of Rebekah's change upon her return to Oxford has, however, not yet been mentioned. Once back at the university, she dropped almost all of the hurly-burly of her previous busy-ness and at last knocked at the door of the Bodleian Library with serious purpose in her eyes. "By special gracious permission of Bodley's Librarian" Rebekah Owen was admitted to read among those venerable shelves where the shadow of woman at that time rarely fell. She read Gervinus, and Aubrey's *Miscellanies* (she later bought a copy of the 1857 edition of Aubrey), and William Stubbs's *English Constitutional History* (he had been made Bishop of Oxford in 1888), and Hare, and others; but in almost all the books that she examined, she read with a purpose and with an eye to Thomas Hardy. She copied a passage in Gervinus to supplement Hardy's reference to Novalis in *The Mayor*. From Holinshed's *Chronicles* she copied a long quotation, not about some Shakespearean passage, but about the Trenchards who appear as the Drenghards of "The Lady Penelope." In Aubrey she found and copied out an account of the appearance of an apparition to a Doctor Turberville, and she later discovered a 1570 edition of the *Poems* of a George Turberville. In the Bodleian she also discovered something else: that in a book entitled *Three Notable Stories* (London, Spencer Blackett, 1890) there was a story called "The Melancholy Hussar" by none other than Thomas Hardy. She had never heard of it before—had never heard Hardy mention it—and she read it, there in the Bodleian, with all the greater interest.

Early in February, Rebekah made a brief visit to London. She used this opportunity to look Stuart J. Reid up at St. Dunstan's House. She had already thanked him for the part he had played in obtaining the introduction to Hardy; and shortly after her first call at Max Gate, she had written Mr. Reid of her excitement at finding herself there in Hardy's presence. Reid had replied as follows:

Dear Madam:

Your note stirs memories of my own holidays. I spent most of June, this year [1892], in Swanage and in rambles around it. Do not forget to see Lulworth Cove. I am pleased to have been of the smallest assistance to you; I felt sure, in spite of your confession that you did not as a rule like authors—in a humble way I am one myself—that Mr. Hardy would prove worthy of forming the exception to your rule. If you are passing thro' London and care to call upon me here, I shall be very pleased to make your acquaintance. I am a biographer of Sydney Smith. Anyhow, I am, Dear Madam,

Yours faithfully,
STUART J. REID.

To this letter Rebekah responded, writing not to "Dear Sir," but to "Dear Mr. Reid," and thanked him for the invitation to call on him in London. She asked whether she might be permitted, when she came, to see where and how Mr. Hardy's manuscripts had been turned into books. In replying Reid made no attempt to point out that the Sampson Low Company had not published any of Hardy's work from the manuscript—that Reid's firm issued mere reprints—but he again urged her to call. His letter is worth quoting, if only as a sample of the sort of response Rebekah Owen was able to elicit from people:

Dear Miss Owen:

If so-copying a kindly example I may be allowed to call you, I beg to thank you for your letter of yesterday. I merely write to say that it will give me much pleasure to make your call upon me a pleasant one, and to unlock—as far as is expedient—the mysterious cupboards of this prison-house of MSS. and unfulfilled dreams of fame. If you wish to see the actual printing of books, that can be easily managed. We do not print at St.

Dunstan's House, but I can show you over a big printing house close by, or give you a letter of introduction to my brother—Wemyss Reid, editor of the *Speaker*, and general manager of Cassells. However, that we can settle when you come.

Only please let me know a few days in advance so that I may not miss the pleasure of your call. As to authors, we can discuss their susceptibilities —they are morbid creatures for the most part, of whom you do well to fight shy, though we both know some charming exceptions in "Wessex" and elsewhere.

Believe me, Dear Madam, to remain
Yours very faithfully,
STUART J. REID.

At last, then, in February, 1893, Rebekah called on Mr. Reid, but her notes do not tell us how many mysterious cupboards were unlocked on that hasty London visit. And from the absence of any further reference to him among Miss Owen's Hardiana, one can conclude that he drops out of her story at this point.

By the eighth of the month, Rebekah was back in Oxford, attending a performance of *Two Gentlemen of Verona* by the Oxford University Dramatic Society, and on February 23 she attended a concert at the New Theatre. But her books and her photographs had come to take precedence over concerts and plays. She bought a three-volume set of James Ingram's *Memorials of Oxford* (1837), but it apparently gave her less delight than her discovery (at Blackwell's?) of a copy of the book that contained "The Melancholy Hussar." This she bought on April 13 and promptly read the story for a second time. On May 2 she bought *A Group of Noble Dames*: it was her first specimen of a Hardy First Edition.

Shortly after the middle of June, Thomas Hardy himself was in Oxford, but the Owens were not there to see or to greet him. Early in June they had again gone north—returning to Mrs. Kate Raven's "Mountain View" at Coniston. In this secluded abode they spent nearly two months. While they were there, the July issue of the *Century Magazine* appeared with an article on Hardy by Harriet W. Preston. The promptness with which Rebekah Owen became acquainted with this article suggests that she was either a subscriber to the *Century Magazine* or —what is, I think, much more likely—one of her New York friends (Mary Drisler?) sent it to her. Miss Owen read Miss Preston's article but thought it highly uncritical. Rebekah noted particularly Miss Preston's remarks about *Two on a Tower*—a tale which "Mr. Hardy's truest admirers must wish most heartily he had left untold." Rebekah Owen had no such wish, nor did she find in *Two on a Tower* the coarseness or the bad moral that Harriet Preston professed to find there:

> In *Two on a Tower* our author may be said faithfully to have tried the effect of combining the two [i.e., coarseness and a bad moral]. The wit of the text, though rather *risqué* at times, is exceptionally keen; but the intrigue, disagreeably implied in the very title, is—let us take courage to say it—insufferably low. The character of Lady Constantine is, properly speaking, a pathological study, fit only for a professional book.

With this view Rebekah Owen did not agree. It was not the first time that she had shown herself capable of digesting stronger meat than some of her Victorian sisters.

After his visit to Oxford, Hardy spent a few days in London, and then returned to Dorchester by the end of July. Curiously enough, Miss Preston—she of the *Century* article—turned up at Dorchester just at this time, and had "a very nice excursion" on Egdon Heath with her "insufferably low" author.

Shortly thereafter, the Owen sisters left the Lake District. On August 1 they paused in Worcester for a brief stay with the Olivers, and while there they came upon another illustration of Hardy's reliability as a portrayer of rural life. The Worcester paper reported a pitiful tragedy: "Two hundred lambs . . . alarmed by some dogs" had been driven to their death. The "hideous sight" described in the newspaper reminded Rebekah of the chapter in *Far from the Madding Crowd* in which Gabriel Oak finds his ewes all dead.

Three days later the Owens again arrived in Dorchester and were soon re-established as the tenants of No. 2 Temple Terrace. Upon making inquiries, they learned that the Hardys were away. They had gone, or were just about to go, on a visit to Wenlock Abbey, and calls at Max Gate had therefore to be postponed. The readings, however, could be continued and the explorations of the preceding year were immediately resumed. On August 5 Catharine and Rebekah drove to Overmoigne, half way on the road to Wool; there they visited and photographed the church of "The Distracted Preacher." They found the orchard, got some good apples, and tried to identify Lizzy's house. Uncertain of the accuracy of their investigations, the Owens returned three weeks later with Hardy himself, so that he could help them. He then told the ladies that "he knew one of the smugglers." Meanwhile they had been reading, anew and aloud, "The Three Strangers" and "Interlopers at the Knap."

At the beginning of this chapter Rebekah's acquaintance with Mrs. Sara Clapcott has been reported. Her daughter Amy, now a Mrs. Williams, was one who moved in circles where the Hardys might be met. Rebekah therefore made inquiries of her and shortly received this note, dated Dorchester, August 12, 1893: "I don't know Mrs. Hardy and from what you told me, feel the opposite of attracted. . . . I am glad you have had such a nice time in the Lake Country and can well fancy how glad the old friends were to see you come back again." Later in the month, the same Amy Williams wrote to say that she had seen Mrs. Hardy at two garden parties, "got up just like 'Charlie's Aunt'—her hat and old-fashioned white lace veil were quite an amusement. She did not seem to me to know any one but her hostesses. Mr. Hardy's little keen face looked rather pale. I wish he would write another book."

With the knowledge that the master and mistress of Max Gate had now returned home, the Owens announced their presence in Dorchester. Immediately came the following note:

Max Gate, Dorchester, Aug. 30 [1893].
Dear Miss Rebekah Owen,

Will you and your sister come to lunch with us tomorrow? We shall be very glad to see you both again, and think you are very appreciative of Dorchester to return to us so kindly. Believe me,

Yours very sincerely
EMMA L. HARDY.

On August 31, therefore, the Owens lunched at Max Gate. Rebekah lost no time in picking up the friendship where it had been dropped nearly a year before. When they came to the table, grouse was served.

"Fancy eating grouse at *your* table!" exclaimed Rebekah.

"Last year," replied Hardy, "after *Tess* had been published, people heaped coals of fire upon my head by sending us quantities of grouse! We ate it all the time!"

There was no need to explain to Rebekah that he was referring to the episode in *Tess* in which the hunters leave the wounded birds to bleed slowly to death. But Hardy later told Rebekah that he had himself heard the blood dripping, just as he had made Tess hear it, and he had seen game-keepers destroying the wounded birds. Some keepers had acknowledged to him that far too many birds are left to bleed to death. Hardy thought he had done a little good by what he had written on this subject in *Tess*.

After the meal, leaving Catharine to talk to Mrs. Hardy, Rebekah and the novelist walked from Max Gate through Came Park, to the "fragment of stone wall in the form of a gable, known as Faringdon Ruin" (in *The Trumpet-Major*, 38). There they sat down, "where once Anne Garland and John Loveday sat," as Rebekah later recorded the fact in her book. But, just as in the case of an earlier conversation about *The Trumpet-Major*, Rebekah soon shifted the talk back to *Tess*. Hardy then referred to the closed house in the New Forest in that novel. Looking at stately Came House, he said: "There are plenty of closed houses where Angel and Tess could have entered and lived for some days. There is Came. If we were to go to Came now, I dare say we could get in."

Then Hardy added something that Rebekah Owen found even more revealing. The idea of having Tess executed at Winchester came to him, he explained, one day when he happened to be in that city. "He had met Lord Houghton's sister, the Hon. Mrs. Henniker, at Winchester and took her to the mile-stone whence Clare and 'Liza-Lu saw the black flag. I reminded him of Sir F. Pollock's letter and statement that a jury would have acquitted Tess." Hardy remarked that another reader, a lawyer who had had a great deal to do with reprieves, had said that it never occurred to him, while reading *Tess*, that she should not be executed.

As they sat at Faringdon Ruin, Hardy pointed towards Overmoigne, home of "the distracted young preacher," and told Miss Owen that he had himself seen the hole into which, or out of which, the smugglers' apple tree was lifted. It was sometimes lifted when in full bloom. Hardy also

pointed out to me a high and solitary house on Came Down, which he said his friend Mrs. Eliot of Weymouth declared was Higher Crowstairs [in "The Three Strangers"]; but the house was evidently a farmstead and not more than three and a half miles from Casterbridge. I said that I had always fancied Crowstairs to the *north* of Casterbridge; Mr. Hardy partly agreed, and said, too, that the hangman would come from the north or north-east, from Sherborne or Salisbury.

The mention of Salisbury brought several things to Rebekah's mind.

"Whose is the jeweller's shop there, which you say in *The Hand of Ethelberta* 'completely outshone every other shop'?"

"Why, don't you know?" replied Hardy. "There is but one: Vincent's."

Thereupon Rebekah recalled her own visit to Salisbury, and remarked: "I never can think of the Wordsworths in the Palace at Salisbury without thinking of *Two on a Tower*." Then she spoke

of Mrs. Wordsworth's sad illness, and wondered if the inevitable second wife of the bishop would be a Lady Constantine.
Hardy laughed.

They then talked about Harriet Preston and her estimate of
Two on a Tower. Hardy said

> he believed she was making a study of the state of morals at Rome under
> the Caesars, and if she could go into that matter, he thought she ought to
> be able to stand Lady Constantine. He knows a lady of rank who is, and
> acknowledges that she is, *exactly* like Lady Constantine.

Rebekah also brought up the subject of the conclusion of *The
Mayor of Casterbridge*. She told him that her American friend,
Miss Drisler, a *very* learned lady in New York, agreed with her
in thinking that the earlier version of the text was better than the
one now printed in the London editions, and the novelist reached
a decision. "Mr. Hardy promised me," so Rebekah wrote later
in her copy of *The Mayor*, "he would restore in a new edition"
those pages which had never yet appeared in any English book.
Rebekah had won a victory, and she felt no doubt about its being
an important victory. "I am sure," she wrote.

As they strolled back through Came Park to Max Gate, Hardy remarked that if Miss Owen liked faithful representations
of reality, he had a book to recommend to her. It was J. M. Barrie's *A Window in Thrums*. Hardy had received his copy from the
author, but if Miss Owen would like to borrow it, he would be
glad to lend it to her. Rebekah accordingly carried the dark-blue
buckram-bound first edition of Barrie back to Temple Terrace.

That evening Rebekah did not read to Catharine. It had been
a red-letter day for her, and before the events of the afternoon
faded from her memory, Rebekah wanted to perform her Boswellian job of writing them up in her diary. This is what she
wrote:

> August 31 [1893]. At 2.45 (after lunching at Max Gate), the Dis-
> tinguished Novelist and I set off together, across Fordington Field to

Came Park and all along the drive to Faringdon Church, which we turned aside to see, and like Anne Garland and John Loveday sat down in what was once the nave, or rather perhaps the chancel, and looked through the ruined window at stately Came House. Mr. Hardy gathered me a lot of flowers. He had not been there since he wrote *The Trumpet-Major* [fourteen years ago]. He quite agreed with me that Anne was not worthy of John and that it was entirely womanly [for her] to take the inferior man. I said people forgot Anne, as well as Elizabeth-Jane [in *The Mayor*] and Marty [in *The Woodlanders*], when they said that he never writes about nice women. Anne was pre-eminently "nice." Once he said "Think of all the people who have sat here, in Church, and lived about here and are buried close by us!" He kept his hat off as if in church. We sat there a long time, and as we left he was very kind [in] helping a frightened sheep through a hurdle-gate, back to the flock.

One of Rebekah's correspondents had recently written her that Mr. Hardy's "little keen face looked rather pale," and it may have been because he was tired that he sat so long with Rebekah at Faringdon Ruin. But as she wrote "We sat there a long time" she may have been able to think of other reasons than fatigue.

September was filled with interest and activity. On the second Rebekah went with Catharine to East Fordington churchyard to attend a military funeral. On the third, the *Dorset County Chronicle* reported a "large hay-rick on fire," exactly as if it belonged in Chapter 6 of *Far from the Madding Crowd*. On the fifth the sisters drove out the Wool road as far as Warmwell Cross, where the excisemen of "The Distracted Preacher" met with disappointment. Whenever their excursions went too far afield for walking, Rebekah used to hire a pony and trap at the Three Mariners Inn in Dorchester. This inn again reminded her of *Far from the Madding Crowd*, and a fresh reading of this novel aloud was begun just as soon as Rebekah had finished reading *Under the Greenwood Tree* aloud "to Tat and Ash" for the seventh time. *Far from the Madding Crowd* took a little longer to read, and the new reading led to fresh questions. The sisters therefore called

at Max Gate, ready with their questionnaire; but they found
Mrs. Hardy out and so did not go in. But they left word that they
hoped that Mrs. Hardy would be able to drive to Bere Regis
with them soon, when the annual fair on Woodbury Hill took
place. The next day this letter came:

Dear Miss Rebekah Owen,　　　　　　　Max Gate, Sept. 10 [1893]

　　I am sorry I missed you yesterday afternoon—in fact we *crossed*, as
letters do. I shall be home from 4 o'clock to-morrow afternoon, perhaps
you and your sister can walk out again. I have engaged the pony-carriage
for Woodbury Hill fair—it seems rather inadequate for the journey, but
the waggonette was previously engaged, and we must have mercy on the
beast and walk up the hills I suppose. Anyway he goes, old [X?] tells me,
and he [the pony] will certainly have a better time with us [than with
some inhumane driver]—at least I think so. This refers to the pony and
not the man. It will be delightful, if [the weather is] fine.

　　With kind regards　　　　　　Yours very sincerely,
　　　　　　　　　　　　　　　　　　E. L. Hardy.

　　Three days later, Rebekah saw Hardy again and this time
she put her questions to the patient author. Was there really an
old Malthouse at Puddletown? Rebekah couldn't find one.
"Yes," Hardy replied, "just as I describe it. But it was long
since swept away."

　　And did such delightfully amusing farm-labourers ever live,
as those that Hardy describes in *Far from the Madding Crowd?*
"Oh, yes," said the novelist. "There were half a dozen such on
our farm." And he added that he could show Rebekah where
Henery Fray and Joseph Poorgrass were buried! "I think," Rebekah wrote in her copy of the novel, "he said Fray's [real]
name was Isaac West and Poorgrass's John Amey."

　　And had he ever really seen the play of "Turpin's Ride and
the Death of Black Bess"? "Yes, I saw it long ago, at Cooke's
Circus. Black Bess was carried out on a board. But I did not see
it at 'Greenhill' Fair." The sheep-fair used to last six days—
time enough for the neighboring villagers to lay in their winter
supplies. Rebekah continued:

In one place, near the end of Chapter 21, he had written: "It has been said that mere ease after torment is delight for a time." Who said that?

"Why, don't you know? Edmund Burke." Hardy still owned the five volumes of the Works of Edmund Burke that he had bought many years ago.

In the chapter where Joseph Poorgrass is bringing the dead body of Fanny back to Weatherbury, he is said to have "looked to the left towards the sea." Ought this not to read "to the right," really?

"Why, yes, certainly!" And Hardy corrected the text in later editions of the novel.

And when Troy plunges down to "Lulwind Cove" where he goes swimming, the book says that the sea stretched in front of him "and round to the left" where the port of Budmouth bristled in the sun. Ought not this too to read "to the right," really?

"Why, yes, certainly!" Hardy said he must change that too. And later on he did.

In her conversations with Hardy about his work, Rebekah did not always confine herself to such *minutiae*. She was quite capable of broad generalizations, particularly on the characters of the novels. Her earlier Shakespearean studies here stood her in good stead. And on this same day, after the quiz on *Far from the Madding Crowd* was over, she discussed *The Woodlanders* with its author. She thus obtained from Hardy one of the most important comments he ever made on this splendid example of his own work, and fortunately the Boswell in Rebekah Owen led her to write it all down promptly.

He said that Grace [Melbury] never interested him much; he was provoked with her all along. If she would have done a really self-abandoned, impassioned thing (gone off with Giles), he could have made a fine tragic ending to the book, but she was too commonplace and straitlaced and he could not make her.

I said I thought her less particular than Giles; she was "willin' " when he was not. I spoke of Marty's very beautiful character, and of her being called by many the one truly noble and womanly woman in his novels.

He said: "Ah, well! She did not *get* Giles, you see. Very likely if she had, it would have been a different matter." (He never wrote anything more cynical than this.)

He further said that he did not make the end as clear as he should have done and perhaps would do in a revised edition. He found that people (I among them) do not see that he means that Fitzpiers goes on all his life in his bad way, and that in returning to him Grace meets her retribution "for not sticking to Giles." Her father hints at it in one sentence ["It's a forlorn hope," in Chapter 48], or forebodes it, but the matter is not made manifest.

This discussion took place during a walk "over Came Down." In a lane Hardy plucked for Rebekah some "leaves from a great hawthorne bough"—leaves which she sentimentally preserved in her copy of the novel. They were still there nearly fifty years later.

On September 17, 1893, one of the characters in *Far from the Madding Crowd* seemed to come alive for Rebekah Owen. "In Winterborne St. Martin's Church I saw the ideal Cainy Ball, bullet-head, shock of dark dust-coloured hair and 'poor dumb felon' complete, or something like it, for his hand was in a sling."

A few days later, the long-awaited trip to Bere Regis took place, and the visit to "Greenhill Fair." Apparently Mrs. Hardy's fears that the pony-carriage would prove "rather inadequate for the journey" turned out to be well founded, for the trip has left no trace among Rebekah's notes. On the twenty-third, however, the Owens completed a fresh re-reading of *Far from the Madding Crowd*. The next day the local *Chronicle* reported "the Going Away of the Artillery," and Rebekah hurried to her copy of the novel and turned to Chapter 10 for Hardy's account of the departure of the soldiers. She wrote: "I saw them go, riding down High West Street."

One other event made this September of 1893 memorable, though in a different way. Rebekah lost the Barrie book that

Hardy had lent her, and found herself in Henchard's predicament, in *The Mayor*, of being unable to find what he had lost without an embarrassing public announcement of the conditions under which the loss had taken place. Later events were to justify a suspicion that the book was stolen and not merely misplaced. In any case, it was later found or recovered and returned to Hardy. It remained in his possession until his death. In 1939 a London bookseller was asking $250 for it.

On October 6 the Owens finished reading *The Mayor of Casterbridge* aloud for the third time in Dorchester. When they came to Chapter 13, with its description of the sycamores on the town walls, Rebekah wrote: "Our lodging looks on those trees, and the bit of Roman wall, and very charming the prospect is in the autumn light." Within a month she clipped from the *Dorset County Chronicle* a notice of a farmer's selling his wife for ten pounds. She tucked the clipping into Chapter One of the novel. In time it came to be joined by nine similar notices of wife-sales. Besides the statement in that chapter: "It has been done elsewhere," Miss Owen wrote: "in Dorchester, for one place. Mr. Hardy told me." And within a few days she was to acquire in a wholly unexpected way a new light on the statement (in Chapter 36) that "in Mixen Lane vice ran freely." For on October 20 the Owens missed a treasured silver knife. It was possibly their mother's, for it had the name "Catherine Owen" engraved on it. Their reading of *The Mayor* had acquainted them with the reputation of some of the Dorchester natives for stealing, and by inquiring among their neighbors in Temple Terrace they learned that Mrs. Emma Hussey at No. 7 had indeed seen such a knife. Mrs. Hussey employed as a servant a fifteen-year-old girl named Charlotte Stainer. The girl had been in Mrs. Hussey's employ only two weeks. On Friday the twentieth, when Mrs. Hussey wanted to cut a cork, the girl produced a silver fruit-knife, saying "This will cut it." Mrs. Hussey asked Charlotte where she got the knife, and the girl replied that her brother had given it to her. When the Owens learned this, they reported the matter to the police. On the following Wednesday, an officer visited the girl's home in Mill Street and there found the silver knife in an old cigar-box in the scullery. The girl was arrested. Rebekah Owen appeared before the Borough Petty Sessions and identified her property, and the girl (who had been convicted of theft in May, 1889, at the age of eleven) was sent to the reformatory school for three years.

Rebekah remembered, of course, Hardy's statement in *The Mayor* that "theft [dwelt] in the mud-walled houses" of Mixen Lane. "I asked the Superintendent of Police if this were so. He said they mostly live by stealing, and if they work, it is *very* little. When he heard that our sneak-thief came from Mill Street (Mixen Lane), he said: 'A pretty place to come from!' . . . Mr. Hardy was amused to hear of our appearance before the Mayor of Casterbridge [Mr. G. Davis], who, he says, is rather like Henchard in some respects." The whole affair was reported in the *Dorset County Chronicle* for October 26 and November 2, 1893.

This unpleasant affair had not been allowed to interrupt the important readings and explorings. Shortly before the theft of the knife, the Owen sisters had gone to Bincombe, half way to Weymouth, in order to visit the grave of the Melancholy Hussar. There they learned that the Bincombe registers for 1801, quoted by Hardy, were now kept at Broadway Vicarage, another mile farther on, on the road to Weymouth. So they made plans to return later, just to see the registers.

On Saturday, October 14, they finished a fresh reading of *A Group of Noble Dames*. On the twenty-third they were on Egdon Heath, "near Blackbarrow" (in *The Native*), and there Rebekah picked furze and heather. On some unidentified previous visit to the heath, in the company of the novelist, she had seen Harry Hardy, Thomas's brother. He was engaged in Clym Yeobright's occupation—cutting furze. On the twenty-seventh Rebekah "walked 7½ miles on Long-Ash Lane," following the road from

Evershot Station in imitation of Tess. On an earlier occasion, when Rebekah had tried (and failed) to find Long-Ash Lane, she came to Piddlehinton. A service was going on in the church. Miss Owen stepped inside, and the congregation all stared at her, just the way the Emminster congregation stared at Tess! Rebekah later reported to Hardy that she had been walking in Long-Ash Lane.

"And did you ever see such another?" he asked.

A re-reading of *Tess of the D'Urbervilles* was completed on October 31—the fourth time (at least) in two years that Rebekah had been through it aloud. Four days later, at Winterborne Abbas, it sounded to her just like an echo out of *Tess* when "John Dunford said to us, touching the going of the old Rector and the coming of the new, 'but 'tis as 'tis, and so it must be.'" On the eighth of November they walked to Broadway Vicarage, a good four or five miles each way, and at last saw the Bincombe church registers for 1801. The Vicar had never examined them, so Rebekah learned, "though he told me that Mr. Hardy the novelist (and he was new enough to the neighborhood to call him so with much respect) had about three years ago examined them in order to write about them. *I* found the entries. The Vicar could not tell me who 'Phyllis' was, but had understood from Mr. Hardy that she was engaged to one of the deserters, or had kept company with him. I suspect myself that she was a relation, one of the Sutton Poyntz or Preston set of Hardys."

A few days later Rebekah met, at Winterborne Steepleton (four miles west of Dorchester) a Major Hawkins, who told her, on learning (as everyone who met Rebekah soon learned) of her interest in Hardy, that "he wished to see Mr. Hardy to tell him some things . . . ; for one, of the shooting of two German deserters from a regiment stationed near Weymouth. He wondered that Mr. Hardy had not used the incident, if he knew it, in *The Trumpet-Major.*"

"He did use it," said Rebekah.

"Where?"

"In a short tale called *The Melancholy Hussar*." Rebekah Owen was glad to be able to make use in this way of the results of her "research" in the Bodleian Library.

On the fourteenth of November the Owens finished their third reading of *The Return of the Native* aloud, and it marked a fitting book with which to conclude their sojourn in Wessex. For the time had come for the Return of these Natives to their own land. They had been away from Madison Square for nearly twenty months and their west-bound sailing date had been set. On the fifteenth Catharine wrote a farewell note to Max Gate, enclosing the results of some of Rebekah's readings in the Bodleian. Two days later there came the following reply:

> Max Gate, Dorchester,
> November 17, 1893.
>
> Dear Miss Owen,
>
> Thank you very much for your little note received yesterday before I was up, for I have not been at all well since I saw you. Driving in the east wind gave me a chill, and I shall have to keep at home a good deal through the winter.
>
> We are both surprised at your "find" of interesting matter about the Turberville subject, and also the very applicable verses for "Betty," which however my husband was not aware of, or I really think he must have added them to the tale [of "The First Countess of Wessex," the first of the stories told about *A Group of Noble Dames*].
>
> "Bon voyage" and thanks.
>
> Yours sincerely
> E. L. HARDY.

From old Mr. Oliver at Worcester came a copy of Thomas Ashe's *Songs of a Year* (1888) to give the Owens something to read on the ocean; and on the day before they left Dorchester, Rebekah received, as a souvenir from her sister, a book inscribed: "For dear Betty, in memory of hundreds of miles walked in Dorset. . . . Casterbridge, November 17, 1893." That word "Betty" (instead of Becky) will call for some explanation later.

On the eighteenth "Miss Owen, Miss R. Owen, and maid" sailed from Southampton on the S.S. "Paris" of the American Line. Their two-years' Wessex idyll was over, and what a lot they had to carry back to New York with them! The frequent contacts with Thomas Hardy had equipped them with autographed copies of almost all his published works, and their minds were stored with information not then available in any book.

If Fate had been kinder to Rebekah than it was, she might have been allowed to see Hardy penning some lines in his study at Max Gate, as the good ship "Paris" fought its way westward across the ocean. Hardy called his poem "A Two-Years' Idyll":

> Yes; such it was;
> Just those two seasons unsought,
> Sweeping like summertide wind on our ways;
> Moving, as straws,
> Hearts as quick as ours in those days;
> Going like wind, too, and rated as naught
> Save as the prelude to plays
> Soon to come—larger, life-fraught;
> Yes; such it was.

It would be pleasant if one could report that Hardy had Rebekah Owen in mind when he wrote these lines about "hearts quick as ours in those days." In fiction that is what he might have done. In fact, however, as well-informed modern readers of course know, Hardy had never a thought of Rebekah in writing about *his* "two-years' idyll." He was thinking of his sojourn (1876-1878) at Sturminster Newton, where he wrote *The Return of the Native*. But as Rebekah Owen mulled things over, on her way back to New York, who can doubt that, to her, the years 1892-1893 had been equally idyllic and triumphantly so. Those years had indeed gone "like summertide wind" and her own part in the idyll was pleasant to recall. In her victorious cry of "Veni, Vidi," she was quite well aware that the last word was "Vici." She had not only met Hardy; Hardy had met *her* and had found her good to know.

Chapter VI

"Some Good Judges Across the Atlantic"

THE steamship "Paris" had hardly cleared Southampton and passed the Isle of Wight when it ran into one of the worst gales ever known in the English Channel. There were 144 wrecks posted at Lloyd's in London all at one time—the greatest number on record. After a very rough crossing, the Owens reached New York in a "rather shaken condition" and soon after Thanksgiving Day were again settled at 26 West Twenty-fifth Street. There the Hardy Perennials went immediately to work. Mary Drisler was invited in to keep Catharine company, while Rebekah read aloud "The Three Strangers," and among the new Wessex material which the Owens were able to bring to Miss Drisler's attention for the first time were the poems of William Barnes. Later on, Hardy himself was to edit for the Oxford University Press an edition of Barnes's poetry, but at this early date Rebekah had to be her own editor. To facilitate her quick access to individual titles, and to lines (or words) quoted by Hardy in the novels, Rebekah made herself an index; and copies of the Barnes Index were promptly dispatched back to England to bear Christmas greetings from Madison Square to Wessex. After Christmas (1893), Rebekah entertained her customary audience—Miss Drisler, "Tat," and "Ashy"—with a reading of *Under the Greenwood Tree* for the eighth time, reaching the end of the story on January 2, 1894.

Rebekah had found time, before Christmas, to write to her many friends in England, and replies began to trickle in to the New York home as the New Year progressed. From Mrs. Sarah Whitaker, wife of the parish clerk at Stinsford, came this letter, postmarked February 26, 1894:

Thank you very much for your nice letter to us at Christmas. We are all very glad to hear that you arrived quite safe in New York. We all thought about you so much during that dreadful storm, fearing what might happen. It was so nice that you did not know the storm was so bad. . . .

Thank you so very much . . . [for the Christmas gift]. My husband said . . . to tell you how well he gets on with reading the book [of] Barnes' *Poems* you so kindly gave him. . . .

We all hope we shall have the pleasure of see[ing] you here again some day. . . . Our dear little Church at Stinsford was so prettily decorated at Christmas. . . .

Other correspondents sent her items from English newspapers, whenever such clippings served to illustrate or enliven the pages of the Wessex novels, and many of these found their way into the books that Rebekah had brought back from England.

From "Margie" Moule came a catty (but doubtless none the less welcome) letter dated March 14, 1894:

We had a visit from Mrs. Hardy lately, in her *most* affable frame of mind. She was rather amusing—she has taken to speak[ing] of "we elderlies"! She also casually alluded to Mr. Hardy's being "with the Jeunes"! It was perfect of its kind.

I have never alluded all this time to your index to Mr. Barnes' Poems. Father is so delighted with it. It *is* clever of you to have done it!

In this same March, Mary Drisler brought a copy of *Two on a Tower* to add to Rebekah's growing collection, and during the first two weeks of April she and Catharine listened as Rebekah read aloud, for the fourth time, *The Return of the Native*. The end was reached on the sixteenth, and on the very next day they tackled *The Romantic Adventures of a Milkmaid*. How their enthusiasm for Hardy survived that dreary ordeal is beyond the present writer's ability to explain; but a Harvard professor has recently (1949) declared that he finds it "hard to understand why Hardy's critics fail to recognize that this is a story of the supernatural—or, at the least, that it was meant to carry supernatural overtones, that it was to be read and accepted as a popular ballad is read and accepted." So perhaps that is the way *The Ro-mantic Adventures of a Milkmaid* was read and accepted at 26 West Twenty-fifth Street in New York City.

The reader may well credit Rebekah with genuine relief, how-ever, when she turned next to *The Mayor of Casterbridge*. She finished reading this novel aloud on May twenty-fifth, and the unusually long time that the reading took on this occasion—the fourth reading aloud—is probably to be explained by the need for discussing in detail, not only the chapter near the end, which Hardy had now promised Rebekah he would amend, but also the numerous other points and details on which the Owens could now enlighten Miss Drisler.

Mary Drisler's father retired at the close of this collegiate year, after fifty years spent in the service of Columbia College. The Alumni Association held a public reception in his honor. The Trustees presented him with a beautiful gold medal and established a Henry Drisler Fellowship, and President Low gave $10,000 to endow a Henry Drisler Classical Fund for the pur-chase of "whatever will make instruction in the classics more at-tractive." Professor Drisler died on November 30, 1897.

From the other side of the water came word that another fine old gentleman had died. The Rev. George Oliver reached the end in May, 1894, at the age of seventy-seven. This date might at first seem to provide an explanation of the mysterious fact that *some* of Rebekah Owen's notes imply that she was in England for about two weeks in 1894. Did she hurry over to Worcester to attend George Oliver's funeral? That possibility is ruled out by the evidence that he died in May and that at that time she was reading *The Mayor* to Miss Drisler in New York. In June she was reading *The Trumpet-Major* (completed on June 18) and *The Woodlanders* (completed on June 28). The notes that seem mysterious and perplexing are dated July, 1894, and suggest that Rebekah was in Dorchester at this time. But in mid-August she was again reading Hardy aloud in New York City, and it would be contrary to all her known habits and all her previous transatlantic experience to imagine that she rushed over to England and back again to New York, all in the month of July. She lived in 1894, not in 1952. The best explanation of those notes of July, 1894, is that they refer to the year 1895, when it is clear the Owens *were* in Dorchester again. In her frequent shuttling back and forth between England and America, Rebekah Owen did not always have her diary and her copy of the novel equally and easily accessible, and notes were sometimes transcribed by her into the printed volumes *after* the date recorded by her had passed. This habit opened the door to error; and while her customary care and accuracy protected her, as a rule, from making mistakes, she did sometimes make them. It is (I think) clear that the "Dorchester, July 1894" notes are wrongly dated. I shall therefore silently transfer them to the year 1895 without further ado.

The New York Hardy readings were, then, not completely interrupted during the summer of 1894. On August 15 "The Withered Arm" and "The Distracted Preacher" were read, and it was not only the text that now had to be read, but also the author's comment on that text, recorded in the margins of the books from which Miss Owen read. On September 18 "Interlopers at the Knap" was the subject of the program, and on September 24 "Fellow-Townsmen." Rebekah Owen's return to New York not only served to revive her friends' interest in Thomas Hardy but it also resulted in an enlargement of the circle that came together to listen to her read. She finally, probably in a jest, came to refer to them as a league—the league of Thomas Hardy Book Lovers, or the Thomas Hardy Book League, whose initials —T.H.B.L.—when they crop up in letters of 1894 and 1895, look strangely anticipatory of our modern alphabetical devices, in these days of O.P.A. and E.R.C. Not only were residents of New York glad to assemble over and over again, to hear Rebekah read and explain the gospel according to Saint Thomas, but la-

dies from Brooklyn and from even more distant places responded to Miss Owen's infectious enthusiasm. The infection reached
at least as far as Burlington, New Jersey, as we shall shortly see.

In October the T. H. B. L. were back at *The Romantic Adventures of a Milkmaid,* and on the seventeenth of this month Rebekah had an adventure of her own. When *The Art of Thomas
Hardy* by Lionel Johnson appeared, Miss Owen acquired a copy
and was delighted to find that it contained a Hardy Bibliography by John Lane. From this she learned that in his early years
in London Hardy had contributed an anonymous sketch to the
pages of *Chambers's Journal.* He was only twenty-four years old
at the time. Rebekah remembered that her father had subscribed
to this *Journal* and that back numbers of the magazine were now
stored in the attic of the house on Twenty-fifth Street. On October 17, 1894, Rebekah climbed the stairs, blew the dust from
Chambers's Journal, and finally unearthed Part XV containing the
section for March 18, 1865. On pages 161-164 she found the
sketch. It was called "How I Built Myself a House." To think
that Thomas Hardy had been there all this time—nearly thirty
years—in the Owen attic! Slight though this four-page sketch
is, Rebekah rescued it, marked it "The first published writing of
Mr. Hardy. Unearthed from our attic," and added it to what
she had by now learned to call her Hardiana.

In November there appeared a new candidate for admission
to Rebekah's list. *Life's Little Ironies* was published at this time,
and Miss Owen promptly read it, though she seems to have put
off until the next year the purchase of her copy. In this same
month, when the December (1894) issue of *Harper's Magazine*
appeared, Hardy's new novel was begun as a serial, first under
the title "The Simpletons," and in the later installments, in
1895, as "Hearts Insurgent." In the very first installment, Rebekah was startled to find in print her own description of Oxford, to the effect that it looked "like the heavenly Jerusalem"
when a flaming sunset illuminated its towers and spires.

"Why, I said that to Mr. Hardy in 1892!" she exclaimed, and thought of his cleverness in adding: "though I should never have thought of it myself."

But as Rebekah read on in further installments, the heavenly light dimmed. She had, before this, learned that Hardy could make cynical remarks, and she was of course familiar with his characteristic tendency to take a tragic view of life. But he had never written anything like *this!* She dutifully finished the story, eventually, but there is no record of her having ever read it aloud. We have since learned to call this story of "The Simpletons" by its book-title *Jude the Obscure.* In spite of all its vivid pictures of Oxford, in spite of all her excellent preparation for following Hardy's own rambles about the streets of that city of colleges, Rebekah Owen was *not* drawn to *Jude the Obscure.* It impressed her with the futility of everything, and the first grain of sand was dropped into the honey of her adoration of the Wessex author. Moreover the discovery of that single grain made her suspicious of others, and she began to look for them even where there were none. A letter from England soon provided the occasion for such looking.

The publication of *Life's Little Ironies* in England led to widespread discussion of its stories; anything by the author of *Tess of the D'Urbervilles* would have received that treatment. Teresa Fetherstonhaugh, of Moreton, wrote to Miss Owen to report that she had been up to London and had there heard people talking about the new book. Lady Jeune, one of Hardy's most loyal supporters and often his hospitable hostess when he was in town, saw nothing amiss in the *Little Ironies,* but Miss Fetherstonhaugh was not so sure. Her own irritation, if that is not too strong a word, may perhaps be traced to Richard LeGallienne's words in *The Quest of the Golden Girl:* "Looking back at the old town [of Dorchester], with its one steep street climbing the white face of the chalk hill, I remembered what wonderful exotic women Thomas Hardy had found eating their hearts out behind the windows of dull country High Streets, through which hung waving no banners of romance." What Miss Fetherston-haugh wanted to know was: *were* Dorset women eating their hearts out behind the windows of dull country houses? or was Lady Jeune right, that all was well in Wessex?

Rebekah rose to the occasion and, writing *en grande dame,* she answered Teresa with the following literary "effort":

I am partly amused, partly chagrined, to find that I must yield to any-one in my capacity for accepting and admiring whatsoever Mr. Hardy puts forth, but I own that I find myself, as to Lady Jeune, in the position of those Turner-followers in the Second Preface to [Ruskin's] *Modern Painters* who, few in number and long faithful, quailed and fell back as he scaled the final heights of his success, one or two only remaining with him. No, I am pushing the figure too far. I accept everything, I follow still, but I must [admit that I] see where now and then, for an instant, a false step is made, and precious time and pains are wasted in turning aside from the outward path to gather what is not worth the stooping for.

And so, among a very few errors of taste elsewhere, in *Life's Little Ironies,* I regret and resent "On the Western Circuit," and what chiefly enrages me in it is the action to which so far I have seen no exception taken, the odious liberty with the woman's hand, which at once suggests one of Leontes' grounds of jealousy. Merely allowing a stranger to take her hand would have been bad enough, but the way in which it was done seems to me very coarse. I blame Mrs. Hardy for letting him print it, but if Lady Jeune sees nothing amiss in it, perhaps she [Mrs. Hardy] did not either. The woman is, to be sure, only a wine-merchant's wife, but she is repre-sented as refined and cultivated. As the scene is laid at Melchester it is possible that the wife of the Bishop of Melchester (in *Two on a Tower*) had influenced the tone of the place!

The ease with which Rebekah, in this letter, brings into play her knowledge of Shakespeare and Turner and Ruskin and *Two on a Tower* will doubtless impress the reader not one bit more than does the supercilious reference to "only a wine-merchant's wife" made by this pen-merchant's daughter!

Meanwhile Miss Owen had spotted and, in February, 1895, copied William Watson's poem on "Egdon Heath." It would be useful, she knew, when the T.H.B.L. got around to *The Return of the Native* again. At the end of this month she received from Burlington, New Jersey, a letter which throws a bright light on the meetings of the Hardy Book Lovers. But before quoting the letter, it may be well to say a word or two about the lady who wrote it.

Among the devoted junior members of the T.H.B.L. was Miss Grace Alexander McElroy. Born in Brooklyn, she was twelve years younger than Rebekah Owen and at this point in our narrative was approaching her twenty-fifth birthday. Her recently deceased father had been a civil engineer, Alexander McElroy (1832-1892), who had worked on the Erie Canal and on various other public works. Among Grace McElroy's friends was Margaret Hamilton, who married Allen H. Gangewer, of Burlington, New Jersey. The Gangewers were the resident managers of "The Burlington." This was originally a fine house which the Episcopal Diocese of New Jersey owned and used as the official residence of its bishop. When, later on, another seat came to be used by the bishop, the Diocese rented the house to a group of Burlington intellectuals for use as a club, and Mr. and Mrs. Allen Gangewer were installed to supervise the property and to attend to the activities of the club. Mrs. Gangewer developed a great liking for the novels of Thomas Hardy, and when one or another of her New York friends discovered this liking, Mrs. Gangewer was invited, possibly by Miss McElroy, possibly by Mary Drisler, to come to New York and meet with the T.H.B.L. She came, and her visit was made additionally memorable for her by the gift from Rebekah of a lily which she had uprooted in the old Roman amphitheater in Dorchester and had brought back to New York. Upon Mrs. Gangewer's return home, she wrote Rebekah the following epistle—one that will transport the reader, if anything will, back into the fragrance of a bygone age:

The Burlington,
Burlington, N. J.
Feb. 27, 1895.

My dear Miss Owen—

The first leisure of my return home shall be dedicated to you and Mr. Hardy—and in furtherance of this election, I enclose the promised list of [magazine] articles bearing upon the subject, which are not already mentioned in the Bibliography appended by Mr. Lane to Mr. Johnson's work—and if you can find it convenient to let me have your list in exchange, I shall be the more your debtor—if that be possible.

I wish I knew how to tell you of the added charm which hangs about my collection of Hardy's works since my brief intercourse with you. The amphitheater lily bore its translation to a New Jersey climate with—I had almost said "heroic *hardi*hood"—but I refrain! Certainly it holds its own. . . .

Very sincerely yours,
MARGARET HAMILTON GANGEWER.

When Rebekah Owen replied to this letter, she not only sent her list of Hardy items "not in Mr. Lane's Bibliography," but also assured Mrs. Gangewer that she would send her other things— and would send them not from New York but from Hardy's own Dorset. For the Owens were already making plans for another trip to England. From Burlington came the following "priceless" letter, dated March 17, 1895. It is one that Emily Dickinson would have enjoyed and understood:

. . . As for the T.H.B.L. you'll find me as innocent as any sucking dove! You could afford to invite seven or eight of me into the ranks, and have never a goose-flesh over the possibly disastrous effect upon the bloom of your own laurels!

But it is not of this I am writing—rather, to hint that my appetite grows with what it feeds upon—that I haven't yet had half enough of you and Mr. Hardy, and that if you could induce yourself to look with favour upon my design, it would give me a vast pleasure to have you come to Burlington for a farewell teacup talk—and if you could arrange to spend the night, it would but augment my happiness. I am remote by only two hours, and if you'll think of it twice, I'm sure it might be compassed. Any day this week would offer itself, if you could accept it without thinking me a vampire with an unhallowed thirst for human blood! I should not promise not to bleed you, but the act would have no ulterior significance, simply genuine pleasure in going over a beloved soil with a sympathetic companion.

Many thanks for your list which I shall try to reach through the Philadelphia libraries, and in advance I make my grateful acknowledgments for the geological and conchological treasures which you promise to send. . . .

In the gloomy event of your finding it quite impossible to give me a day before you sail, may I not hope to have tidings of you when leisure and desire open the way? for I should be very loth to regard our intercourse thus far as only "A Mere Interlude."

Very sincerely yours,
MARGARET HAMILTON GANGEWER.

Rebekah, however, had no time just now to visit the banks of the Delaware. She had been away from Wessex for nearly sixteen months and was eager to return. "Oh, to be in England, now that April's there!" By April 14, the Owen sisters, accompanied by the ever-faithful Caroline Ash, were once again in Oxford. There Rebekah clipped the *Oxford Times* and read the further installments of *Jude* "on the spot." Before the month was over, they had learned a new way of seeing the Hardy landscapes. They experimented with the new craze for bicycling and found that they liked it. Catharine was now forty-four, but under the urging of the energetic thirty-seven-year-old Rebekah, she managed not only to learn to ride but even to achieve surprising distances. On April 29 they cycled to Woodstock and on the thirtieth to Yarnton.

Thomas Hardy was at this date in London, overwhelmed with proofs for the new collected "Uniform Edition" of his works which Osgood, McIlvaine & Co. were shortly to issue. Rebekah was to see marks of her own achievements in many a volume of this set of Hardy's Works.

A brief visit to Worcester to call on the widowed Mrs. Oliver gave Rebekah a chance to pick up in a bookshop there a copy of Annie Macdonell's *Thomas Hardy*. This little book had been published the preceding year but news of it had, apparently, not reached Rebekah in New York. It may, I think, be safely assumed that Miss Owen and Mrs. Gangewer continued to exchange comments and bibliographical information about their favorite author. While the Owens were still abroad, *The Chap-Book* (published by Stone & Kimball in Chicago) appeared with an article on Hardy in its issue for January 15, 1896. It was entitled "Without Prejudice" and signed by "I. Zangwill." This article (really a review of *Jude the Obscure*) found its way into Miss Owen's Hardiana and one may suspect Mrs. Gangewer's help in getting it there. In return, Rebekah may have been able to offer the Burlington lady a copy of a similarly obscure item: *The Eagle* for December, 1895. This was certainly *not* an item likely to become known to Hardy enthusiasts in America; it was "a Magazine supported by Members of St. John's College, Cambridge" [Wordsworth's old college], and the issue just referred to contained a long discussion of "Thomas Hardy" signed by A. H. T.—probably A. H. Thompson. Miss Owen spotted this little magazine, probably in Blackwell's bookshop at Oxford. Rebekah Owen's bibliographical services to future students of Hardy make a story in themselves.

Early in July the Owens went again to Dorchester. There, on July 11, they noticed an announcement in the *Dorset County Chronicle* that Higher Waterson Farm had been sold; the notice reminded Rebekah of the day when she had gone there and watched Mrs. Hardy make her sketch of "Bathsheba's house." Next there was a notice in the *Chronicle* about the Mayor and the Petty Sessions, which recalled the time when Rebekah had had to appear before the Mayor and identify the silver knife which Charlotte Stainer had stolen. Hardy was still absent from Dorchester and the Owens did not have to ask why. The newspapers explained. Arthur Waugh's "London Letter," dated July 18, 1895, printed in the New York *Critic* (which Rebekah had learned to read), told them that "Thomas Hardy is busily engaged upon the dramatization of *Tess*. It seems that the task is giving him a deal of trouble. .... It is clear that, for stage-purposes, the development [of the plot] must be considerably re-arranged." When Hardy had rented a flat in Westminster for the 1895 London season, he had—so it was reported—chosen one "in an adjoining block" to one occupied by the actress Mrs. Patrick Campbell. It was rumored that she was the one among a number of applicants that he had selected for the part of Tess. "If the play goes on," said the papers, "that may be convenient."

The play, however, did not go on, and Hardy eventually returned to Dorchester with a rejected manuscript. It was an old story—at least, he thought so. Some one *might* have come along to help him to a successful and profitable dramatization of his novel, but no one did come, because no one does. What was worse, Mrs. Campbell blamed *him* for her failure to get the part and never forgave him for the collapse of her efforts to appear as Tess.* The experience made Hardy all the more grateful, or at least *ought* to have made him all the more grateful, for a sympathetic and understanding reader like Rebekah Owen. "I spoke to Mr. Hardy," she recorded of one of her talks with him (presumably this summer), "of Tess's dreary life beyond the river Brit and her return through Chalk Newton. .... He said I was the only person, to his knowledge, who had seemed to notice, or take in, the wearing anxiety and growing despair of those days to her when her little stock of money was wasting."

That must have been music to Rebekah's ears. "I was the only person." There can, indeed, have been few readers of Hardy like her. To a New York friend, Mrs. Scott, Rebekah wrote the following involved but well-argued defense of *Tess:*

* For her subsequent visit to Dorchester on January 3, 1896, and for her purchase of one of the 225 copies of the Kelmscott Press edition of Rossetti's *Hand and Soul* which she presented to "Thomas Hardy from Beatrice Stella Campbell in dear remembrance, January, 1896," see the *Colby Library Quarterly* for January 1946, pages 201-208. The "dear remembrance" book is now in the Colby College Library, a close neighbor of Rebekah Owen's Hardiana.

You may bring up what heavy artillery you like to demolish *Tess;* in real life I dare say we should all cast stones at her for her first misfortune—unless she had been a married woman of high position and had done much worse—and though after the second [offence], which was in my opinion her first real fall, but to which I contend that circumstances and despair and even a sort of feeling of moral obligation* drove the poor girl, no one in actual life could call [such] a woman pure, I must yet hold Tess by the purging of her love and the expiation of her dreadful death to have attained such rank among the great and beloved heroines of tragedy as is given to Clarissa, Francesca, Lucrece, and Philomela.

R. O.

Rebekah thought well enough of this critical essay on *Tess* to transcribe it into her journal, and then, for her own eyes alone, she added:

Then too (this I did *not* send Mrs. Scott!) I hold that Tess was really purified—rarified, so to speak—by that first sorrow and humiliation, that the three years of shame and seclusion were years of development, and she came from that hiding into the light and new life and budding love at Talbothays as a hyacinth or lily springs the better and blossoms more exquisitely for being buried at first in ashes in a dark cellar. The lily could do this and bear no stain. A weed would die of the damp foul air, or but grow coarser when brought to the light. I can entirely understand Tess being a far nobler woman than she would have been, had she never fallen into Alec's hands.—As Mr. Hardy himself says, in *A Pair of Blue Eyes,* XIX, "There is nothing truer than that people who have always gone right don't know half as much about the nature and ways of going right as those who have gone wrong."

In August and September, the papers were full of notes and announcements about Mr. Hardy's collected works "in the Uniform Edition," for which the author had written a series of new prefaces. On September 21 a newspaper report of a child-suicide might have prepared Rebekah for the tragic episode in *Jude the Obscure* which was shortly to startle the world, but at the time she was busy with other things. If a note dated "Wareham, No-

* Her union with Clare must have seemed such a mere dream, her experience with Alec such an evident reality.—[Footnote by R. O.]

vember 10, 1895," is to be trusted, she remained in Dorset until that late in the year and visited "Anglebury" at that time. But the date of that note is probably an error. For the Owens seem to have returned to Oxford early in November, and on the fifth Rebekah cycled to Kidlington, on the eleventh to Abingdon, and on the eighteenth to Islip.

In Oxford Rebekah at last bought (for six shillings) a copy of *Jude the Obscure*. The book was dated "1896," but the notoriety of the serialized version of the story had created such a demand that the first edition was released two months before the copyright date of 1896 had arrived. For the first time in England, a Hardy novel was issued, in its First Edition, in one volume. Throughout the rest of November and December, almost every paper that Rebekah took up contained some comment on, or reminder of, *Jude the Obscure*. But to her it still seemed a novel of futility. She liked the descriptions of Oxford; the landscapes were inviting; but as a story—no! Back in America, not all the members of the T.H.B.L. were similarly repelled. Margaret Hamilton Gangewer gave her friend Grace Alexander McElroy, as a Christmas present, a copy of *Jude the Obscure*. Miss McElroy proceded to write in it a record of whatever she learned from "Miss Owen" about the book and its author.

On December 2 Rebekah enjoyed another bicycle trip to Woodstock, and on the seventh she again walked to Headington with her sister. On the twenty-third she visited Nuneham. Even the wintry months of January and February did not stop Rebekah's cycling. On February 17 she "biked" once again to Woodstock and back, and throughout March, April, and May, she lost no opportunity, even on Sundays, to explore "with cycle" the countryside which, by this time, she knew almost by heart. On March 31 she made the trip to Woodstock for a fourth time, to see the Duke and Duchess of Marlborough return to their "seat" at Blenheim Palace.

Meanwhile, Hardy too was affected by the cycling craze, and

even Mrs. Hardy, at the age of fifty-five took it up. The novelist reported that he had seen "the loveliest 'byke' for myself—the 'Rover Cob,'" and thought that he *must* have it.

The Bodleian Library and the bookshops of Oxford gave Rebekah an easy opportunity for seeing the Uniform Edition of Hardy's works, and for examining the new prefaces as they appeared from month to month. Every reader of this book will regret, as I do, that we lack her comment on the new edition of *The Mayor of Casterbridge;* but it is easy to imagine with what pleasure and satisfaction she found the goldfinch chapter restored to the text and was able to read in the new preface that

The present edition ... contains nearly a chapter which has never yet appeared in any English copy, though it was printed ... in the American version. The restoration was made at the instance of some good judges across the Atlantic who strongly represented that the home edition suffered from the omission.

"Some good judges across the Atlantic": *that* certainly gave Rebekah something to write Miss Drisler about; and how the T.H.B.L. could buzz now! And when *Wessex Tales* appeared in the new edition, what must Rebekah Owen have thought—or said—on discovering that Susannah (in "Interlopers at the Knap") had disappeared from the text and that a Rebekah had taken her place!

Well, if Mr. Hardy could make use of *her* name, she could make use of one of *his*. For some reason or other, Rebekah began shortening her name, not to "Becky," but to "Betty"—the name of the First of the Group of Noble Dames. From this time on, she inscribed her books "Betty Owen," and people eventually learned to call her Betty, Mrs. Hardy among them. "Tat" seems to have been the first person to call Rebekah Betty and it may well be that Catharine was responsible for her sister's acceptance of the name. As we have seen in a previous chapter, Catharine inscribed a book to "dear Betty" at the conclusion of their two years' idyll in Dorchester. Whether Catharine found any of Countess Betty's characteristics in Sister Rebekah we shall never know.

Meanwhile, let no one think that the readings aloud had come to an end. On March 15 an otherwise unknown Miss Pennell heard "The Three Strangers" read before the Owen fire, and in April "dear Tat and Ash" listened to one after another of the stories in *Life's Little Ironies.* When the Easter number of *Munsey's Magazine* appeared in America, some member of the T.H. B.L. promptly clipped "A Study for Elfride" and sent it to Rebekah. It found a place in her copy of *A Pair of Blue Eyes.*

Now that *Jude the Obscure* was in their hands in book form and its geography could be more easily studied, the Owens were glad to turn their bicycles in a new direction. On May 15 they cycled out the Wantage road, all the way to the region of Jude Fawley. There Rebekah took pictures of the Brown House, the well-curb, the church, and the village green—places in which Hardy had aroused their interest in spite of the gloom of the story. Remembering young Jude's experience in Chapter One, Miss Owen tried to drink from the well and found that it appeared "a shining disk," *exactly* as it is described in the novel. She reported this and similar experiences in the Jude country to the T.H.B.L. back home, and Grace McElroy promptly wrote it all down in her Christmas-gift copy of the book. For her own record Miss Owen was more specific, even though she wrote in telegraphic haste:

Cycled part of the way; then from "Alfredston" [Wantage] walked. Such a hill we had to climb! On top were Jude's milestone, where he cut the hand pointing toward "Christminster" [Oxford], and "Thither J.F.", and the Brown house whose roof he climbed to see Christminster. Thereabouts he and Vilbert met. Thereabouts he was often with Sue. Not quite a mile from there we passed the house where he lived with Arabella, and where the pig-sticking took place. ... Just there, I saw a cart track which I felt sure was the correct Jude one, leading across the hollow field

to Marygreen ... , all up-and-down rolling downs. Fawley, a pretty little place. Back by cart-track to Jude's and Arabella's house—quite a ruin.
An old bedstead still there.

In August the Owens once again took up their residence in
Dorchester. This time they found quarters at Albert Lodge, at
the corner of St. Helen's Road. They paid the usual calls on
Curator Moule, on the Bankes couple at Wolfeton House, and
on Miss Fetherstonhaugh at Moreton. The Hardys were away,
enjoying a much-needed vacation on the continent.

Miss Fetherstonhaugh wanted to know what Miss Owen
thought of Mr. Hardy's latest book. In October (1896) Rebekah wrote the following discriminating comment:

In *Jude* I think the rapidity of the movement obscures the motif, which is
therefore not so clear as the motif of *Tess*. Zola's book, *La Faute de l'Abbé
Mouret* [is] healthier than *Jude*, though more openly sensuous. Though
the hero dies, though the Priest goes on in his baffled ascetic life, one feels
that the tone of the book is sane and beneficent, that a great law of Nature
is exemplified and justified, and that the catastrophe of the tale comes about
because the hero tried to thwart it. One feels broader and wholesomer for
realizing that the universal impulse to love is a great and sacred law of life.
In *Jude* one feels nothing but the futility of all impulse, lofty or base.

This is an interesting illustration of Rebekah Owen's ability to
rise above the petty details of text in which her close study so
often involved her. She went through the novels word by word,
line by line; she wanted to know what each word and each line
meant. But she never allowed herself to be engulfed in an ocean
of triviality, and was always—as here in her comment on *Jude*
—able to scan the entire horizon, to take a broad view, to imitate Jude's own example in climbing to the roof of the Brown
house in order to see the beckoning spires of the distant City of
Light.

The readings went on through October: on the seventeenth,
"The Three Strangers"; on the nineteenth, "The Withered
Arm"; on the twenty-first, "The Distracted Preacher"; and on

the twenty-third, "The Melancholy Hussar." Every other day, as in many a college course, there was a Hardy assignment.

When Mr. and Mrs. Hardy got back from their trip to Belgium, the Owens promptly communicated with them. Among other questions, Rebekah asked whether Hardy would be willing to autograph some more of her books. Upon receiving his assurance that he would, she went on November 12 for another interesting call at Max Gate, carrying three of her volumes with her. *Jude* was not one of them. The omission was a small thing, but like the ear-ring in *A Pair of Blue Eyes*, it was enough; it served. Hardy noticed that *Jude the Obscure* was not one of the books brought for him to sign. Whether he asked "Why?" point-blank, or whether he merely lifted a quizzical eyebrow, is not clear; but Rebekah obviously felt herself on the defensive. Without indicating any enthusiasm for the story—for she was honest enough not to pretend—she could at least announce her ownership of a copy of *Jude*; and to prove the care with which she had read it, she proceeded to talk about some of the things she had noticed.

"Who was the prelate who apologized for the Church in Latin?"

"I declare, I cannot recollect!" Hardy replied.

"You make the policeman say 'What med you be up to?' Is that right? Would an Oxford policeman really say *med*? I fancy not."

"Berkshire people do," replied Hardy. "Perhaps this policeman was a Berkshire man! It is *med* there; *mid* here in Dorset."

Hardy then asked if *she* had noticed a discrepancy about which he had received numerous letters. "Every writer fancied himself the first to discover the error." On page 49 Jude "suddenly closed" his book and went out. On page 55, he returned, and "there lay his book open, just as he had left it"! Hardy laughed. He would have to change that. Betty Owen had to confess that she had not detected the contradiction. If she had read the book aloud, the point would doubtless have come to her notice. She said nothing to Hardy about her having read this one book of his in silence.

Hardy could not help sensing her displeasure with *Jude*, or at least the absence of her usual enthusiasm over what he had written. He remarked wryly that *Jude* had found at least one supporter. Only a week ago, the poet A. C. Swinburne had written him that "the tragedy [of Jude] is equally beautiful and terrible in its pathos. . . . There has been no such tragedy in fiction since Balzac died." Hardy showed Swinburne's letter to Miss Owen. She asked whether he would permit her to copy it. Hardy consented and supplied her with a sheet of Max Gate stationery. She thereupon copied out the letter. The second Mrs. Hardy afterwards printed it (in *The Later Years of Thomas Hardy*, p. 39) with the omission of the first sentence in the letter: "Thank you most sincerely for the gift of *Jude*."

Perhaps, after all this, Rebekah felt sorry that she had not brought her own copy of *Jude* along for Hardy to sign. She asked if she could bring it, or send it, later, and Hardy promised to sign it if she would get the book to him.

She was back at Max Gate on November 23, and again she brought a book for autographing. Hardy very "faithfully" affixed his signature in her copy of *Life's Little Ironies*, but again there was no *Jude*. In signing the *Ironies*, Hardy told Rebekah that he thought "The Son's Veto" was his best short story, and was taken aback when she frankly said she couldn't agree with him. "Mr. Hardy seemed surprised," she wrote later, "that I placed 'The Three Strangers' far above it, and above all his and other people's short stories." Miss Owen knew her own mind, and in this instance, at least, she was right and Hardy was wrong.

While making a call on Curator Moule, Rebekah learned from him of a passage in a book which would, she thought, help to illustrate her copy of *The Trumpet-Major*. She accordingly borrowed Moule's copy of *Memories and Traditions* by Lucy B. Horn (1806-1891) and made her transcript.

As the end of her stay in Dorchester approached, Miss Owen thought better of her unautographed *Jude the Obscure*. After all, it was by "the adored one." At the last minute, she tried to correct the omission and sent the book to Max Gate for Hardy's signature; but before it was returned, her date of departure arrived. On December 12, 1896, the Owens sailed from Southampton, again on the S.S. "Paris." They arrived home shortly before Christmas. Hardy took his time about signing the copy of *Jude*, but at last he added his name to the frontispiece and on January 10, 1897, dispatched the book to "Miss Betty Owen, 26 West 25th Street, New York."

What he did *not* send her was a copy of the poem he had just written. It bore the revealing title:

To a Lady
Offended by a Book of the Writer's

Now that my page is exiled,—doomed, maybe
　　Never to press thy cosy cushions more,
　　Or wake thy ready Yeas as heretofore,
Or stir thy gentle vows of faith in me:
Knowing thy natural receptivity,
　　I figure that, as flambeaux banish eve,
　　My sombre image, warped by insidious heave
Of those less forthright, must lose place in thee.

So be it. I have borne such. Let thy dreams
　　Of me and mine diminish day by day,
　　　　And yield their space to shine of smugger things;
Till I shape to thee but in fitful gleams,
　　And then in far and feeble visitings,
　　And then surcease. Truth will be truth alway.

When Betty Owen received her copy of *Jude*, she had no knowledge that this sonnet had been written. But if she had been able to look over Hardy's shoulder as he sat at his desk, and had been able to see him write the words "Let thy dreams of me and mine diminish . . . and then surcease," she would perhaps have been startled, perhaps have been incredulous. Doubtless vanity would have prevented her thinking that her own doom was sealed. But it was. Not that her immediate extinction as a welcome guest at Max Gate was decided on, but the decline and fall of her friendship was but a matter of time. In thought, if not to her face, Hardy had called her smug. She was later to call him by a much harsher name.

Knowing nothing of all this, Rebekah Owen doubtless had a happier Christmas. She must have been welcomed by all the members of the T.H.B.L. and must have received with pleasure their half-envious congratulations on her "honorable mention" in the new preface to *The Mayor of Casterbridge*, with its public even though anonymous recognition of her as one of the "good judges across the Atlantic."

Chapter VII

"Cheek by Jowl to Max Gate"

A S soon as Rebekah received her copy of *Jude* enriched with the autograph of its Distinguished Author, she performed a characteristic act: she sent Hardy a gift to show her appreciation of his kindness in signing the book and mailing it back to her. She bought some little trees and shipped them to Max Gate. Hardy's reply, however welcome it may have been to Rebekah, cannot be called effusive. He sent a post-card which read:

> MAX GATE, DORCHESTER
> Feb. 15. 97
>
> Have planted little trees, which arrived uninjured. Many thanks.
>
> T. H.

The card was postmarked "Feb. 17," two days after it had been written; and, for some reason or other, there was a further delay in its delivery, once it had reached New York. Rebekah also sent another little present to Dorchester—a gift of appreciation to "Margie" Moule for providing storage for a bicycle during its owner's absence from England. For Rebekah was sure she would return and would want her bicycle again. Miss Moule, like Hardy, wrote in reply, but she sent a letter, not a card:

> Trinity Street, Dorchester,
> Feb. 5, 1897.
>
> My dear Betty,
> Very many thanks. . . . Your bicycle is flourishing in its private apartment! Now what would you like to hear about next? The Hardys, I should think!
> Just before Christmas Father and I walked over and found them both "to hum" and very agreeable, nay affectionate on Mrs. H's part. I devoted myself to her and let Thomas severely alone for a change. I thought

it would be a pleasing variety as he is so much "made of." When we arose to depart, however, he addressed me and was very gracious and said how long it was since we had met. I did *not* rejoin as Mother once gaily did to someone else: "Oh! do you think so? It doesn't seem long to me!!" ...

MARGARET E. MOULE.

By the time these communications reached Rebekah Owen, Thomas Hardy was being advertised in New York in a new manner. On Tuesday, March 2, 1897, Mrs. Minnie Maddern Fiske opened, at the Fifth Avenue Theatre, a dramatization of *Tess of the D'Urbervilles* by Lorimer Stoddard. Catharine and Rebekah were present on the opening night.

I do not know how much information the Owens had brought back from England with them about the complicated attempts in which Hardy had been involved, in trying to get *Tess* onto the London stage. Probably Hardy had told them very little, perhaps nothing at all. He knew how to keep his mouth shut. But the plan that involved Mrs. Patrick Campbell had fallen through —chiefly because Forbes-Robertson did not like Hardy's manuscript and proposed reshaping this attempt at a dramatic adaptation of the novel. Hardy thereupon gave Harper & Brothers permission to arrange for an independent American dramatization, even if that involved a modification—"a reasonable modification"—of his own version. A contract was accordingly signed with Mrs. Fiske and she in turn called on Lorimer Stoddard, the thirty-three-year-old son of Richard Henry Stoddard, to write the script. Stoddard was a fast worker. He wrote his play in five days, between a Friday noon and the following Wednesday night. A copy was rushed to England, so that Hardy could copyright the play there; and on the morning of the same day on which the Owen sisters went to see Mrs. Fiske at the Fifth Avenue Theatre in New York, Hardy and two or three friends went to the St. James's Theatre in London and carried through the farcical procedure by which George Alexander, manager of the London theatre, gave a "private performance" and thus helped

Hardy, at a price, retain his copyright. It proved to be a valuable piece of property.

Catharine and Rebekah Owen were delighted with the play. So were the critics. "It is one of the most pregnant happenings of recent years," declared the *New York Journal;* "it is revolutionary." William Dean Howells (with whom Rebekah Owen was later on to have some correspondence) wrote the play up for *Harper's Weekly* (March 20, 1897). Rebekah herself clipped the *New York Tribune's* account of the opening night's performance and tucked it into her copy of *Tess.* In addition to the praise which almost all the critics were heaping upon Mrs. Fiske— "marvellous," "wonderful," "her acting was perfect,"—the Owens had high praise also for Annie Irish, the actress "who did Marian so well." As soon as Rebekah could compose a proper report, she sent a detailed account of Mrs. Fiske's performance to Thomas Hardy, and she could not possibly have done anything so certain to interest him and dispose him to unwonted action as this. Result: for the first time he wrote her a letter, a long letter (long for him); it was addressed to "Miss Betty Owen."

MAX GATE, DORCHESTER.
March 16. 1897

Dear Miss Owen:

I received on Sunday [14th] your interesting letter and its vivid description of the first night of the play. It was really kind of you to go, and still more kind to put yourself to the trouble of sending me such a full report. You may well imagine that, though I have not taken very kindly to the idea of having the story dramatized at all [that is, by any one other than myself!], I was much entertained, as my wife was also, by your account of how it was done, since it had really been accomplished.

Mrs. Fiske seems to be a clever and energetic woman, to whom much credit is due for her persistence in bringing out the play and for the fervour with which she has thrown herself into it. Did you notice whether her intonation was sufficiently near the English to pass on the stage here as that of an English girl without seeming discordant to London ears, in case she should bring the play to England?

I am sorry you had a difficulty about the post card. We send our united

kind regards to you and your sister; and with renewed thanks believe me,
Sincerely yours
THOMAS HARDY.

This was one letter which Rebekah did *not* tuck into a book. It was too precious for that. Other additions to her Hardiana came from other sources. On April 10 a package arrived from Mrs. Allen H. Gangewer of Burlington, New Jersey. It was addressed to Catharine Owen. On opening the package, she found some flowers and a book. A card which was enclosed read: "The violets for Miss Owen, and the book for Miss Rebekah, in grateful memory of many happy hours." The book was a copy of *Desperate Remedies*, in which Rebekah wrote: "Betty Owen from M.H.G." (i.e., Margaret Hamilton Gangewer). It would appear that neither sister had previously known this early anonymous production of their novelist. They now read it, but not aloud. It was obviously not to their taste, and whenever a book was not to their taste they wasted little time on it. They made no notes in *Desperate Remedies* and wrote no comments upon it.

The title of the book had, however, a certain timeliness and pertinence. New York had become less and less attractive to the Owen sisters. It seemed noisier than ever, each time that they returned from England. The streets were busier, the traffic thicker and thicker, and life on West Twenty-fifth Street had become so unalluring as to demand desperate remedies indeed. The duration of their stays in their native city had of late become shorter and shorter, and in spite of the satisfaction that Rebekah—and Catharine too—must have found in the "many happy hours" spent with the members of the T.H.B.L., their hearts were really in England. Why not go and *stay* there? Why involve themselves with the expense of frequent ocean-crossings and the difficulties of looking after property in New York City during prolonged absences abroad? Why not sell the house near Madison Square and cut the American anchor? Before the end of 1897, that is exactly what the Owens decided to do. Old Professor

Drisler had just died and Mary Drisler promptly set about disposing of the home on Forty-sixth Street. The Owen house on Twenty-fifth Street was now even less attractive as a place of residence.

Meanwhile the contacts with Hardy books continued. "Betty" had subscribed to the *Dorset County Chronicle*. In September she noticed in this newspaper an announcement of the marriage at St. Peter's Church, in Dorchester, of "Mr. Shiner." It reminded her of Dick Shiner in *Under the Greenwood Tree*. In November she clipped a picture from *Country Life* to illustrate the heath-cropping ponies in *The Return of the Native*. There was, however, rather little time left just now for reading. The sale of the old home meant moving everything—all the familiar books, the pictures, the furniture, the accumulation of old magazines in the attic—everything had to be crated or sold or destroyed. The reader will doubtless approve of our drawing the curtain on the enactment of this dusty scene, and of not raising the curtain again until the actors have arrived in the land of heart's desire—back in Wessex.

Having cut their American cables, Catharine and Rebekah Owen crossed the Atlantic for the last time in the Spring of 1898. I judge that, on their arrival in England, they headed as usual for Oxford; but one cannot be sure, because the books and papers which usually carry the record of Betty's peregrinations fail us here. Rebekah of course wanted to reside in the Hardy country, in Dorchester or near it. But she knew enough about "Casterbridge" to know that a suitable dwelling would be hard to find. Thomas Hardy himself had learned that fact fifteen years earlier. He had looked diligently for a place in which to live and finally had to give it up and build his own house. The construction of brick or stone residences in England was (and is) a very different thing from the building of wooden houses in America: Rebekah was well aware of that fact. While residing at Oxford (or elsewhere), she appealed to Curator Moule for help and he replied on July 27, 1898, that possibly Upwey Manor House could be rented. Betty's spirits rose.

Mr. Moule, however, had apparently written without having seen the place, for a few days later he wrote again: "Dear Miss Rebekah: I don't think that there is any chance of your liking it as an abode." He had been to see the house; it had "very low rooms," and he was now sure it would not suit. Betty and "Tat" decided that they had better see for themselves, so to Dorchester they went. This gave Rebekah a chance to reclaim her bicycle from the storage the Moules had been giving it. Rebekah also had a chance to talk with Hardy, but he was of very little help in house-hunting. Mrs. Hardy had learned of old what a "chore" Thomas made out of the annual Spring search for a flat in London, and what an unhappy choice he often made. Rebekah did, however, pick up from Hardy one idea, the fact that real estate was often advertised in certain magazines and newspapers; and she carried off from Max Gate, on loan, a paper listing some "possibilities" that might be investigated. The summer went by, however, with no results. The only other harvest from the visit to Dorchester was a trip to the churchyard at Stinsford, where Betty photographed the graves of Hardy's grandfather and grandmother.

While waiting like Micawber for something to turn up, the Owens decided to have another look at the Lake District. So, taking their bicycles with them, they returned to Coniston and from that lovely spot Betty wrote, in the middle of September, to return the paper she had borrowed from Hardy. She also reported that an accident to her bicycle had, for the moment, prevented any touring among the Lakes. Hardy replied:

MAX GATE, DORCHESTER.
20. 9. 98 [i.e., September 20, 1898]

Dear Miss Owen:

Many thanks for the return of the paper. Would that all borrowers were so conscientious. I hope that, with the exception of the mishap to the bicycle, your return to Coniston has been delightful.

Yours sincerely

T. HARDY.

In reply, Rebekah wrote a letter consulting his opinion of the relative merits of two houses which the Owens were considering. She also made some reference to *Tillotson's Journal* (or some such title), which she had apparently borrowed from Hardy. On October 13 he addressed another postcard to "Miss Betty Owen" at Coniston:

Just one line before going out, to acknowledge receipt of kind letter. Keep *T.J.* till read. As for the houses, I should say the *second*—but can't advise!

T. H.

Miss Owen wrote also to other friends in England. From Mrs. Norah E. Bartlett, daughter of the Stinsford Church parish clerk, she received a note dated October 20, 1898: "I am delighted to think that you expect to live in England. I hope you will find a nice house that will suit you."

Betty was at least still trying! Even while sojourning among the Lakes, she still nursed the fond hope that she would be able to find a house in the Hardy country. Signing herself "X., Coniston, Lancashire," she advertised in the *Dorset County Chronicle* on October 20, 1898, for an "Unfurnished or Partly Furnished HOUSE within 5 miles [of] Dorchester." The advertisement produced no results, and the Owens continued in their Coniston lodgings. Thus the months dragged by.

Fortunately the post office enabled Rebekah to maintain a contact with the outside world. When the magazines and newspapers made references to Hardy's latest (and, as it turned out, his last) work of fiction, she was able to order a copy of *The Well-Beloved*, issued in London the previous year by Osgood, McIlvaine & Co. She thus acquired another Hardy First Edition. In reading it, *not* aloud, she was moved to make just one note. The very solitude of this note, on page 237 of Rebekah's copy, gives it all the more significance. In reference to Hardy's statement that Avice the Third "wore a large-disked sun-hat," Miss Owen wrote: "like Sue Bridehead. See *Jude* [II, 1]."

These two passages invite our attention for a moment. In *The Well-Beloved* the hat is described as having "a brim like a wheel whose spokes were radiating folds of muslin lining the brim." In *Jude the Obscure*, Hardy had written that Jude had one day observed "the photograph of a pretty girlish face, in a broad hat, with radiant folds under the brim like the rays of a halo. . . . It haunted him. . . ." The similarity between Sue's hat and Avice's hat is quite in keeping with Hardy's habits of repetition. He had done that sort of thing before. In the opening chapter of *The Return of the Native* he had written the simile: "like the parting-line on a head of black hair," and ten years later, in the opening chapter of *The Woodlanders* (serial version), he had used exactly the same figure of speech. In writing a review of Barnes's *Poems* in 1879, Hardy had written a description of "the beautiful Vale of Blackmoor"; eight years later he repeated the description in an article in *The Athenaeum*, and five years after that, he copied it for its third appearance, in Chapter II of *Tess of the D'Urbervilles*. No, Hardy was not averse to repeating himself. Rebekah Owen's close reading of his texts had acquainted her with many of his habits of composition. But that is not the chief point here. In addition to Betty's notice of the similarity of the two hats, there is the startling fact that, laid in at page 92 of her copy of *Jude the Obscure*, there is a picture of Rebekah Owen herself, identified and dated 1879. The photograph shows "a pretty girlish face, in a broad hat," with "radiating folds of muslin," "like the rays of a halo." Both descriptions were written by Hardy after he had become acquainted with Miss Owen. Had he seen this photograph of her "pretty girlish face in a broad hat"? Had it haunted him, in the way Sue's photograph haunted Jude? The suggestion is rendered less improbable by the evidence found elsewhere in Hardy's writings of his indebtedness to Rebekah Owen, and also by the evidence found among *her* papers that photographs were, on at least one occasion, the subject of discussion at Max Gate. The first portrait of Hardy published in America showed him with a beard, but when Rebekah Owen saw him for the first time, in August, 1892, the beard had disappeared. Inquiry of Mrs. Hardy would have produced the information that Hardy had shaved off the beard only the year before; Mrs. Hardy herself had never seen him without a beard until then—except, of course, in photographs taken when he was quite young. Whereupon she (or he?) produced one, showing Hardy at the age of twenty-one. The second Mrs. Hardy reproduced this same picture, many years later, at page 46 of *The Early Life*. But Betty Owen had seen this same photograph long before. She had sketched a small copy of it to insert in one of her books. It makes one wonder all the more whether a picture of herself, also at age twenty-one, was produced by her for Hardy's viewing at this same time. In any case, there the photo is, at the appropriate place in *Jude*. And "it haunted him."

After Miss Owen had bought, and read without enthusiasm, her copy of *The Well-Beloved*, she noticed in Osgood, McIlvaine's list of the titles now available in the new Uniform Edition of Hardy's works one title—*A Laodicean*—that was new to her. The novel itself was not new: it had, in fact, been before the public for seventeen years; but it was, clearly enough, not one of Hardy's successes. Miss Owen of course knew that there is always a reason for neglect and that it is usually a good reason; but she had, long before this, reached the point in her devotion to Thomas Hardy at which his mediocre or even his inferior work interested her. She therefore wrote to London and ordered a copy of *A Laodicean*. By this time Harper & Brothers had taken over the business of Osgood, McIlvaine—Osgood having died (as we have seen in Chapter IV)—and the copy which Betty received from London bears the 1898 Harper imprint instead of the ear-

lier 1896 Osgood mark. When the book finally reached Coniston, Miss Owen had other things to claim her attention—more
immediate and more pressing things—and *A Laodicean* was put
aside without being read at all.

In December Rebekah bought a copy of Hardy's *Wessex Poems*
and had the new experience of finding out that her novelist was
also a poet. The reader of the present book will want to know
what Rebekah thought of the sonnet "To a Lady Offended by a
Book of the Writer's." Alas, all that can be told with any certainty is that *Wessex Poems* reached Betty Owen's hands just a
week before Christmas, that she noticed the title of the poem
"To a Lady" in the table of contents, and that she wrote something under it. But the words are now illegible, and I shall not
risk making any guess about what the words may have been.
What *can* be reported is that Rebekah took Hardy's first venture
as a poet quite seriously: she studied the poems with her usual
care, she listed some thirty-six titles among them, and early in
1899 she wrote him a letter about them.

When, after a reasonable time, no reply came from the poet,
Rebekah wrote again, telling Hardy that she was (in the American phrase) "mad at him" for not replying. She told him also
that they—the Owen sisters—had at last settled upon a house
and would move into it just as soon as they could get some modern plumbing installed. The house was situated between Hawkshead and Ambleside, and only four miles from Coniston. But
the chief point Rebekah made in her letter was one that went
straight to Hardy's heart. Nothing, absolutely nothing, could
have pleased him more than Rebekah's comment on his poetry.
We have independent evidence of this fact. Eighteen months
after Rebekah wrote her letter, Professor William Lyon Phelps
turned up at the door of Max Gate. He has left us his report on
what he and Hardy talked about, and on what Hardy obviously
wanted to talk about (in Phelps's *Autobiography*, page 391):

He asked me what I thought of his poetry. .... I wish I had then liked the poems as I do now. I could not believe they stood so much higher than the novels in his own estimation, that they were so close to his heart. .... He spoke quite strongly about this. He thought they were far superior to any of his novels and that many of his more discerning friends had told him so. .... He wished to be considered and remembered only as a poet.

One would like to know whether, in talking to Professor Phelps, Hardy included among "his more discerning friends" the American lady who had recently written him about his poems. For Rebekah Owen had waxed enthusiastic over the glowing emotion which she found in his verses—a warmth and fervor which so delighted her that she was, she said, quite ready to forgive him for not answering her previous letter.

Her own cordiality so thawed the ice in Hardy's pen that he wrote her the longest letter she ever received from him—four holograph pages which he mailed to "Miss B. Owen" on Valentine Day:

MAX GATE, DORCHESTER.

14. 2. 99 [i.e., February 14 ,1899]

Dear Miss Owen:

I should be a more uncivil and neglectful person than I am at the worst times if I did not reply to such a pleasant letter as your last, with its flattering opinion of the *Wessex Poems*. With regard to the previous one, I am hopelessly guilty, and you were quite within the bounds of reason when you were "mad" with me (we use that excellent expression here, too, with great success). One small extenuating fact was that the residence question was puzzling. That you have settled where you have is doubtless best, but Dorset would have found you a nook, I am quite sure, if you had had patience.

Perhaps your own vivid imagination warmed up the verses to a glow they had not naturally: though it is a fact that all poetry must be met half way by the reader, and not treated as a critic boasted in one of the reviews that he had treated mine—read it before breakfast on a cold dismal morning—to arrive at a true judgment!

You ask me to mention some reviews. I remember a few—one in *The Bookman* for Feb. (a sixpenny monthly)—another in *The Outlook* for Jan.

28. (a 3d weekly)—one in the *Saturday* [*Review*], Jan. 7, giving me a set down (It goes without saying that the last was written by a fool or knave—authors all know that, in such cases). Also one in *The Academy*, &c. I regret I have no copy of either to send you.

I pity you in the operation of plumbing: you should learn to do a little yourself. A London physician told me he learnt, and saves pounds annually now, plumbers being the most expensive workmen of any.

My kind regards to your sister, and with best wishes I am,

Sincerely yours

T. HARDY.

This letter shows that by February, 1899, the Owens had been at last able to make up their minds. With the help of a local young man named William Heelis, they had finally (even though, in Hardy's eyes, impatiently) brought their search for a house to a conclusion. Heelis was a member of a firm of Hawkshead-and-Ambleside solicitors, W. Heelis & Sons, who had dealt with property transfers and other legal affairs of the Lake District for two generations. We are to hear more about Mr. Heelis in a later chapter of this book. With his help, then, early in 1899, Catharine and Rebekah Owen became joint tenants of Belmount Hall, Outgate, Ambleside, Westmorland. Some years later, Rebekah bought the property and retained possession of it until 1937.

It was a large, old, stone dwelling, with high-ceilinged rooms. It faced south and had fourteen large windows which took full advantage of this southern exposure. There were stables nearby, and a large, high-walled garden where flowers and vegetables were well protected from the cold winds that often blew in from off the ocean or the Irish Sea. "Ambleside" was the post-office address, but the "Hall" was nearer to Hawkshead than to Ambleside—in fact, it was within easy walking distance of Wordsworth's old school at Hawkshead. Belmount was well named, for it was situated on a fine rise overlooking the whole vale of Esthwaite. The position of Belmount Hall is indicated on the

map of the Lake District in the 1930 edition of Muirhead's Blue
Guide to *England*.

Once they were installed in their new abode, the Owens were
delighted with the place. They moved thither from Coniston at
a time of year when wintry blasts were over, and when the abun-
dance of daffodils and other spring flowers gave them great joy.
Then came the trunks and boxes and crates from America; and
by the time that the familiar books had been put on the shelves,
and Daniel Huntingdon's oil painting of "Roman Charity" had
been hung over the chimney-piece in the drawing room, and
some of their New York furniture had been uncrated and put in
place, the Owens were able to look about them and call it good.
The Hardy books were placed in a fine old Sheraton bookcase
in the large drawing-room to the right of the front door. But
just as soon as the house had been put in order, the Owens left
it! For Betty's heart was still in "Casterbridge" and she would
not be satisfied until Mr. and Mrs. Thomas Hardy had been invited to visit her and "Tat" in Belmount Hall. A written invitation would not do, so off to Dorset they went. For the past sev-
en or eight years, whenever the Owens were not in New York,
August had been a favorite time for making a pilgrimage to
Dorchester, and this year there was a special reason for going.

At Max Gate, then, Catharine and Rebekah extended their
invitation to the Hardys to come and visit them, now that they
had a home of their own in England. And to Max Gate "Betty"
carried her copies of *The Well-Beloved* and *A Laodicean*, her mail-
order harvest from those recent months of waiting in Coniston.
In both these books Hardy wrote his name. He apparently remarked to Betty that *A Laodicean* was not worth reading; it had
been composed when he was seriously ill and much of it was dictated to Mrs. Hardy from his sick-bed. It was a book he was not
proud of; the manuscript of this book was the only one he had
ever destroyed. Rebekah took the author's advice and never read

the book. She never even cut the leaves open. They remain uncut to this day. The only mark of writing in the book is on the title-page; it reads: "Yours truly Thomas Hardy."

Upon their return to Westmorland, the Owens busied themselves with beautifying the grounds at Belmount Hall. After a while, Catharine wrote to Mrs. Hardy, repeating the invitation to pay them a visit, if not this Fall, then next Spring. She explained the best railway connections, and assured the Hardys that they would not find the trip north an arduous one. For some time no answer came, but "Tat" at last received the following letter:

MAX GATE, DORCHESTER.
Sept. 12, '99.

Dear Miss Owen,

It is very kind of you to renew your invitation, and if we had been accepting two others lying [in] your direction—and beyond, we certainly should have been delighted to accept it. But we have declined all for this year; and as for the Spring, we are much too uncertain in our movements to plan so far ahead, and especially to promise—as so many of our friends do—but we are erratically-minded and *actioned!* rushing off, when it occurs to us to be quite easy and nice, every way. Thank you many times over, for showing us the best way to come, and trying to make us feel that it is not troublesome at all, but to us the journey seems *great.*

I am kept home by having my nephew and niece, on a long visit, and household affairs are rather pressing. The latter enjoys going to parties, and we have been therefore somewhat lively in that way, lately, at home, and elsewhere. The days fly by, and the hot weather is enjoyable, but exhausting. T.H. is content to journey with his bicycle [he was then 59!] and is off this week to a house-party which he will meet at Stonehenge. He is not very strong just at present. He desires me to thank you, for him.

Now I must apologize for delay in replying, "nothing extenuating." I am a procrastinator, I know, and it is very bad of me; but I really have had every minute occupied, and letters have been a pressing business as well as other matters. Perhaps you may like to read a letter I wrote some days ago which appeared in the *Daily Chronicle.* Ask "Betty" if she likes Blake's "Tiger" and feels my disgust at Exhibitions of wild animals. The letter came under the Bull-Fights—a propos, so they inserted it.

We have been having tea out of doors almost ever since we returned from London and have decorated our middle lawn, quite finely for us. I know your place is just exquisite and the feeling which prompts you, as it does me, to have others to enjoy things; and I am thinking of those spring flowers you and your sister tell me of.

With kindest regards,

Yours very sincerely

E. L. HARDY.

I do not know whether the Owens saw the London *Daily Chronicle*, and Mrs. Hardy's vague reference to "some days ago" would not give much help in ordering or searching for a copy. But doubtless other papers too had carried comments on the Bull-Fights mentioned by Mrs. Hardy. They were held at Boulogne-sur-Mer, on the French coast; the first fight was on Tuesday, September 3, and the second on Sunday the eighth. A steamer carried many English excursionists from Brighton, and it was this British participation in the brutal sport that led the *Daily Chronicle* to publish an article on the subject. Many readers wrote their views, and among those that got published was the letter of Mrs. Hardy. It appeared in the issue for September 8, 1899:

Many Englishwomen must have felt a painful shock on learning that a thousand English men and women could so far forget their English birth and breeding as to go to the disgusting spectacle at Boulogne. Can it be found out who were the English men and women who have thus trailed our national reputation in the dirt, that decent people may keep clear of them?

—An Old-Fashioned Englishwoman.

The months rolled by, and gave the Owen sisters abundant opportunity to discover that Belmount was indeed different from Madison Square. Life was very quiet in the Vale of Esthwaite. When Rebekah couldn't get what she wanted in Hawkshead or in Coniston, she knew what friend to write to. When she learned that some paper or other had printed a new Christmas Eve poem by her author, she wrote to Margaret Moule for help, and in time "Margie" ran the poem to earth. On March 10, 1900, she addressed a card to Betty at Belmount Hall, copying Hardy's

"A Christmas Ghost-Story" from the *Westminster Gazette* for December 23, 1899, and saying: "I expect [*sic*] these are the lines you wanted."

The New Year brought renewed invitations to Belmount Hall, and if the Hardys did not accept, the Moules did. Curator H. J. Moule, Mrs. Moule, and Margie visited the Owens late in May or early in June. They enjoyed a picnic at nearby Tarn Haws, where Betty took pictures of them all. On Hardy's sixtieth birthday, June 2, 1900, the Moules and the Owens joined in sending him a congratulatory telegram. Hardy knew them all well enough to pick out the ring-leader. It was to "Miss Betty Owen" that he addressed this reply:

THE ATHENAEUM,
PALL MALL [LONDON] S. W.
5. 6. 1900 [i.e., June 5, 1900]

Dear Miss Owen:

A telegram expressing good wishes, which reached me on my birthday, and which bore the somewhat cryptic signature of "Owen Moule," may possibly have hailed in part from you, dated as it was from Hawkshead. If so, many thanks, both to yourself and "Moule" for your remembrance of me. If otherwise, please thank him, her, or them when you see the same, since he, she, or they must be in your neighbourhood.

We are suddenly plunged into warm weather here, and to make us warmer there is news of the entry [of the British troops under Lord Roberts] into [the Transvaal capital in South Africa,] Pretoria.

No doubt your estate is looking leafy now; Dorset was when I left it. With kind regards, I am,

Yours sincerely
THOMAS HARDY.

A month later, when Harpers announced a new London edition of *Tess*—a cheap six-penny edition in paper covers—Rebekah promptly got a copy and on July 25, 1900, wrote her name on it, adding, no doubt with pride, "Belmount Hall."

If, however, Mohammed wouldn't come to the Mountain, the Mountain would have to go to Mohammed. The residents of the Mountain-and-lake District would have to go to Wessex. In October, Betty Owen wrote to Mrs. Hardy to say that she and Catharine were planning to come south and would hope to see her (and of course Mr. Hardy) in Dorchester. Weeks went by but no answer came from Mrs. Hardy. Rebekah wrote again, and on November 9 Hardy himself sent this explanatory postcard:

> MAX GATE,
> DORCHESTER.
> Nov 9, 1900
>
> Mrs. H. has returned today from a month's absence with sick relative, which will account for her silence. She is rather broken down, but will reply to your letter as soon as possible. We shall be glad to see you and sister when you come.
> T. H.

At the last minute, however, Caroline Ash (now eighty years old) was taken sick and could not leave Belmount Hall. Catharine stayed behind to look out for her old nurse, and for the first time Rebekah went to Dorchester alone. Upon her arrival, she put up at the Antelope Hotel, where Lucetta (in *The Mayor of Casterbridge*) had stopped. Doubtless to her surprise, and probably to her keen enjoyment, Rebekah shortly found herself provided with an unexpected opportunity to imitate Lucetta in other ways as well. Mrs. Hardy was not at home, but her young niece Lillian Gifford was there, and Max Gate proved to be a very different place with Madame away. Nor was Max Gate the only house where Rebekah found herself not at all far from the madding crowd. She was invited everywhere by the host of friends who were delighted to have the vivacious American lady back in their midst again.

"Ashy's" sickness has proved a boon for us modern readers who are interested in getting a vivid impression of Rebekah Owen in action. If Miss Ash had been well enough to accompany Rebekah, the story of the latter's doings would have been told Miss Ash orally. But because "Ashy" had had to stay behind at Belmount Hall, Betty wrote her a long, chatty letter—one writ-

ten on the installment plan—and it survives to give us a picture
of what went on in Dorchester in November, 1900. Not until
Thursday, the twenty-second, did Rebekah find time to tell her
story. Then, from the Antelope Hotel, she wrote:

"It is a crime to be in[doors] a moment this heavenly mild
brilliant day, but I want to consume a little time before meeting
the adored one at Max Gate for a walk. . . . I have just met Mrs.
Moule and left her in fits of laughter, saying she should write to
my sister that I was not to be trusted. . . . Mrs. Sheridan [met on
a previous occasion at Max Gate] has invited me out to Frampton Court again. . . . She seemed very glad to see me, and so was
Mr. Hardy. He says it must agree with me in the North, I look
so well. . . . Mrs. Sheridan and Mr. Hardy so wish we had [set-
tled] or would yet settle in Dorset. My pink waistcoat, hat and
long coat are much admired. The roads are dry and good here. I
shall borrow a skirt from Miss Moule and try cycling. Mr. Hardy wants me to. Mrs. Hardy is away, and the little niece is to
chaperon me! . . . [Later, that same night:] Just there a parcel
came from Miss Moule, containing two skirts. I put on one, liked
myself in it amazingly, hired a bicycle and went off to Max Gate.
Mr. Hardy, Miss Gifford and I then biked by way of Came Park
and Herringstone . . . to the Weymouth Road, to the top of the
Ridgeway Hill, which I got up and they did not. [Rebekah was
then 42; Hardy was 60!] Two ladies stood watching me do it.
Then we spun back down it like anything. . . . I left my bike in
South St. (it only cost one shilling) and hurried out after them
to Max Gate to tea, and again Mr. Hardy walked home with
me. . . . To-morrow Mr. Hardy goes to Frampton if [it is] fine,
so I hope to visit Whitaker [at Stinsford]. . . . I *love* cycling here.
. . . I hardly dare think how I am enjoying myself. . . . Mr. Har-
dy is too funny over his cats, [as] bad as we [are] about the dogs.
. . . Mr. Hardy says I look exactly the same. . . . Friday noon
[November 23]: . . . It is a draggly dirty day . . . and I fear Mr.
Hardy won't go to Frampton to-day but [will] put it off till to-

morrow and so I shall lose my ride with him and niece. . . . So far I have enjoyed myself hugely since I came here. I don't think Hawkshead would know me. I am so lively and make people laugh so. . . . Dorset people are so *pleasant* as well as of superior birth and fashion, to Lake District people, . . . but I should be sorry to live in or near the town in a small place, unless cheek by jowl to Max Gate."

At the same time that Rebekah was writing the above letter to "dear Ashy," Mrs. Sara Clapcott, of South Walk, Dorchester, was addressing a note to "Dear Miss Owen":

We have only this morning heard that you are in Dorchester. *Do* give us the pleasure of seeing you. . . . We only wish your sister were also with you and are sorry to learn from Miss Moule that your old Nurse's illness keeps her at home.

Rebekah's fears that she would lose her bike ride with Hardy were borne out when she received the following note from Mrs. Hardy's niece:

MAX GATE, DORCHESTER.

23rd Nov: [1900]

Dear Miss Owen:

My uncle finds he will be unable to cycle to-morrow, but will be glad to see you here to tea. I shall be delighted, if [it is] fine, to cycle a shorter distance with you, and bring you back. Will you come about 2 o'clock if this is agreeable.

Your sincerely

L. GIFFORD.

Rebekah found it "agreeable" and thus paid another visit to Max Gate. Her record for Saturday, November 24, 1900, reads:

"Mr. Hardy wrote in my books and carried one of them home for me. We looked over *Wessex Poems* together. I think he said that Swinburne rated his three best poems thus: 1st. Friends Beyond. 2nd. The Dance at the Phoenix. 3. In a Wood. . . . Swinburne also much liked the picture of Leipzig. I said I liked 'Middle-Age Enthusiasms' very much. He said he liked it himself but that no one else had said so. A lady, very intellectual, liked 'Thoughts of Phena' best. I like it but not so much as 'Middle-Age Enthusiasms' or 'In an Inn.' I showed him lines which showed Browning's and James Thomson's influence. He admitted it, then said What an advantage it was to be Shakespeare, who borrowed where he liked from men long since forgotten."

On November 24, then, the author signed his name—"Yours truly, Thomas Hardy"—on the title-page of Rebekah Owen's copy of the *Wessex Poems*. While he sat and "looked over" its contents with her, one would like to know whether he noticed her pencilled comment on the poem "To a Lady Offended by a Book of the Writer's." If he did, he apparently said nothing; or, at any rate, she wrote nothing further on this subject in her copy of the book.

Before separating at the Antelope, Betty and her adored one agreed to meet again on Monday. Miss Owen wanted to see Mill Street—the "Mixen Lane" of *The Mayor of Casterbridge*—but she wanted to see it after dark and couldn't go alone. Hardy offered to escort her through this slum region, and on Monday evening they carried out this plan. On parting, they agreed on a bike ride for the next day. But on Tuesday the cycling was called off, unexpectedly, and Rebekah thus found herself with unanticipated leisure for penning the following bulletin, for dispatch to the Lake District. She wrote from the home of Curator Moule, to which she had moved from the Antelope Hotel:

[Tuesday, 27 November 1900:] It is much warmer down here than [in the] north . . . [but] it is vexing [that] it isn't cycling weather to-day. How like T.H. to back out of going. He looks better than two years ago, less scrawny. Niece is as fat as butter and the image of a China doll, with bushy frizzy dark hair, round red cheeks between which the tiny nose is scarcely visible. . . . [I was] delighted to talk over . . . Lord Roberts with . . . Mr. Hardy. . . . [Later, on the same day:] No action of Emma Lavinia's ever surprises me and probably does not her husband; but niece, just gone, says "Auntie took us by surprise and returned last night." I expressed myself delighted and sent her my love, and niece says I am to come up to tea to-morrow. . . . I haven't a doubt it is niece's letters telling of my being here which has brought Madam home. Mrs. Sheridan says "She leads him a Hell of a life," so I expect he caught it if she arrived while he was traipsing through the slums with me. . . .

The *Standard* speaks of "Enter a Dragoon" [a short story in the December *Harper's Magazine*, just out] as an event, it being some time since the greatest living novelist has written [any prose fiction]. . . .

Mrs. Moule . . . is so quick and amusing with her quotations, as quick tho not as widely read as Miss Drisler, and far better company. . . .

[Later:] We all think it so rude in Mrs. T.H. not to invite Margie and me out. Margie says for me to go to-morrow, if I don't go to Frampton. If I do [go to Frampton], she will go [to Max Gate] with me on Saturday, and between us we can quell her from any open hatefulness. She is so uncertain, she may be gushing. Mrs. [Sheridan?] thinks her half-cracked, and Mrs. M[oule] says she is the deevil. Mr. Moule's emphatic "Poor woman, she is phenomenally plain!" and his outbursts against her general unbearableness amuse us all. I must stop now. Fondest love. . . .

BETTY.

Rebekah was certainly having her eyes opened to an overcast if not stormy aspect of the background against which the works of her Distinguished Author were set. While waiting for the hoped-for invitation to Max Gate, she turned back to *Wessex Poems* and read them anew. On the twenty-eighth she wrote in her journal: "I never noticed until to-night that the charming 'Ditty' dated 1870 on pages 39-41 is inscribed to E.L.G.—Emma Lavinia Gifford herself. They were married next year."

Here Betty Owen was wrong. Hardy did not marry Miss Gifford until 1874. Rebekah's journal continues: "He told me the story of 'Her Death—and After.' I had a little forgotten it, and he said it would have made a prose tale. . . . My dear 'Middle-Age Enthusiasms' is, I think, dedicated to his sister, Mary Hardy, M.H."

On December 5 Rebekah finally obtained her copy of the December *Harper's Magazine*, the London edition of course, and read "Enter a Dragoon." On the seventh she clipped a column from the *Dorset County Chronicle* which dealt with Hardy's "Tradition of 1804," and this in turn sent her back to *Life's Little*

Ironies. Then, seeing that the door of Max Gate was not going
to swing open for her, at least not just now, she packed her bags
and headed north. She left word that mail could be forwarded
to Radley, in Berkshire, and after that to Worcester. Amy Williams, daughter of Mrs. Sarah Clapcott, of Dorchester, wrote
her the following note, dated December 9, 1900:

> I was sorry not to see you again. . . . I hope Mrs. H. only amused you, in-
> stead of annoying you. I suppose those who live with her know how to dis-
> count anything [she does] and I doubt if she knows many of her im-
> mediate neighbours much. At any rate I hope you added to your former
> pleasant associations with Dorchester.

Upon her return to Belmount Hall, Rebekah wrote to thank
Lillian Gifford, the China doll with the round red cheeks and
the invisible nose, for the rides and the teas Betty had enjoyed
with her. On December 30, Miss Gifford replied from Max Gate,
but without a single mention of Mr. Thomas Hardy or of Mrs.
Thomas Hardy. Word got around later that Hardy returned
home one day to find that the lively niece had been banished from
the premises.

The nineteenth century came to an end on December 31, 1900.
It was a day made memorable by the publication of a poem by
Thomas Hardy. In the opinion of some people it is the greatest
poem he ever wrote. The world has since come to know it by its
later title, "The Darkling Thrush." I do not know whether Rebekah Owen saw the poem when it appeared in newspaper print
on the last day of the year; but if she did see it, she had some reason to understand why Hardy had expressed the feeling that
"little cause for carolings . . . was written on terrestrial things,"
and why, as the century came to its "desolate" end, "every spirit
upon earth seemed fervourless as I."

Rebekah Owen's return to the quiet and the isolation of Belmount Hall must have reduced her also to a "fervourless" state
of mind, markedly in contrast to the intense excitement of a

month before, when she had written "I hardly dare think how I am enjoying myself." Doubtless part of her pleasant Castle in Spain was built upon a very sandy foundation. In moving to England and setting herself up as a Landed Proprietress, she cannot have failed to see herself as a more-or-less Noble Dame living "cheek by jowl [close] to Max Gate." On the night when Rebekah's Distinguished Author squired her through the slums of Fordington, her ego unquestionably pranced gallantly along on a very high horse, and her fall from that high position was as inevitable as it was sudden. Hardy had enjoyed the momentary exhilaration of her company, but that was all and it was soon over. At the age of sixty he was too old to slough off old habits of moody introspection, of shrinking into his shell; and he doubtless had not forgotten that Betty Owen was "a lady offended by a book of the writer's."

Thus before the Owen sisters had been two years in residence at Belmount Hall Rebekah had her own reasons for fervourlessness and for a sharper appreciation of Life's Little Ironies than she had ever had before.

Chapter VIII

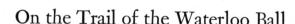

On the Trail of the Waterloo Ball

AFTER the partial refrigeration of her cordial relations with Max Gate, Rebekah Owen retired to the Lake District where she had already discovered the people to be "of inferior birth and fashion." Doubtless there was less admiration of her pink waistcoat in Hawkshead than in Dorchester, and the mistake she had made in settling at Belmount Hall was already becoming apparent to her. But the illness of Caroline Ash rendered the Owens powerless to do anything more just now than contemplate the possibility of a change later on. Meanwhile they could read.

When Spring came, Catharine managed to find someone— probably Norah Barton—to stay with "Ashy" while she accompanied Rebekah on a trip south. They went, not to Dorchester where they might be cold-shouldered, but to London. There they attended the 1901 exhibition at the Royal Academy. Among the pictures exhibited was one by Sargent entitled "Daughters of A. Wertheimer, Esq." (a painting now, I think, in the Tate Gallery). Rebekah was immediately reminded of her visit with the Hardys to Wool, nearly ten years before; for what she called "the repellant, defiant, audacious beauty" of the Wertheimer women recalled the portraits she had seen in the old manor-house used by Hardy for Tess's honeymoon. The Sargent portraits thus served to inspire a wish to re-read *Tess*, and when the Owens got back to Belmount Hall, the readings began. On August 8 Rebekah reached the chapter that gives Hardy's description of the "two life-sized portraits" and found that it brought the Wertheimer women vividly before her again, "age only excepted."

While they were in London (or possibly on some previous visit to the big city), the Owens had met Rhoda Broughton. She was now an elderly lady of sixty-one, whose earlier reputation for writing audacious novels had faded with her youth. The Owens invited her to visit them at Hawkshead, and on September 3 she called at Belmount Hall. Rebekah was true to her first love, however, and the conversation ignored Miss Broughton's books entirely and dealt with Hardy's. Rebekah had recently come upon an article which reminded her of *The Trumpet-Major*, and while Miss Broughton sat there almost within sight of Wordsworth's old school and within an hour's walk of Ruskin's Coniston, she was given no choice but to discuss Hardy's Napoleonic novel. As soon as Miss Broughton had gone, Betty was ready to begin a re-reading of that work. She read it aloud "to dear Tat and Ash" and reached the end on September 30.

Meanwhile she had heard from Margie Moule, but August and September went by without any communication from Max Gate. In October the occupants of Belmount Hall turned again to *Under the Greenwood Tree*, and the ninth reading of this story aloud was completed on the twenty-eighth of the month. Their feeling of isolation at Hawkshead was somewhat mitigated by the arrival from time to time of letters from America, from one member or another of the league who had not yet lost her enthusiasm for Thomas Hardy. One sent a clipping from the *New York Times* for November 2 and another clipped the November issue of the New York *Bookman*, but it is clear that the ties with America were growing weak. The *Times* clipping was about "Thomas Hardy's new volume of verse" which had been first announced by Harpers for fall publication under the title *Poems of Feeling, Dream, and Deed*. Rebekah Owen sent off her order for a copy of the book, but when it came, on November 21, she learned that the title had been changed to *Poems of the Past and the Present*, publication date "1902." Doubtless with some misgivings, after the long silence at Max Gate, she mailed the book to

Dorchester, requesting Hardy's autograph. He dutifully signed his name on the title-page and mailed the book, without comment, back to Hawkshead.

On receipt of the *Poems,* Rebekah cannot have failed to read "The Darkling Thrush" with its December, 1900, date. But she did not read it aloud to "Tat." She wrote no comment in the book, neither on this memorable poem nor on any other. She never read any of the book aloud. Not that she had lost interest in Hardy's poetry; on the contrary. From the Christmas *Graphic* she extracted "The Dead Quire"; in the *Lakes Herald* she found (early in 1902) a reprinting of the "Song of the Soldiers' Wives"; and on January 19 she found in the *Westmorland Gazette* a reprint of Hardy's wistful poem "An August Midnight." This poem refers to "the beat of a clock from a distant floor" of Max Gate, and Rebekah may well have wondered when, if ever, she would hear that clock beat again.

One of the *Poems of the Past and the Present* was entitled "To Flowers from Italy in Winter." If the reader is willing to spin with me the fine gossamer of pure conjecture, he can picture Rebekah's reading of this poem—she had long been interested in flowers—and can imagine her deciding that, since Italy had now appeared in Hardy's poetry, she would sooner or later have to acquaint herself with that country. In any case, as if the Owens felt the need for a change of scene, Rebekah and Catharine spent some time in 1902 on the continent. It was apparently their first venture into a non-English-speaking land. But the shadow of Thomas Hardy followed them even there. In the Paris Salon, Rebekah was startled to find Sargent's "Daughters of A. Wertheimer" again on exhibition. Again she was reminded of Hardy's description of the Turberville women, and again Rebekah felt the desire to read *Tess* all over again. Not having her copy of the book at hand, her resolve had to be postponed; but they returned to Belmount Hall eventually, and in April, 1903, a re-reading of *Tess* aloud was begun. The black flag went up on Tess's execution on May 7.

It was Browning's birthday. Rebekah Owen knew Browning's poetry well enough, as we have seen, to make instantaneous detection of Browning's influence on Hardy's metrical composition: she is probably the first to have detected this influence. (The present writer knows at least one person who unwittingly trailed Miss Owen by at least forty years in noting Hardy's close study of Browning.) But on May 7, 1903, Betty Owen had no time for Robert Browning or his birthday. As soon as the reading of *Tess* was completed, she turned to *The Hand of Ethelberta,* and for the next three weeks Tat and Ash listened to this reminder of a former visit to Swanage.

On July 11 Rebekah clipped from the *Daily Chronicle* a review of Lawrence Hutton's *Literary Landmarks of Oxford.* She promptly ordered a copy. When the book came, one glance at the index showed that Mr. Hutton had made the totally incomprehensible mistake of saying not one word about *Jude the Obscure.* Hardy's name wasn't even in the index. Rebekah at once put the book aside; its pages remain uncut to this day. Not discouraged by this failure, she tried again. When she read a review of a new "Annual of Art and Literature edited by Laurence Housman and W. Somerset Maugham" called *The Venture* (published in London by John Baillie in 1903), she ordered a copy and this time fared better. For at page 10 she found Hardy's poem "The Market Girl."

In January, 1904, Miss Owen learned of the publication of Part I of *The Dynasts.* She ordered a copy and again used the formula she had tried in the case of *Poems of the Past and the Present.* She sent *The Dynasts* to Max Gate with a polite request for Hardy's autograph. He signed the book and returned it on February 20 with the following letter:

Max Gate, Dorchester

Dear Miss Owen: 20: 2: 04 [February 20, 1904].

I have signed the book as requested, and send it back herewith. I should have returned it sooner if it had not happened that I have been particularly pressed for time lately, and in my hurry overlooked it.

It is interesting to hear of your social functions among the misty mountains up your way—mistier than ever this damp year, I surmise. But after all, anything is better than frost and snow, according to my views at present.

My wife has been very well this winter and sends her kind regards. I hope your sister is well likewise.

Yours sincerely
T. HARDY.

On March 13 her old friend Curator H. J. Moule died; a long obituary notice appeared in the *Dorset County Chronicle* on the seventeenth. Three weeks later, on Easter Sunday, April 3, Thomas Hardy's mother died, at the age of ninety-one. Catharine and Rebekah both wrote at once to express their sympathy, and ten days later Hardy acknowledged their letters. It was done, however, quite impersonally. He addressed an envelope on April 14 to "The Misses Owen, Belmount Hall," and in it inserted a printed card with mourning border, which expressed "sincere thanks for kind sympathies" from "the family of the late Mrs. Hardy." The novelist's comment on his mother was printed in the Dorchester newspaper on that same day; Rebekah clipped it, for insertion in her copy of *Under the Greenwood Tree*. Later on, she made a note of the fact that *Memories of a Vicarage* by Handley Moule, the Bishop of Durham, "contains twenty-seven references to Thomas Hardy's mother." Has anyone else ever noted this fact?

During the summer of 1904, the Owens did a great deal of traveling. Their tour of France and Italy must not here detain us longer than is needed for us to note that their trip resulted in their adding to the Belmount Hall library T. A. Cooke's *Old Touraine* (1898), Maurice Hewlett's *The Road in Tuscany* (1904), and a number of other titles. The sisters eventually assembled at Hawkshead forty or fifty books on Italy, France, and Spain, in addition to thirteen volumes in The Mediaeval Town series. Their continental travels failed, however, to drive Hardy from their minds. By September they were back at Belmount Hall, and on the twenty-eighth they finished reading *Two on a Tower* aloud. In October they decided to give *Desperate Remedies* another chance, but it was slow going. Rebekah noticed, however, that it alone, among her Hardy volumes, lacked the author's autograph. She therefore sent the book off to Max Gate, with the request that Hardy once again, for the second time this year, affix his signature for her. It was weeks before the book was returned; but it came, at last, with the following perfunctory note of explanation:

Max Gate, Dorchester.
Nov. 28: 1904

Dear Miss Owen:

I must apologize for having neglected till now—owing to the many demands upon one's time—your request for my signature in your book—returned herewith.

I am glad to hear that you have been doing a great deal of travelling, etc. this year, and hope that you and your sister are well.

Yours very truly,
T. H.

While waiting for the return of the book, Betty had been busily reading. On November 15 "The Three Strangers" was the title chosen; next, "The Distracted Preacher"; and after that, *Life's Little Ironies*. But Belmount Hall was proving to be a highly unsatisfactory place of residence, especially in the winter time. "Ashy" was now eighty-five and Catharine, in her fifty-fourth year, was not well. Rebekah decided not to fight the winter and the servants (such as could be found) at Hawkshead, and the first three or four months of 1905 were accordingly spent at Oxford. Here they lodged at a familiar old address, 34 Wellington Square.

The Oxford bookshops offered Betty an irresistible temptation. She got quotations on a fifteen-volume set of Cowper; and, reverting to her father's old habit of wholesale purchasing, she bought seventeen volumes of Madame de Sévigné's *Letters*—in French.

When the July sun had warmed up the cold walls at Belmount, the Owens returned—glad to get back to the Hardy books in the Sheraton bookcase. Tat and Ash listened once again to the reading of *The Return of the Native;* and when autumn fires had been lit, *The Mayor of Casterbridge* was read aloud. Before the year was over, Betty added a new book to the collection: F. R. and Sidney Heath's *Dorchester and its Surroundings*. This volume, in the Homeland Handbook series, had a Foreword by Thomas Hardy. Early in 1906 there was yet another addition: H. J. Moule's *Dorchester Antiquities* by Rebekah's old friend, the curator. This volume had a double claim upon her interest, for it contained (pages 7 to 13) Hardy's "H. J. M.—Some Memories and Letters." Here again Rebekah Owen got ahead of many a Hardy bibliographer. On January 28, 1906, she read "The Three Strangers" to "Ashy and Norah," and on February 22 she celebrated Washington's birthday by another courageous (and incredible) reading of *The Romantic Adventures of a Milkmaid*. By March 12 the reading of *The Trumpet-Major* aloud was completed. And Part II of *The Dynasts* was now added to the Owen library.

In August the Owens were invited to Auckland Castle, the "seat" of the Bishop of Durham. There on September 26, 1906, the bishop's daughter, Isabel Moule, was married. Rebekah sent a silver spoon, which the bride described as "a lovely little spoon from America." Six weeks later, Isabel's cousin also married: Margie Moule became Mrs. Edward Leslie. Rebekah sent another silver spoon and Catharine sent a "cream ladle." The Owens came down from the Lakes to attend the wedding, which took place in Dorchester on November 6. The *Dorset County Chronicle* two days later reported that Mrs. Thomas Hardy sent the bride a "plated toast rack," while "Mr. T. Hardy" sent her a book of his poems. Mrs. Hardy sent the bridegroom a pocket-book, and Hardy gave him a copy of *The Return of the Native*. The county newspaper obviously thought that the wedding was *much* more important than *The Return of the Native* or the un-named book of poems by Mr. T. Hardy.

Rebekah did not linger long in Dorchester after the wedding. She afterwards wrote friends that she was "uncomfortable" and her letter doubtless referred to physical discomfort. She was now forty-eight and not inclined to repeat her bike ride up to the top of Ridgeway hill. But there may also have been other reasons why she felt "uncomfortable," and if there was any call at Max Gate, I have found no trace of it. Catharine and Betty hurried on to Bath, where they lodged a while at 14 Widcombe Crescent, and then they returned to Belmount Hall.

The Leslie-Moule wedding had, however, provided the opportunity for some thawing out of ice and Rebekah knew how to follow it up. She was a great believer in the wisdom of Samuel Johnson's advice to Boswell on how to court a Great Man: "You must not give a shilling's worth of court for six-pence worth of good; but if you can get a shilling's worth of good for six-pence worth of court, you are a fool if you do not pay court." Rebekah remembered the little trees she had sent Hardy from New York, and she remembered the books she had given the Bodleian. As soon as she got back to Belmount Hall, she sent Mrs. Hardy a Christmas present. The novelist's wife could, at times, be a fast worker: she did not wait until Christmas to acknowledge the gift. On Christmas Eve Rebekah had her reply. A postcard came from Max Gate saying: "Many thanks for your kind present, and wishing you and your sister a Happy New Year. Will write soon. E. L. Hardy." Only that and nothing more. If any further letter came from Emma Lavinia Hardy, Rebekah did not preserve it, and she had preserved all her other communications from the same source.

The year 1907 did, however, prove to be a happy new year for the Owens. One of the reasons was their acquisition of a motor-car. Both sisters were now beyond the age for cycling, and even though automobile engines in 1907 were not always equal to the demands of the hills in the Lake District, the new car did make it possible for Catharine and Rebekah to see many landscapes previously inaccessible to them. They eventually bought eighteen volumes of Macmillan's Highways and Byeways series, five volumes by Charles G. Harper on English roads, and several eighteenth-century volumes on *Seats of the Nobility*.

When summer came, the Owens made one more attempt to get the Hardys to visit Hawkshead. Rebekah apparently did not write but put Catharine up to sending Mrs. Hardy an account of the beauties of Westmorland, which the Owens were now prepared to show the Hardys in greater ease and comfort. Mrs. Hardy retaliated—if that is not too strong a word—by sending Catharine a set of postcards illustrative of "Beauty Spots of Dorset." It wasn't a very direct or formal kind of invitation and in 1892 it certainly would not have served. But fifteen years had passed, and Rebekah (who forgot nothing) had not forgotten that she had once declared: "I should be sorry to live in a small place, unless cheek by jowl to Max Gate." So this time the postcards served. To Dorchester the Owens went in their new motor-car, ostensibly on their way to the Continent but quite willing to see the "Beauty Spots of Dorset" on the way. They paid a call at Max Gate. It was a brief call; no books were autographed, no letters were copied, but it helped to clear the cloudy skies.

Rebekah found her poet deeply involved with plans for bringing *The Dynasts* to a conclusion. Parts I and II, which Rebekah had already bought, were (Hardy explained) to be followed by a concluding volume, if he could only get a few final points settled. At present he was busy with the Brussels ball on the eve of the Battle of Waterloo. He was, so he told Rebekah, struck with the curious historical uncertainty as to the exact place where the ball was held. He had himself looked the ground over, more than thirty years before, but had been unable to come to any assured conclusion.

Miss Owen saw her chance to be of service. Before she and Catharine left England for their September and October tour on the continent, she wrote some hasty letters, to friends who might (she thought) be of service, and by the time the sisters had returned to Belmount Hall—that is, by November first— there were answers and suggestions. One writer whom Rebekah had consulted sent her a clipping that contained a small map of Brussels, with a mark that purported to show the exact spot at which the famous ball took place. Rebekah hurried off a letter to Max Gate, passing the information on to Hardy and expressing the hope that it would not arrive too late to be of any service to him.

Hardy's reply is among the most interesting and the most instructive letters that Rebekah Owen ever received from him. It is one more illustration of her service as a bibliographer, or (as a chemist might put it) of her value as a catalyst. Hardy wrote her as follows:

MAX GATE, DORCHESTER
6. Dec. 1907

Dear Miss Owen,

My best thanks for what you have sent (which I return herewith as you request). Anything about the Brussels ball on the Eve of Quatre Bras is interesting.

In respect of *The Dynasts* it does not matter that you write too late, (the proofs of the ball room scene were returned to the printers some time ago) the question of where the ball took place being of no importance to the drama. But, as I told you, I had been struck with the curious historical uncertainty about the spot, when one would have supposed it would not have been forgotten. My opinion is still that, though well-guessed at, it has never been *proved* to be at any guessed place—despite Sir W. Fraser

whose book (containing the plan reproduced in the newspaper cutting
you send) I read when it came out, but was not convinced by it, having
visited the same hospital, coach-house, etc., myself in 1876—years before he investigated the buildings. It is, of course, *possible* that he may be
right. But I prefer that the site of the room should remain unknown, as it
helps the romance of the event—unless, indeed, it could be where Byron
puts it—at the Hotel de Ville, the only place worthy of the occasion.

I am glad you have got back safely. Your hills must try the motor car
a little. With renewed thanks I am

Sincerely yours

T. HARDY.

It is clear from this letter that Hardy promptly identified the
source of the newspaper map which Betty Owen had sent him:
it was from a book by Sir W. Fraser. But Hardy's statement that
he had read the book "when it came out" did not tell Miss Owen
what the title of the book was or how long ago it had been published. Interested readers may not find the identification of the
book an easy matter, and few libraries are equipped with copies
of it. It may be well, therefore, to supply such information here
as may prove useful to the reader, whether he be a student of
Hardy or of Byron or of Napoleonic history.

The Waterloo Ball by Sir William A. Fraser appeared in London in 1897 under the imprint of F. Harvey. This book is quite
specific in disagreeing with Hardy's contention that "the Hotel
de Ville [is] the only place worthy of the occasion." Fraser ex-
plains (on page 15) that this misguided idea originated with Byron's visit to Brussels in 1816: "he was shown . . . an apartment
in the Hotel de Ville which answers precisely to his description."
But Fraser points out that there is "clear and distinct evidence
[which] contradicts the possibility of such a thing." That the
Duke and Duchess of Richmond would give a private ball in
the Town Hall is, says Fraser, "all nonsense." He states that
he had known the daughter of the Duke of Richmond during the
greater part of his life and that she had assured him that there
was no "high hall" in her father's house, and that the ball had

been given in an old building nearby, once used as a coach-maker's stock room. Lord William Lenox, a son of the Duke of Richmond, is also quoted (on page 30) as saying that "the ball given by his mother was *not* in the Hotel de Ville but in an . . . adjacent . . . house." Fraser himself reports (pages 13-14) having gone to Brussels, to Number 40-42 Rue de la Blanchisserie, and finding there "a very large room . . . , a long, barn-like room, with . . . the floor . . . polished to complete smoothness. [It was] 'the Waterloo Ball Room'—there could be no mistake about it." Hardy reports that he visited this coach-house in 1876, but Fraser quotes the daughter's statement that she looked in vain for it in 1868 and was told that the house had been pulled down. Hardy's desire that the site remain unknown is likely to be granted. On May 1, 1950, when the present writer visited the spot where Sir William Fraser says the house of the Duchess of Richmond once stood, he found there a modern medical clinic, with a sign reading "Clinique Chirurgicale S.S. Jean-Elisabeth." And at 40 Rue de la Blanchisserie, where the adjacent coach-house once stood, there is now nothing resembling a barn, and No. 42 is gone altogether. One house is marked 40; the next, 46. Perhaps the most useful result of Miss Owen's having elicited the letter just quoted from Hardy is the fact that the student of Part III of *The Dynasts* now knows why there is a footnote to Act IV, Scene II. Although *The Waterloo Ball* (London, Harvey, 1897) is not mentioned in this footnote, Fraser *is* mentioned, and the student now knows to whom to turn for authoritative and detailed information. Fraser's book is a closely argued piece of work, well worth looking up.

Miss Owen might, on her return from the continent, have been expected to read *The Dynasts*. She now owned Parts I and II and she had recently been talking with Hardy about the projected Part III. But old custom was too strong. On November 5 she read "The Three Strangers" to "Ashy and Barton." The absence of Catharine's name from the record suggests that she was not in good health at this time. But there was another reason, too, for Catharine's not listening to Rebekah read, and also another reason why *The Dynasts* was not a book to which Rebekah Owen at this point in her life was inclined to turn. She had never been drawn to Hardy's philosophy, in so far as she deemed him to have a clearly defined and systematically organized philosophy of life; that was one reason why she didn't like his *Jude*. And in the emotional and physical disturbances through which she had recently been passing, ever since that night, years ago, when she traipsed through the slums of Fordington with her adored one, she had come, more and more, to feel the need of spiritual anchorage, and she was certainly not likely to find Hardy's Phantom Intelligences, his Spirits Sinister and Spirits Ironic, now to her taste. In the year 1908, when she became fifty (and wouldn't admit it), she reached an important decision. Betty eventually broke the news to "Margie," who was now Mrs. Leslie, and she promptly relayed it to Max Gate: "Betty Owen has become a Roman Catholic, much to her sister's distress."

The disturbance of the peace of Belmount Hall and the rift in the affectionate relations of the sisters left their mark. The year 1908 is a total blank among the Hardy records, and not until the summer of 1909 are there signs that the stormy weather has subsided. In August, when Betty read *Under the Greenwood Tree* to "Ash, Edith, and Barton," Catharine was not in the audience. In September *Two on a Tower* was read, and in October *Far from the Madding Crowd*. Fortunately for all concerned, at this point a new interest turned up and blew a breath of fresh air into the stale atmosphere of Belmount Hall. The newspapers announced that on November 17 and 18, 1909, the Dorchester Dramatic and Debating Society would give a dramatic version of *Far from the Madding Crowd* by Alfred H. Evans. He was the father of Maurice Evans, the Shakespearean actor who has since become known to thousands of Americans.

If Rebekah Owen had not been otherwise occupied in 1908, either with her own spiritual unrest or with her strained relations with her aging sister, she would doubtless have learned about the activities of this Dorchester Dramatic Society sooner than she did. A scene from Hardy's *Trumpet-Major* had been arranged by Alfred Evans as an "interlude" on a program at Dorchester in February, 1908; and the success of this one-act performance led Hardy to urge Evans to dramatize the entire novel. This he did and the play was given in the Corn Exchange at Dorchester on November 18 and 19, 1908. It excited great interest and was an immense success. If Miss Owen read the statement in the *Dorset County Chronicle* a week later that "leading dramatic critics had come down from London especially for the occasion," she must have keenly regretted that she had not been there with them. She must have promised herself that if there were any repetition of Hardy plays in the future, she would be on hand to see them. And she was!

It was now twelve years since she and "Tat" had seen Mrs. Fiske as Tess. They doubtless felt that it was high time they again saw Wessex come alive behind the footlights. They motored to Dorchester in November (1909) and showed what keen interest the play aroused in them by going to see it twice. Hardy liked it too, and (according to his second wife, in *Later Years*, 1930, page 140) he "thought it a neater achievement than the London version of 1882 by Mr. Comyns Carr." Mrs. Florence Hardy's phrase, "by Mr. Comyns Carr," calls for comment. Did Mrs. Hardy really think that Carr was the author of "the London version of 1882"? In that year the second Mrs. Hardy was only three years old; probably she never saw the London *Times* of that year. In its issue for January 2 there is a letter from Thomas Hardy in which he referred to "a manuscript play of my own based on the novel." "*I* dramatized the story," he declared, and complained that "my drama is rendered useless" by reason of its having been anticipated by a plagiarizing play of Pinero's. Hardy sought help from Carr, and after Carr had done some revising of Hardy's manuscript, their play was given at the Globe Theatre in London in May, 1882, but it lasted only three weeks. After this failure, if it can be called that, Hardy was quite satisfied to have the play called Carr's, just as, after the success of Alfred Evans's *Trumpet-Major* in 1908, Hardy was quite satisfied to have it reported that the play was "practically written by Mr. Thomas Hardy."

Rebekah Owen was quite unacquainted with this side of her adored author's history. It was perhaps while she was still in southern England—in Oxford or in London—that she learned of the publication of a new volume of his verse. She obtained a copy of *Time's Laughingstocks* and once again Hardy dutifully wrote his name in her book. On page 160 he made a correction in the text. But after the Owens had returned to Belmount Hall, Betty read—not the new poems, but the old and familiar *Trumpet-Major*. She read it to "dear Ashy," now nearly ninety. The novel was completed on December 13. After Christmas *The Hand of Ethelberta* was undertaken and the reading completed by February 1, 1910. It was the last time that Rebekah's old nurse was able to lend her patient ears to a reading of Thomas Hardy. She had certainly earned her rest—by her many years of listening to *The Romantic Adventures of a Milkmaid*, if in no other way. Caroline Ash died at Belmount Hall, at the age of ninety, and was buried four miles away at Coniston, near the spot where John Ruskin had been buried only ten years before. Hereafter the name "Ash" or "Ashy" will not appear in the record of Rebekah's readings, but it remains in the previous lists as a touching tribute to the sisters' loyalty to their old nurse, as well as a mark of her ability to retain their affection into extreme old age. "Dear Ash," "dearest Ashy": the words are a credit to both sides.

By October, 1910, Catharine Owen had once again taken her old place in Betty's audience, and on the eighteenth and nineteenth she listened as her sister galloped through *Under the Greenwood Tree,* reading "to dear Tat, Mrs. Raven, and Snowdrop." On the twentieth Rebekah read "The Three Strangers" aloud for at least the eleventh time, and in early November *Two on a Tower* provided the text for the readings. Of these titles *Under the Greenwood Tree* was the one to stir the liveliest interest this autumn, for the Dorchester Dramatic Society had announced that they would this year give a play called "The Mellstock Quire"—a dramatization of *Under the Greenwood Tree,* again by Alfred Evans. Rebekah promptly wrote to reserve seats and also, in her typically thorough way, to ask whether a copy of the text of the dramatic adaptation were available. It so happened that there were only four typed copies of Mr. Evans's prompt-book, but Rebekah eventually had her way: an officer of the Dramatic Society forwarded a copy of the book of "our forthcoming play" to Belmount Hall, and the Owens were able to study it before they set out for Dorchester.

"The Mellstock Quire" was presented on November 16 and 17, 1910. The Owens were in the fifth row of the audience on the first night, but some of the zest of Dorchester seemed to have departed. The sisters called at Max Gate and found Mrs. Hardy at home. She invited them to a formal "tea" she was about to give, but there was no mention of the novelist-and-poet and he did not appear. As Rebekah had—perhaps all too obviously— little interest in calling on Mrs. Emma Lavinia for her own sake, the sisters declined the invitation to the tea and decided to move on. By December the first they were back in their cold rooms at Belmount Hall, and there Catharine received from Mrs. Hardy the following letter. Betty noticed that it was chiefly about the weather. If she had been acquainted with Laurence Sterne's letters, she might have recognized here a modern revival of his publicly announced formula for letter-writing: "begin with the first sentence—and trust to Almighty God for the second."

MAX GATE, DORCHESTER,
Nov. 30 [1910].

Dear Miss Owen,

It was a disappointment not to see you both again, at my "Tea" which was a pleasant gathering with this exception! I feel the cold of winter is upon us already—a keen East wind to-day keeps us in, with a kindly eye on our hearths, but there is much to do always as one waits for the Spring again, and Winter trees are beautiful. I hope this crisis in the nation will be passed through without any [thing] terrible coming worse than any before.

Yours very sincerely, with love to both,

E. L. HARDY.

Not a word about Mr. Hardy. The political "crisis" thus glanced at by Mrs. Hardy was brought about by the death of King Edward VII. The coronation of his son and successor, George V, took place in June of the following year, with nothing more "terrible" happening than the embodiment of a change in the King's accession-declaration.

But all was not well at Belmount. There was trouble with servants, there was trouble with the man who drove their motor-car, the roof leaked under the incessant rains of the Lake District, and Catharine's health was not good. Thus the year 1911 dragged along, with never a trace of Thomas Hardy. No letters from Max Gate; no readings aloud. Now and then a letter came from New York, with which the old ties were not yet completely broken. In July, 1911, reports from New York that the "heat here is terrific" reconciled them for a brief while to their residence in Westmorland, but a year went by without leaving much to show for itself. In October, 1912, one of the faithful in New York clipped a review by P. P. Howe of a new book on Thomas Hardy—the work of Lascelles Abercrombie—and sent the review to Rebekah. She promptly ordered a copy of the book and it came in time for her to read it before she and Catharine set out for Dorchester. They were planning to attend the performance of the "Hardy Players"—as the Dorchester Dramatic Society was coming to be called. This year there was to be a repetition of their first success—*The Trumpet-Major*—which the Owens had not seen in 1908. They were therefore all the more eager to see it this time. The play had been somewhat revised by Mr. Evans, because the 1908 performance had been too long. Rebekah had written to reserve the same fifth-row seats they had occupied in 1910, and in mid-November they set out.

Leaving Belmount Hall in the care of Mrs. Dickinson, wife of their chauffeur, the Owens drove down from the Lakes via Oxford, and thence across the Chiltern Hills to "Wessex." As they came through Wallingford, on the Chilterns, they paused to admire an ornate staircase at Britwell House, and in this way became acquainted with a Miss Gertrude Smith who lived there with her sister. Rebekah Owen never wasted an opportunity to preach the Hardy gospel, whether she was in New York, in Oxford, or on the wing. Before the Owens and the Smiths separated in Wallingford, the English sisters had been informed that the American sisters were on their way to Dorchester to see the Hardy Players; and the information was presented in such an alluring way that Gertrude Smith and her sister decided, almost on the spot, that they too would have to visit "Casterbridge" and see *The Trumpet-Major* for themselves. Rebekah promised to play guide if they would come.

On arriving in Dorchester, the Owens found lodgings at Mrs. Way's on Royal Terrace. As soon as they were settled, they drove over to Wolfeton House to call on Mr. and Mrs. Bankes but found them out. Shortly after their return to Dorchester, Miss Owen received the following note from Mrs. Bankes:

Wolfeton House, Dorchester.

We were so very sorry that we were not at home when you were kind enough to call. On Sunday next Nov 24th you will find us at tea at about 4.30 should you and your sister care to drive over. We shall be so very pleased to see you both again.　　FLORENCE BANKES.

On Monday the twenty-fifth the Owens went to Max Gate. The maid who answered their knock said that Mrs. Hardy was not well, but Rebekah sent her card in and the maid shortly returned and admitted them. After some delay Mrs. Hardy appeared. When they saw her, they thought she "seemed very ill" —so ill, in fact, that they got up to leave. Mrs. Hardy insisted, however, that they stay and have tea, and (just as she had done two years previously) she urged them to come back on Friday, *after* they had seen the play, so that they could talk further about it. It was to be given on Wednesday and Thursday nights.

Rebekah of course lost no chance to talk with her author. He was at work in his study and had given orders that he was not to be disturbed. But Rebekah played the rôle of Margaret Catchpole, and Hardy eventually gave in and came down. Rebekah told him that she had just been reading a new book about him, by one Lascelles Abercrombie. Hardy had not yet seen it. Oh, yes, he *knew* about it. "Mr. Hardy said Mr. Abercrombie came to see him one day, 'a young man on a bicycle,' and as he did not know him, he feared he was 'a little short with him.' The preface [however] leads one to think Mr. Hardy had admitted him to friendship and confidence." Since Hardy had not seen the book, Rebekah offered to lend him her copy. On Tuesday afternoon she accordingly carried it to Max Gate and left it for Hardy without seeing him. It was returned to her on Thursday morning—unread. Much had happened in the interval.

When she got back to her room in Dorchester, Betty found a note from her old friend Teresa Fetherstonhaugh, the "Tess" whom she had met at Max Gate twenty years ago. Miss Fetherstonhaugh obviously wrote in answer to a recent letter from Rebekah.

Oakers Wood, Dorchester
Station: Moreton
Nov. 26. 1912

My dear Miss Rebekah,
    Thank you very much for your letter and refutation of Mrs. Hardy's

charges against her poor old patient husband. She is a queer woman and I never thought her quite right in her upper story! ...

TERESA FETHERSTONHAUGH

The next day was the date set for *The Trumpet-Major*. In the afternoon, the Reverend Mr. Leslie, "Margie" Moule's husband, now rector of Came Church, came hurrying to Royal Terrace to say that Mr. Hardy had asked him to let Rebekah Owen know that Mrs. Hardy had died at seven o'clock that morning.

Chapter IX

"An Infinite Waste of Life"

REBEKAH Owen had rarely, if ever, been so shocked as she was at the news of Mrs. Hardy's death. She could not rid her mind of the thought that she and Catharine had been the last persons (outside of the Max Gate household) to see Emma Lavinia alive. She wondered if the play that evening would be called off. Her chauffeur came with a report that he had seen a placard in the town announcing that, in accordance with the wishes of Mr. Hardy, there would be no postponement of the performances. As usual, the Owens had planned to attend on both days. Rebekah hurried off a note to Mrs. Leslie at Came Rectory, near Dorchester, and (by means of that promptness which has so often made Americans envy their British cousins the superiority of the service rendered by the Royal Post Office) she shortly had this reply postmarked Dorchester, November 27, 1912: "Shall be so very glad to see you both any time in the morning. ... How appallingly sudden the news of poor Mrs. H."

Unfortunately the Owens had already engaged themselves for the morning of the twenty-eighth. Rebekah therefore had to write again. She suggested that she and Catharine come with their car on Saturday, pay a brief call on the Leslies, and then take them to Mrs. Hardy's funeral. Back came this reply:

Came Rectory, Dorchester
Nov. 28 [1912]

My dear Betty

We shall be so glad if you and Miss Owen will lunch with us on Saturday [the 30th] at 1.15 before going to poor Mrs. Hardy's funeral. Edward and I will be very glad to go with you. ...

MARGIE E. LESLIE

Even before these arrangements had been completed, the Owen sisters received their expected callers—the Smith ladies from the Chilterns—and arranged to sit with them at the play that evening, and in the morning to show them something of Hardy's Casterbridge. This plan was carried out. Public announcement of Mrs. Hardy's death was made from the stage Wednesday evening. What the Owens did with the Smiths on Thursday will appear from a letter written by Gertrude Smith, to be quoted a little later; but what any of them thought of the play, *The Trumpet-Major*, I am unable to state. For the death of Mrs. Hardy, the rushing about from one spot to another, the letter-writing, and eventually the funeral—all this pushed the play so completely into the background that not a word of comment on it got written down.

At last, on Thursday evening, after her second visit to the *Trumpet-Major* performance, Rebekah found time to write out the following detailed account of the events of this crowded week. Writing to "Dearest Mrs. Fauty" (apparently some one at Belmount Hall not otherwise identifiable) and dating her letter at Dorchester on Thursday, November 28, 1912, Rebekah announced:

"We have postponed our return, from Saturday till Monday. Yesterday Mr. Hardy was so very good as to send Mr. Leslie to tell us of the death of his wife yesterday morning. I was almost never so shocked in my life. We called on her on Monday and the servant said she was not well and was not seeing anyone, but I wrote on my card, 'Would you not see *us?*' and word was immediately brought that she would. And soon, and *very* slowly, she came into the drawing room, saying how glad she was to see us and that she would not have seen any one else. She had been out in an open car the week before, and since Friday had felt too unwell to eat, and suffered great pain in her back. She had not had a doctor, did not want to be cut up, etc. We thought it as likely to be nerves and melancholia as anything. She was furtively wiping her eyes. She *would* give us tea, and really seemed at moments better and calmer for talking, but yet most visibly depressed and *op*-pressed. She held out no hopes of his appearance, said he had been told [of our call], but that he usually had tea in his study: so I told the maid myself to tell him that the Miss Owens would feel very hurt if he did not see such old friends. She still cast doubts, but down he came, most evidently delighted to see us, and saying so twice over. And then he talked to me in the old delightful way, and Tat talked a little to her, but often they both [i.e., Tat and Mrs. Hardy] sat and listened. She was no worse for seeing us, but better, I think. Only the pain came on now and then. We didn't stay nearly as long as usual, for Tat fancied Dickinson [the chauffeur] was sitting out in the rain and dark, but he was in the kitchen. Mrs. Hardy came as far as the door to see the car, and then went back, but he stayed and talked while the lamps were being lighted [oh, those auto lamps of 1912!], and it was arranged that we should go there again on Friday. We begged her over and over to see a Doctor. I wish we had begged him.

"It appears that the following day, as she still felt so ill, the Doctor was sent for, but she allowed no examination. The next morning he was sent for again, but she was dead when he got there—had died about 8 a.m. in the Cook's arms, who was trying to lift her. This was only Wednesday morning early, and we had been with her at 6 p.m. on Monday. We both said, after we got back, 'She will die or go insane, she can't go on like this.' I don't gather that she took any remedy or went to bed, except for the night. Poor thing, poor thing!

"Her death on the day of the Hardy play shocked every one inexpressibly. Many learnt the news only from the placards of the play which said simply: 'In accordance with the wishes of Mr. Thomas Hardy there will be no postponement of the performances.' Dickinson saw that and wondered what it meant and then he met the Max Gate servant who told him.

"There was no reason she should not die first, and she certainly looked awfully, yet one had always the feeling that she would survive him, tho' I strongly fancy she was no younger. [Actually, Mrs. Hardy was five months younger than her husband; he was then 72.] She was so marked a personality no one could meet her in the street without saying at home, 'I met Mrs. Hardy to-day.' We had known her well, I may say uncommonly well, for 20 years and four months. It is incredible to me that she is gone. I think we must see her laid to rest, and it will be kindness to take the Leslies.

"We have so far much enjoyed our stay, and have done more lunching and tea-ing and calling in five days than we should do in five months at Belmount. . . . The charming ladies whose fine staircase was the beginning of our acquaintance came down for the play. They came to see us first, and we sat together at the play [last night], and this morning we took them to some of the localities of the novels. They were in love with the beautiful villages, and want us to rendezvous with them here in the summer, and to pay them a visit at their fine old place on the Chilterns. . . .

"We were at Wolfeton house . . . on Sunday. Mr. Bankes was lamenting that Mr. Hardy had three times refused a knighthood, he (Mr. B.) wishing 'dear old Mrs. Hardy' to be Lady Hardy. My own opinion is that he [Hardy] had a low opinion of knighthoods as rewards for literature: he *had* to accept the O.M. [Order of Merit, in 1910].

"To-day at the play (we went last night and to-day both) Mr. Bankes was full of Mrs. Hardy's death and much interested to hear we were the last people—outside her own household—that she saw.

"People keep on [saying], as they always do, 'Give up your house in the North and come here where you seem to belong.' And if I show pictures of Belmount they say they don't wonder we find it hard to leave such a view and such a garden. . . .

"Keep this letter . . . and give it me back, for . . . I should like . . . a little record of my last of many visits to her—I hope not our last to him. . . .

"I doubt if anyone but myself and of course Mr. Hardy thinks of the exceeding pathos of her being buried just where she will be [in the Hardy burial lot in the Stinsford churchyard]. Very few people know, or will connect, the ideas and associations. She would have done [so]. They both often said no one knew the books as I did. Poor thing, poor thing. I am crying for her now. They had been married 38 years. It must be a great shock to him. I believe his fidelity to her to have been *perfect.*

With our fondest love,

Your

BETT.

Rebekah's comment on "the exceeding pathos" of Mrs. Hardy's being buried "just where she will be" shows that she knew of Emma Lavinia's disdain of what she regarded as the peasant origin of her husband. Mrs. Hardy had refused to call on her husband's parents at Bockhampton—and now she was to be buried beside them at Stinsford! Rebekah didn't miss a thing! And who else besides Betty Owen had learned, or has until now learned, that Hardy had three times refused a knighthood. And "no one knew the books as I did." Of that there can be no doubt.

As soon as "the charming ladies" from the Chilterns got back from their trip to Dorchester, Miss Gertrude Smith promptly wrote Rebekah as follows:

Britwell House, Wallingford.

Thursday night [28th].

[Postmarked Nov. 29, 1912.]

Dear Miss Owen,

After you left us, we clambered to the top of the Amphitheatre and let *the* apple roll from top to bottom by mistake! We retrieved it [in] a muddy state, washed and brought it home in triumph.

Since our return we have pulled out all the literature appertaining to Hardy we possess and have enjoyed ourselves *nearly* as much as we did last night and this morning, thanks to you and [your] sister's great kindness. I feel we have a new interest in life, to prepare ourselves for meeting again in the Hardy country. I am reading *Under the Greenwood Tree* again at once. It was most good of you both to help to give us so much enjoyment and I only wish we could have stayed one more night and had a few more hours.

With again many thanks to you both from myself and sister, I am

Yours very sincerely

GERTRUDE G. M. SMITH.

Given a little more time and under more favorable conditions, Rebekah would doubtless have been able to organize a British League of Thomas Hardy Book Lovers to vie with the one she had left to wither in New York.

Mrs. Hardy's funeral took place at Stinsford on Saturday the thirtieth. The event can be best described in Rebekah's own words, written down two days after Christmas when the Owens were back in the privacy and quiet of Belmount Hall:

We and the Leslies went to the funeral. I was greatly touched by the scene, the lonely Churchyard, the pale November sunlight, the very few who were there—Mr. Hardy, his brother and sisters, a deputation from some Dorchester society, a very few villagers, the Leslies and ourselves. She who was in many respects Elfride [of the *Blue Eyes*] was laid to rest near the great vault described in *A Pair of Blue Eyes*. To those who knew her as well as we did the sad inscription on Mr. Hardy's wreath had double pathos—"From her lonely husband—with the old affection." I think it was meant for all who *had* known her,—this one outspoken word of a silent man.

The Owens sent some flowers for Mrs. Hardy's grave and, upon their return to Hawkshead, wrote a letter of sympathy to the lonely widower. A week before Christmas he penned them this reply:

Max Gate, Dorchester.

Dear Misses Owen, 18:12:12 [i.e., December 18, 1912].

I send a line to thank you sincerely for your kind letter on my loss, and for the beautiful wreath you were so good as to send, which was duly placed on Mrs. Hardy's grave. I hope you made the return journey without mishap, a journey that was undertaken with such a different object from its event.

Most truly yours

THOMAS HARDY.

Rebekah also received another letter from Teresa Fetherstonhaugh at Moreton. It expressed the hope that "this may find you and your sister comfortably established at your own fireside after your cold journey north. It was nice that you happened to be in Dorset just at the time of poor Mrs. Hardy's death and that you were able to attend her funeral. I am sure your presence there must have pleased and comforted Mr. Hardy. What beautiful and well chosen words he put on the wreath."

The New Year brought Rebekah Owen little except reminders of the past. When the London *Times Literary Supplement* printed (on February 6, 1913) a review of Lascelles Abercrombie's *Thomas Hardy*, she could compliment herself on being three months ahead of the *Times*. On April 5 an unidentified Barbara Collingwood wrote to Betty: "Being in Dorset makes me think so much of you." And in Belmount, Betty herself kept thinking of Dorset. With the passing of time her thoughts drifted from the death of Mrs. Hardy and the sad funeral, back into more familiar channels, and the old studious habits gradually reasserted themselves. During the summer Rebekah got out the program of *The Trumpet-Major* performance and studied it more carefully. She noted that there were three "Wessex Tunes"—musical settings for poems by Hardy, two from *The Dynasts* and one from *Wessex Poems*—the composer of which was not named. She wondered who had written the music, especially the rousing "Rolli-cum-rorum." She wondered, too, what the Hardy Players proposed to do *next* November, now that the giving of a "Hardy play" had become, as it were, an annual affair. Early in September, when her curiosity could wait no longer for a newspaper announcement, she addressed an inquiry to the secretary of the Dorchester Dramatic Society and drew an immediate reply:

Dorset County Museum, Dorchester

Miss Owen,   10 Sept. 1913.
  Belmount Hall
    Outgate, Ambleside.
Madame:

Permit me to thank you for your letter of the 9th inst. and for the very kind interest you and your sister have shown in our amateur efforts to portray some of the characters of our great Wessex Writer. Although it has not been my privilege to personally meet you, I have frequently heard of the support you have both given us [nectar! nectar!], and it is a rare satisfaction to all of us, to know that we have been able to give some pleasure to our audience. . . .

The song you are good enough to admire was set to music by a Dorchester organist, the late Mr. Boyton Smith, who achieved some reputation . . . as a writer of music.

This year we hope to perform an adaptation of *The Woodlanders,* in three acts. The adaptation is by Mr. A. H. Evans, but it has been revised to a great extent by Mr. Hardy himself, and in the production the Master is taking his usual kindly, if retiring, interest. The play will be produced here, all being well, on Wednesday to Thursday, November 19th and 20th, and in London, at the Cripplegate Institute, City, on Monday, December 8th. I greatly fear these dates may be too advanced for you, for the journey to your beautiful Lakeland is a long one if the weather proves bad. If, however, you can again witness the play, the Cast would feel honoured if they can make your acquaintance, and we should be delighted if both you and your sister would take tea with us after the matinée. We are glad to know the plays have interested your chauffeur.

Believe me,
                Very faithfully yours,
                H. A. MARTIN
                Hon. Secretary.

In October Rebekah clipped from the *Times Literary Supplement* an article entitled "A Happy Surprise: Mr. Hardy's Short Stories." The notice reported the publication of *A Changed Man and Other Tales* and explained that in this volume Thomas Hardy had collected a number of his previously published short stories.

Rebekah immediately ordered a copy. When it came, she discovered the book to contain at least two old familiar tales, "A Mere Interlude," and "The Romantic Adventures of a Milkmaid." The latter reminded her of the old American copy of this work, which she had used on previous occasions when she had read the *Adventures* aloud. She hunted it up, noticed that she had never obtained Hardy's autograph in this particular book, and decided to carry it, as well as *A Changed Man*, along when she went to Dorchester in November.

Catharine's health was failing and, when the time for the Hardy Play arrived, she had to remain at Belmount Hall and see Rebekah depart without her. Some of the natives thought that Rebekah was pretty "short" with her sister, and they remembered long afterward her impatience with "Tat's" inability to show the physical vigor she had once had. Betty carried her books to Dorchester with her.

The Woodlanders was given on the nineteenth and twentieth and Miss Owen had her usual seat in the audience. When she went to take tea with the cast, as Mr. Martin had invited her to do after the matinee, one of the actresses who was presented to her was a seventeen-year-old girl named Gertrude Bugler, the daughter of a local baker and confectioner, who had played the part of Marty South with great success. Miss Owen was told that Gertrude Bugler was Hardy's own "find" for the part. Martin himself played the part of Giles Winterborne. In *The Trumpet-Major* of the preceding year, he had had the part of Bob Loveday, the trumpet-major's brother.

Rebekah Owen paid her usual call at Max Gate and at the proper time produced the books she had brought along for Hardy's signature. He readily signed *A Changed Man*, writing "Thomas Hardy. Nov: 1913" on the half-title. But when he saw that Betty's copy of *The Romantic Adventures* was a cheap and flimsy American piracy, he declined to legitimize it, as it were, by his autograph. Betty expressed the opinion (certainly erroneous) that it was a rare piece of American printing, but Hardy remained unimpressed.

Betty's visit to Max Gate provided her with a surprise in a wholly unexpected way. She found the household functioning smoothly and happily under the efficient administration of a Miss Dugdale—a young woman not yet thirty-five—whose words and attitude gave Miss Owen the feeling that Max Gate would not be long without a second Mrs. Hardy. The cats of the first wife had disappeared and their place was taken by a young, restless, wire-haired, noisy terrier called "Wessex," or "Wessie." Rebekah didn't like the dog, even though she had several of her own at Belmount; but she concealed her dislike, or even her fear of the animal, by complimenting him on his affection for Mr. Hardy and Miss Dugdale. Then they talked about Hawkshead and about how cold it was up there at this time of year, and about the absence of a Catholic church there, and about her plan to drive North by way of Bath where she had friends. The prospect of the long cold ride back to Westmorland made her wish anew that she had succeeded in finding a house in Dorset.

Before leaving Dorchester, Miss Owen drove out to Moreton to call on Teresa Fetherstonhaugh, and to Frampton Court to call on Mrs. Sheridan. And, in order to leave a pleasant reminder behind her at Max Gate, she ordered two François Guillot rosebushes delivered there with her best wishes. On November 30 Miss Fetherstonhaugh wrote her this good-bye note:

... Mrs. Sheridan writes me that she was going to Max Gate yesterday. I am so glad you found all going so happily and harmoniously there. I shall like to think of dear Mr. Hardy [he was now 73] happy and comfortable and in good hands. What glorious weather you have for your motor trip to the North!

The rose bushes arrived at Max Gate; and on December 11, by which date Betty had returned to Belmount Hall, she received the following letter:

MAX GATE, DORCHESTER.
10th Dec: 1913.

Dear Miss Owen:

Thank you so much for your extremely kind gift. We are looking forward with great anticipation to a feast of creamy-white roses. The two trees are to be planted against a little conservatory that is now being built —and we will rechristen them, and call them by your name, which will mean so much more to us than François Guillot.

Mr. Hardy wishes you had told us how your return journey prospered —how long you stayed at Bath, and so on. He says he could and would gladly find you [a] house, but he knows you wouldn't live in it, if he did. He is, I see, quite inclined to "sniff" a little at your pirated copy of the *Milkmaid*, which he doesn't love, rare and valuable though it may be.

We have had a great excitement this week—great to us, who live so soberly and remotely. Sir Hubert Herkimer's son has been down, arranging with Mr. Hardy for the production of a film of *Far from the Madding Crowd*, and he hired the local "picturedrome," and gave a little private entertainment of Herkimer films to ourselves and Mr. Hermann Lea, who was invaluable in finding scenes, properties, etc., for the film. Mr. Herkimer hopes to induce our excellent Mr. Pouncy to be the Joseph Poorgrass in the film.

An extraordinary case of witchcraft has occurred in Higher Bockhampton—in the very next cottage to Mr. Hardy's birthplace. Everyone in the village believes firmly in witchcraft—including, I believe, Mr. Lea himself.

It must be exceedingly difficult to practice Catholicism at Ambleside. If one had need of a religion, that, I am sure, is the only one.

With kind regards from Mr. Hardy and all of us,

Yours very sincerely

FLORENCE E. DUGDALE

P.S. Wessex sends his love. He grows dearer every day, and is to have his photograph taken this week.

"Wessie" lived for fourteen years and left his mark in Hardy's poetry as well as on the postman's leg, but he added nothing to the attractiveness of Max Gate for Rebekah Owen. As for "our excellent Mr. Pouncy," he had played the part of Robert Creedle (the factotum of Giles Winterborne) in the 1913 performance of *The Woodlanders;* and in *The Trumpet-Major* of the preceding year, Pouncy had appeared as Corporal Tullidge, a beacon-watcher. The film version of *Far from the Madding Crowd* was finally finished and shown on November 16, 1915, at the West End Cinema in London. Hardy wrote a brief synopsis of his story for use in the program printed for this occasion. This program is one of the very few bits of Hardy's writing that seem to have escaped Miss Owen's eagle eye.

One thing, however, had *not* escaped her. She had read the signs in the matrimonial sky quite correctly. On February 10, 1914, at Enfield, near London, Hardy married Florence Emily Dugdale. She was thirty-five; he, nearly seventy-four. Rebekah Owen sent the bride "a very charming and uncommon piece of silver as a wedding present"—her own modest words (written in her private record)—and she wrote to her friends in the South to ask for "all the news" about the not-unexpected event. Teresa Fetherstonhaugh replied from Moreton on March 5 to say:

I spent a delightful time with the Hardys yesterday. I think I must have been with them nearly an hour and a half. I thought her a dear little gentle thing but what a melancholy face she has! He looked most cheerful and unworried. I have seldom seen him with such a happy expression. The house is so improved. He has built on a little conservatory or rather small winter garden to the drawing-room and I caught glimpses of meadow lilies and daffodils. The room itself smelt very sweet of hyacinths and everything looked redolent of comfort and peace. She seems very fond of flowers and natural history. I must get her books. [Mrs. Florence Hardy had written a number of books for children, for example *The Adventures of Mr. Prickle-back.*] Mr. Hardy was at his best and we discussed so many interesting subjects, from the habits of jays and woodpeckers to the intentions of the Prime Minister. . . .

I wish I knew of a house to suit you in these parts. Which do you prefer —isolation with books or the society of very second-rate little-minded people? My sister-in-law who writes enjoys the latter plight. She says she gets copy for her stories. . . .

With love to your sister. . . .

TERESA FETHERSTONHAUGH

Mrs. Margaret Leslie, who had now moved from Came Rectory to Brighton, also wrote on March 5:

My dear Betty,

I have thought of a letter to you ever since Mr. Hardy's nuptials. . . . We really know no more than the papers [have told us], except (and this is really entre nous) I was much touched by a letter from Mrs. Hardy the day after the wedding, hoping we didn't "disapprove," as Mr. H. "had such an affection" for me and my Father and Edward that she "couldn't bear to in any way separate him from such old friends!" I hastened to assure her that we were delighted to think of their happiness, and only prayed God to give them His Peace and Joy in their lives. I think it was a marvellously *humble* thing to do, don't you, and very sweet of her. I think he wrote to Edward as if he were very happy. I *think* she has more definite religion than he. I don't a bit know how people take it. One friend wrote that everyone was surprised, but many think she is a relative of a very good and rich Mrs. Blodgett,—which is just as well!! . . .

I can't help thinking you would both be better *elsewhere* than Belmount. . . .

MARGIE E. LESLIE

Rebekah's distaste for a prolonged sojourn at Belmount Hall was a familiar story to everyone who knew her. In the spring of 1914, she planned an excursion to Italy with Catharine, but the latter's failing health forced them to remain in England. They did not, however, remain at Belmount. In April, having read the review of "Mr. Hardy's New Poems" in the *Times Literary Supplement*, Betty obtained a copy of *Satires of Circumstance* and checked fifteen of the titles among the "Poems of 1912-13." The relation of these poems to the late Emma Lavinia Hardy was, of course, obvious to Rebekah Owen, and they reinforced the call of Wessex which would not be denied. Betty persuaded Catharine to set out in the motor-car for what proved to be "Tat's" last visit to Dorchester, and early in May they were installed at No. 1 West Walks, not far from their old abode of twenty-two years before. There were the usual calls at Max Gate. Rebekah asked about the Mr. Hermann Lea who had been so invaluable in finding properties for use in the filming of *Far from the Madding Crowd*. She learned that he now occupied the house in which Hardy had been born. Would he let them see it? Hardy promised to see if it could be arranged, and within a few days the following note was delivered to the sisters:

> Upper Bockhampton, Dorchester.
> 17/5/14 [i.e., May 17, 1914].
>
> Dear Ladies,
>   I hear from my friend Mr Thomas Hardy that you would like to see Mr Hardy's birthplace. I shall be at home tomorrow about 4 o'clock and if you will honour me by drinking a cup of tea I shall be very charmed.
>   Yours very faithfully
>   HERMANN LEA.

On the morrow they drove to Bockhampton, taking Mrs. Hardy with them. Thus Catharine and Rebekah Owen became acquainted with the thatched-roof dwelling where Hardy had been born on June 2, 1840, and where he had written *Under the Greenwood Tree*, *A Pair of Blue Eyes*, and *Far from the Madding Crowd*. They found it in 1914 as isolated a spot as Hardy had known it to be during his boyhood. They also found an opportunity, with Florence Hardy's help, to make the acquaintance of Hardy's sisters, Kate and Mary, and of their brother Henry. The Owens made a brief call on them all at Talbothays, near Dorchester, and Rebekah recognized that the name of the estate was that of the dairy in *Tess*.

Meanwhile, Betty Owen had not failed to make inquiries about the plans of the Dorchester Dramatic Society. Was there to be another Hardy Play next November? She went to ask Mr. Martin, the secretary, and took him a picture—a colored print —of an English farmer who, she thought, looked very much like Mr. Martin himself when he was dressed for the rôle he had played in the 1909 performance of *Far from the Madding Crowd*. He apparently was out when she called, but her "court" (to use Dr. Johnson's word) resulted in this reply to her inquiry:

4 Alexandra Villas, Dorchester

Miss Owen   11 May 1914
    No. 1, West Walks,
        Dorchester.

Dear Madame,

I much regret that I was unable to thank you in words for your most kind gift. My friends tell me there is a striking resemblance to my poor self in the part of "Boldwood," in the fine plate, which I shall always treasure, as the part was one in which I took great delight, although I felt painfully aware of my limitations.

The sustained interest shown by the Misses Owen in our work will long be gratefully remembered by those who have been privileged to take part in the Hardy Plays.

With my very grateful thanks,

Believe me
Yours very faithfully
H. A. Martin

With the approach of warmer weather, the Owens apparently motored back to Lakeland, and on June 6 Teresa Fetherstonhaugh addressed the following letter to Belmount Hall:

My dear Miss Owen,

. . . I had such a very nice letter today from Mrs. Hardy. They both came one afternoon to see the bluebells and she writes that he was thrilled with the beauty of the wood. She says, referring to his [74th] birthday [on June 2, 1914]: "I think he must really be 24—he is ever so much younger that I am." She is sending me a poem of his in the *Fortnightly:* "Channel Firing." I wonder if you have seen it? It has not reached me yet.

I suppose you never were able to find that quotation "No heart is pure that is not passionate"? I asked the Hardys. They did not know. . . .

Teresa Fetherstonhaugh

When the Owens got back to the Lake District, they doubtless had to drive around the northern end of Lake Windermere as they approached Belmount, because the ferry across the lake would not accommodate their motor-car. But if, like Wordsworth, they *had* been able to take the short cut and use the ferry, and thus had returned to Belmount Hall via Sawrey and Hawks-

head, they would have been attracted by a scene which, without
any doubt, would have carried their thoughts back fifteen years
to the time when they were preparing to make their first entry
into Belmount Hall. In 1914 any traveler in that region would,
after leaving the Lake Windermere ferry and after mounting
the slope up to the village of Sawrey, have noticed, just off the
road to the right, men at work on the so-called Castle Farm,
where a low white-washed cottage was being put in readiness for
new occupants. If Rebekah had inquired, she would have learned
that her former real-estate agent, Mr. William Heelis, was about
to marry the fifty-year-old woman who owned the Hill Top
property on the other side of the road—a writer who (as the
neighbors had been gradually finding out) had written a number of very successful books for children. But Mr. Heelis's bride-
to-be didn't talk much about her books, and after she became
Mrs. William Heelis she would talk even less about them. And
everyone who knew her, there in the Vale of Esthwaite, knew
that she would never express any admiration for Rebekah Owen's
pink waistcoat. Just at this time, Mr. Heelis and his bride-to-be
were doubtless as little interested in the Owen sisters as the latter
were in the renovations being made at the Castle Farm cottage.
Rebekah's heart was still in Dorset, even though her books and
her motor-car were here in Westmorland.

A few days after her return to Belmount, Betty wrote to Dorchester to ask again about the possibility of a Hardy Play in November. Several weeks went by before she received this reply:

> 4 Alexandra Villas, Dorchester.
> 2 July 1914
>
> Dear Madame,
>
> I delayed writing you in reply to your kind letter of the 11th ult. in the
> hope that I might be able to report something definite as to a Hardy Play
> for November next.
>
> I much regret to say no arrangements are yet made for one, and I fear
> that it will [not] be possible to present one at all this year.
>
> Should, however, we be able to get a suitable play and cast, you shall be

one of the first to be informed, and the seats you mention shall be reserved
for you.

Again thanking you most sincerely for your kind interest, I am

Yours very faithfully

H. A. MARTIN.

Mr. Martin could assure Rebekah that she would "be one of
the first to be informed," but it is very evident from the paucity
of communications at this date from Hardy himself that *he*
would not have assigned Rebekah this high priority. He had
known her now for more than twenty years: the freshness and
vivacity of 1892 were no longer there, and it was becoming increasingly clear to him that she had less and less to offer him in
return for the autographs she was continually asking for. Not all
American ladies were like that: Hardy had had some opportunity for comparing his New York friend with other American
types. Three or four years before Rebekah Owen turned up at
Max Gate for the first time, Hardy had met Louise Chandler
Moulton and had enjoyed a dozen or more years of friendly
contact with her in London. He had found her "a sympathetic
critic," and on the very day of Rebekah's first arrival in Dorchester, he was writing to Mrs. Moulton to suggest that she desert
Boston and "live in London altogether. You might thus please
us your friends, and by sending to America letters of a higher
and more thoughtful kind than those we usually see . . . , go on
. . . raising the standards . . . of journalism." Mrs. Moulton died
in Boston in 1908, but Hardy's memory of her—and of her
poetry (which he found "penetrated by the supreme quality,
emotion")—lingered with him and enabled him to measure the
New Yorker in Rebekah Owen with a Bostonian yardstick.

Moreover, only a few days after Rebekah's visit in 1914, Fate
handed Hardy another American yardstick, another basis of
comparison. The Owens had hardly got back to Belmount Hall
when Hardy received a letter from London: two other American
ladies wanted to come and call. They, like the Owens, proposed

to motor to Dorchester; they too were obviously persons of means: one didn't stay at the Berkeley Hotel in Piccadilly without money. Hardy himself had usually stayed, when he was in London, at the West Central Hotel in Southampton Row, not far from the British Museum; and he knew London well enough to know the difference between Southampton Row prices and Piccadilly prices. In answering the letter he had received, Hardy appointed a day when he would be glad to welcome Miss Amy Lowell of Boston and her friend Mrs. Russell; but—two days before the proposed call—Miss Lowell sprained her ankle and could not leave London. Ten days later, she had improved enough to be able to resume the plan to motor to Dorchester. A day was set. Neither she nor Hardy ever had any difficulty in later years in recalling that day, for on Saturday, August 1, 1914, the first World War began. Hardy later wrote her of "this hideous European tragedy" and of "the barbarousness of the German methods." But even a World War did not crowd Amy Lowell out of the picture that day left in Hardy's memory. Amy Lowell wasn't easy to crowd out. She and Hardy "got along beautifully." She later sent him a copy of her *Sword Blades and Poppy Seed*, published that year, and it was not long before he was writing her letters of a length and cordiality he never displayed in any of his letters to Rebekah Owen. He took to calling Miss Lowell "Cousin Amy," explaining that it was "after the lady in *Locksley Hall*," and at the age of eighty-five he was able to write: "My dear Cousin Amy: It has been a great pleasure to me to receive this valuable book—your *Life of John Keats*."

What would not Rebekah Owen have given to receive a letter like that! Instead, it was typical of her to go to Max Gate with her copy of *A Changed Man* or the *Milkmaid*, asking for an autograph, asking for an introduction to Hermann Lea, asking whether she could call on his sisters Kate and Mary, asking—asking—asking! Obviously, she wanted the center of the stage, and obviously she expected her Distinguished Author to be just off stage, ready for her to summon him. At the age of seventy-four one doesn't like to be peremptorily called with a "What ho, Horatio!"

After the return to Belmount Hall, Rebekah ordered a basket of fruit sent to Talbothays, and then wrote to Mary Hardy and asked her to pass some of it on to her famous brother at Max Gate! Sister Mary replied:

Talbothays, near Dorchester
3 Sep[tember]: 1914.

Dear Miss Owen,

Many thanks for your present of delicious fruit, which we did not send on to Max Gate but ate ourselves. . . . My elder brother and his wife have not been down here for the last fortnight, but my sister met Florence one day and told her about the peaches, and she begged us to thank you for them. Tom is deeply affected by the appalling march of events, as day by day the news of this momentous and terrible war reach us.

I am sorry you have reason to be anxious about your sister. I saw she was not looking very well, also her gentle acceptance of her weak state of health, when you were here. I hope that with rest and as the seasons get a little cooler she may recover some of her lost strength.

With kind regards from us all to you both, I am,

Sincerely yours,
MARY HARDY.

Catharine, however, did *not* recover her lost strength, and in September took to her bed. On September 9 Betty clipped from the London *Times* Hardy's poem, "Song of the Soldiers," and during the last few days of Catharine's life, Rebekah read this poem to her sister over and over again. What a strange death-bed consolation and comfort! On September 15, 1914, Catharine Owen died at Belmount Hall and was buried near "Ashy" at Coniston. John Ruskin now had two American neighbors.

Rebekah hurried the news off to Max Gate, but even this act had to be accompanied by a request: what was the address of "Margie" Leslie in Brighton? for Betty would like to notify her too that "Tat" had died. On September 17 Hardy sent the following telegram from Dorchester:

OWEN, Belmount Hall, Hawkshead, Ambleside: Much grieved. Wife away. Will send Leslies' address when ascertained.

HARDY.

In that "much grieved" Rebekah got her six-pennyworth of "good" for her peach-basket of "court."

Miss Owen now had her chance. All her life up to this moment had been a superb preparation, and now she was free: no more responsibilities to Ashy or Tat, no family obligations, no exposure to the havoc of war, no need to work for a living; she had a home, and health, and wealth. Even the war had a beneficial aspect, for Rebekah's isolation at Belmount gave her a splendid opportunity for achieving that detachment without which there can be no truly enlightened *at*tachment—at least not for the student of literature. Once upon a time her old friend, the Reverend George Oliver of Worcester, had written her: "You must have enjoyed the introduction to Thomas Hardy, and we expect you will write a book some day." The time had now come to write it. She had excellent qualifications for the task. Even the Hardys knew that—Thomas and Emma Lavinia both knew it. "They often said no one knew the books as I did." Rebekah Owen now had her chance.

In earlier days Betty had taken the idea seriously enough to jot down notes for the not-impossible publication. In addition to facts about Hardy, his family, his books, and his friends, she also wrote down some memoranda with which she may have intended to enliven her book. One of her anecdotes offers a sample of Dorset "native humor" which Rebekah picked up in some "cottage interior" such as she had visited at Stinsford or at Bere Regis:

American lady (to old woman with the plaintive expression): "And your husband has a brother in America! Is he pleased with it? Is he getting on well?"

Old woman: "Well, miss, 'e do write as 'ow 'e is, but I says to my old man, we ain't there to contradict 'im!"

Rebekah now had her chance to get out all her notes and go to work. She *ought* to have been able to produce a valuable work on Thomas Hardy—a better book than Miss Macdonell's. Samuel Johnson once remarked that biography is rarely well executed, because of two facts: "they only who live with a man can write his life with any genuine exactness and discrimination; and few people who have lived with a man know what to remark about him." The great Boswell didn't always know "what to remark." He tried to record everything and sometimes allowed his ship to founder in an ocean of triviality. But Rebekah Owen did know what to remark and rarely permitted her eyes to wander from the important object of her study—Hardy's books. The contrast between the two is worth detailing.

Boswell's first meeting with Johnson led him to record that the great lexicographer was a worthy man, but instead of remarking on the evidence of his worthiness, the *London Journal* of 1763 tells us that "Mr. Johnson is a man of a most dreadful appearance . . . , very slovenly in his dress and . . . with a most uncouth voice." After "remarking" on the two bottles of port wine which Johnson drank with him on 14 July 1763, Boswell wrote: "I take pleasure in recording every little circumstance about so great a man as Mr. Johnson. This little specimen of social pleasantry will serve me to tell as an agreeable story to literary people." With all her vanity, Rebekah Owen never looked into the mirror to see herself in action as a teller of agreeable stories to literary people. She must have observed that Hardy could be just as slovenly as Johnson, but she did not stop to record the fact; and although she took tea at Max Gate on many an occasion, she did not think it important to record whether Hardy drank two cups or ten, or whether he took sugar in his tea or not. She was quite appreciative of "social pleasantry" and Hardy had found her good company, but Rebekah Owen had little of Boswell's self-conscious dramatization of himself.

Johnson once remarked (in the *Rambler*, No. 60) that "more knowledge may be gained of a man's real character by a short conversation with one of his servants than from a formal and studied narrative, begun with his pedigree and ended with his funeral." Miss Owen acted in accordance with this view. She talked with everyone who could tell her what she wanted to know; servants, housekeepers, gardeners, chauffeurs, editors, friends, curates, actors, writers, housewives, noblemen and "noble dames"—all were tapped to provide her with the knowledge she craved. And for thirty years she had been scribbling her notes —always scribbling. When Edward Gibbon brought a copy of the second volume of the *Decline and Fall of the Roman Empire* to the Duke of Gloucester, the Duke (we are told) laid the book on the table and with a good-natured smile said to the author: "Another damned thick book! Always scribble, scribble, scribble! Eh, Mr. Gibbon?" Well, if it is not fair to Miss Owen's assiduity and zeal to call her notes scribbling, it is certainly true that by 1914 she had been writing long and much about her adored author. Even at the date when he composed his statement about "some good judges across the Atlantic," it is quite likely that Rebekah Owen knew more about his life and literary career than anyone then living, and she had not been idle since that date. By her careful reading of his books, by haunting his footsteps, by quizzing him at Max Gate, by gleaning all she could from him during numerous trips afoot and awheel in his company, by her conversations with those who knew him, by her letters from both wives of the novelist, by her exploration of every inch of the Hardy country, Miss Owen had certainly served her literary apprenticeship conscientiously and well. Her little essays on the futility of *Jude*, on the expiation and purification of Tess, on the artistic quality in the termination of *The Mayor*, serve as exam-

ples of the critical insights of which she was capable. Here she
was certainly James Boswell's superior. The girl who had corrected Longfellow's misguided reference to Shakespeare's children had developed into the woman who could set Hardy against
Zola, who could quote Gervinus and Bishop Stubbs, and who
had sense enough to put *Desperate Remedies* aside and to leave *A
Laodicean* unopened.

Yet, in spite of all these favorable winds, her ship never left
the harbor. Why? There is, first of all, the obvious fact that it
is easier to plan an ambitious project than to carry it out. If Miss
Owen had merely shied away from an irksome task, she would
not be the first person to do so. After all, she was fifty-six years
old when "Tat" died, and fifty-six is an advanced age at which
to *begin* an arduous task. Boswell was dead at that age. Moreover,
he would never have achieved his *Life of Johnson* if it had not
been for his friend Malone. The *Boswell Papers* show how great
was his indebtedness to this friend. Without Malone's encouragement and help, without his constant and unwearied prodding,
Boswell would in all likelihood never have seen his famous book
in print. Such a thing *has* happened. Charles Whibley (we are
told) got together a vast lot of material about W. E. Henley and
had all the knowledge necessary for "a biography of Boswellian
proportions," but he never wrote it. Boswell might easily have
remained equally silent. He was quite equal to brief spurts of
energy, but it takes more than a spurt and a spasm to produce a
book. Boswell planned other literary projects as ambitious as
the great biography, but he never found the will-power to bring
them to fulfillment. Fortunately, Edmond Malone was on hand
(while the *Johnson* was a-making) to poke and prod, to coax and
urge. *Un*fortunately, Rebekah Owen had lost all her Edmond
Malones. George Oliver, who had expected her to write a book
and who could have encouraged and helped her in doing one,
died twenty years too soon. When the Owens turned their backs
upon New York, they sacrificed their stimulating contact with

Miss Drisler and with Columbia University. When they bought Belmount Hall, they denied themselves the occasion for long sojourns at Oxford such as had previously brought them into intimate relations with the dons there and had gained special favors for Rebekah in the Bodleian Library. When Rebekah resigned her presidency of the Thomas Hardy Book League and expatriated herself in the attempt to set herself up as a Noble Dame, she laid the foundation for the futility that now settled down upon her. The World War gave her her great chance—isolation, solitude, quiet—but she was not equal to its demands.

Other women, no better equipped, wrote their books on Hardy, but not Rebekah. Unlike Annie Macdonell, she wrote no little primer to arouse the interest of members of some future Thomas Hardy Book League. Unlike Harriet Preston, she made no attempt to introduce Hardy to readers of the *Atlantic Monthly* or of any other magazine. Unlike Jeannette Gilder, she published no review of *Jude the Obscure*. Unlike Helen Garwood, she wrote no study of Hardy's philosophy. Rebekah had heard Hardy talk so often about "The Withered Arm" and about the ghostly coach in *Tess;* but, unlike Ruth Firor, she wrote no study of *Folkways in Thomas Hardy*. Unlike Mary Ellen Chase, she wrote no book on *Thomas Hardy from Serial to Novel*. Unlike Rebecca West, Rebekah Owen wrote no account of *The Dynasts* nor any appraisal of Hardy as an "Interpreter of his Age." Unlike Irene Haworth, she wrote no Introduction to *The Return of the Native*. Unlike Elizabeth Hickson, she made no analysis of *The Versification of Thomas Hardy*. Unlike Phyllis Bentley, she wrote no account of "Hardy as a Regional Novelist." Rebekah Owen inquired about the music of Boyton Smith; but, unlike Elna Sherman, she wrote no account of "Music in Hardy's Life and Work." She went to the Hardy plays over and over again; but, unlike Marguerite Roberts, she wrote no study of Hardy's connection with the theatre. Here are the names of a dozen English and American women who were in no way better qualified or better equipped than

Rebekah Owen for rendering useful service in the Hardy vineyard; yet *they* produced, whereas *she* lapsed into sterile and self-
ish uselessness. In the days of World War II, a German bomb
landed in a field near Belmount Hall, breaking a window and
killing a sheep. If this bomb had destroyed Miss Owen's Hardiana, all her years of "heroic hardihood" (to quote Mrs. Gangewer) would have forever dropped out of sight without leaving a trace.

As the end of the year 1914 approached, Rebekah wrote to
the Hardys, telling them that she was sending her copy of *Satires
of Circumstance* to Max Gate and would be glad if the author
would insert his usual autograph. In reply, she received (on
December 30) a curt picture postcard from Florence Hardy:
"Letter just received, Every good wish for 1915 from us both.
May you soon see this spot again. F.H." But no book! Rebekah
wrote again. Finally, in the second week in January, there came
another card from Max Gate, unsigned but in Mrs. Hardy's
handwriting. It said: "Am so sorry for the delay. Your book . . .
will be sent off today, with others. Bad weather and servants ill
with colds have prevented anyone going into Dorchester for
days." (Max Gate is a mile or so out of town.) The *Satires of
Circumstance* eventually came back with "Thomas Hardy" autographed on the half-title. Before adding the book to the collection in the Sheraton bookcase, Rebekah looked at the familiar
signature, but she did not notice the handwriting on the wall.
Hardy was obviously becoming increasingly impatient with her,
but she continued, blindly, to pay court.

On the first anniversary of Florence's wedding, Miss Owen
sent her a check for two guineas to buy a suitable present with.
Then, as soon as the weather permitted travelling with the motor-
car, she drove south and in April made the inevitable call at Max
Gate. Wouldn't Mr. Hardy like to take a motor-ride? Hardy
declined, but Mrs. Hardy accepted, and eventually Kate Hardy

was included in the party. They drove to Talbothays to get her. The party then followed a route which Hardy himself drew up for the chauffeur: "To Talbothays. Stafford; Woodsford; across mead to Waddock Cross, thence to Puddletown. Come out of Puddletown by New Street, or Cow Lane; past Coom to 'the Duck'—(view of heath)—'Duck' to Bockhampton Cross; turn down through Lower Bockhampton," and thus back to Talbothays and Max Gate. As Rebekah Owen listened to the minute directions Hardy gave, she had abundant reason for understanding why William Archer had once exclaimed to Hardy: "What you don't know about this Wessex of yours isn't knowledge! ... It seems to me there isn't a contour of the country that isn't mapped in your mind."

They took the ride but it wasn't a success. Perhaps Rebekah's ardor was dampened by the discovery that the Hardys were not wholly unfamiliar with the uses of a motor-car. Although the poet-novelist had none of his own, Mr. Lea at Bockhampton owned one, and Hardy often made some arrangement with him when he needed to drive some distance.

Upon her return to Belmount, Rebekah took out the old familiar copy of *Far from the Madding Crowd* and read it once again, reaching the end by May 13. But it was an empty performance, with both Tat and Ashy gone from the audience. When the geraniums and fuchsias in the Belmount garden could be handled, she had her gardener cut some and sent them with a note to Mary Hardy. At the end of the month a reply came:

Talbothays, Dorchester,
24 May, 1915.

My dear Miss Owen,

I am so sorry not to have replied at once to your kind letter accompanying the kindly present of the flowers. Henry planted them at once. ... I must thank you for the kind attention of reading *Far from the Madding Crowd* in the evenings. My brother and Florence were here yesterday and in the course of a week they are going to London for a little time. My brother's health will not stand it there long, and he seems much depressed about this terrible war. . . .

Most sincerely yours,
MARY HARDY.

Rebekah tried yet once more reading the Wessex Works aloud. On June 7 she finished reading *Tess of the D'Urbervilles* to an unidentified Nelly Dennis, but it was "no go." The joy had gone out of such performances, and Betty never tried another oral rendition. Then she lost Dickinson, her chauffeur. Many years later, people in Hawkshead said he went mad, but all that can be stated now with any assurance is that Rebekah found herself with a car but no driver. She eventually appealed to Hermann Lea at Bockhampton. On September 22, 1915, he wrote to say: "I have just heard of a man who may possibly suit you." But nothing came of it. Rebekah was finally reduced to staying at home, reading to herself, clipping the newspapers and magazines, receiving and answering letters. She also sent presents. Sometimes she got results, sometimes not.

On December 14, 1915, she received from Mrs. Florence Hardy a fulsome and effusive letter beginning "Best and Belovedest Betty." As the unrelieved routine of life at Max Gate settled down upon the second Mrs. Hardy, she found Rebekah Owen a useful and willing person to turn to. Much of what she wrote is not worth printing; some of it ought never to have been written. In the year 1916 alone, Miss Owen received thirty-three letters from Florence Hardy. A few samplings must here suffice:

January 18: My husband went out today for a walk for the first time, but not very far. He gets soon tired. . . . I keep a diary . . . but when I remember the *awful* diary the first Mrs. T. H. kept (which he burned) full of venom, hatred, and abuse of him and his family, I am afraid to do more than chronicle facts.

February 4 [after Rebekah had written that she hoped to get down to Dorchester soon]: It will be delightful to see you here . . . but your visit last year seemed so disappointing to you.

February 16 [after Rebekah had written on the second anniversary of Hardy's second marriage and had sent a two-guinea book about Botticelli]: Thank you ... for your kind letter on the second anniversary of our wedding-day. On the whole—in spite of my profuse grumbling—I think no two years could have been happier.

June 13: We are expecting a visit this afternoon from ... a first cousin of the "late espousèd saint."

September 22: When I married, I remember how it was impressed upon me that I must "keep off" people [i.e., keep people off].

October 23 [after Rebekah had written asking Florence to get her a seat for the November performance of "Wessex Scenes from *The Dynasts*"]: Kate Hardy has the seat directly behind you.

October 29: The play has had to be postponed.

November 22 [after learning that Rebekah was on her way to call on Mrs. Leslie at Brighton]: I am so glad that you have at last managed [to get away]. . . . Give our love to Mrs. Leslie.

November 25: It is going to be a most difficult job to find you any lodgings whatever. . . . [Army] officers are giving high prices and so many of them have their wives and families here too. [Rebekah eventually had to take a room at 14 Royal Crescent, Weymouth, eight or ten miles away from Dorchester. There she was near the little theatre she had once written about in her correspondence with Mary Drisler. See page 235.]

December 1 [after Rebekah had called at Max Gate]: Sorry not to see you this afternoon.

December 2: Shall be at home all day Monday [4th]. Come when you like.

December 6: My husband is in bed [on this first day of the performance of *Wessex Scenes*]. . . . Will you have tea with me [tomorrow]?

December 14 [after Rebekah had called on the 7th and had then returned to Belmount Hall]: Your visit seemed so short, and I had so much to tell you. . . . How is your cold?

If all the years of Miss Owen's life had been as unprofitable as the year 1916, the present book would never have been written. Not that all years can be like eighteen-hundred ninety-two. And not that a period of idle waiting may not be a good thing. Hardy's old editor in the *Cornhill* office, Leslie Stephen, once declared that "no man is a real reading enthusiast until he is sensible of the pleasure of turning over [the pages of] some miscellaneous collection, lying like a trout in a stream, snapping up with the added charm of unsuspectedness any of the queer little morsels of oddity or pathos that may drift past him."

If Rebekah Owen had been lying like a trout in her Belmount stream, snapping up little morsels that might drift past her, she might even yet have achieved something useful. But as she approached the age of sixty, she did very little snapping up of anything except idle gossip. One morsel of pathos came to her in a letter from Florence Hardy, dated June 24, 1917: "My husband says that he wishes your visits to Dorchester would be in the summer. He thinks of you when we walk across the field . . . up to Came Plantation, for you walked there once with him, I think."

Yes, Rebekah could say to herself, I walked there once with him, and we sat there a long time. The memory of that day doubtless resulted in her sitting in Belmount Hall a long time— thinking—thinking—thinking of what might have been. On July 18, 1917, she penned this sad and lonely note:

"To think how long and familiar [twenty-five years, to be exact] the intercourse has been, how unchanged it is [or seems] whenever I go to Dorset, and what an infinite waste of life my eighteen years at Belmount have been!"

Chapter X

They Resolve to Say No More

AS Rebekah Owen penned the sad confession of her sense of wasted life, she doubtless thought that the important tell-tale words in her statement were "at Belmount." The great mistake had been the purchase of that property back in 1899. In another environment her life might have been quite different. The ablest and most energetic of farmers will find it impossible to raise in Arizona the crops that are produced by the soil and climate of Minnesota. Rebekah Owen had found out that here in Lakeland it was just one fight after another. If it wasn't the rain it was the rats; if it wasn't the rats it was the servants; if it wasn't the servants it was the plumbers. Male workmen didn't like to be ordered around by a woman, especially by an imperious American woman.

"I had rather a row with the plumber—or perhaps I ought to say I lost my temper! . . . If he won't take orders from a lady, I may pack him off and get one from Kendall."

It so happens, however, that those are not the words of Rebekah Owen but of a near-neighbor of hers in Sawrey—they are the words of Mrs. William Heelis who had moved into the cottage on Castle Farm a few weeks after the death of Catharine Owen. Like Rebekah, Mrs. Heelis knew from experience that plumbing and servants and rain could cause endless trouble. And the rats! Mrs. Heelis knew them too. Said she:

A most painful tragedy happened last night. I woke up at the noise of a poor chicken screaming. It stopped, and [as] it was extremely cold . . . I did *not* get out of bed. I went, directly I got up, and found a horrid big old rat in the hutch on the lawn. It was eating one chicken and had hurt two others. . . . The dogs killed the rat, and the lame ones are recovering. But next time I hear chickens at night, I shall turn out. I feel ashamed of my-self: I was half asleep.

When Rebekah Owen read about "a most painful tragedy" like that, it touched her heart. That is, if she read about it in a book. The episode which she had rescued from the discarded chapter of *The Mayor*, that "beautiful and most touching" chapter in which occurs the slow starvation of the caged goldfinch, this epi-sode she had called the "saddest incident in fiction." And there were other "painful tragedies" which touched her heart as she read one or another of the Hardy novels. Rebekah could recall one such scene in *Jude the Obscure*—the description of a night when Jude had retired to rest early, and then had an experience very much like that of Mrs. Heelis:

At some time near two o'clock . . . , he was aroused by a shrill squeak. . . . It was the cry of a rabbit caught in a gin. . . . Almost half-an-hour passed, and the rabbit repeated its cry. Jude could rest no longer till he had put it out of its pain, so dressing himself quickly he descended, and by the light of the moon went across the green in the direction of the sound . . . of . . . the writhing animal. . . . Reaching the spot he struck the rabbit on the back of the neck with the side of his palm, and it stretched itself out dead.

And how many times had Rebekah read that painful chapter in *Far from the Madding Crowd* in which Gabriel Oak learns of the loss of all his sheep: "two hundred mangled carcases represent-ing . . . the untimely fate of those gentle ewes and their unborn lambs." In *books* Rebekah Owen had ears to hear, and "the noise of a poor chicken screaming" could stir her tender feelings. But if the noise came, not from a book but from the Belmount gar-den, she was deaf. Unlike Mrs. Heelis, she did not resolve to "turn out." The result of this difference in the two women is very striking: living in exactly the same region, facing exactly the same problems, confronted by exactly the same difficulties, one woman continued to lament what an infinite waste her life at Hawkshead had been; the other proceeded to put even the "hor-rid big old rat" to work; and thus, by the transforming power of her imagination, she made Mr. Samuel Whiskers into one of the most successful of her animal villains. For Mrs. William Heelis was none other than Beatrix Potter, who (before her marriage) had become the author of the most delightful series of animal stories ever composed for children.

The contrast between these two neighbors in the vale of Esthwaite appears clearly defined when we compare their productivity. In Rebekah Owen's eighteen years at Belmount Hall (1899-1917), she had produced nothing but some nostalgic scrapbooks and some photograph albums. In contrast with this stunted harvest, Beatrix Potter had, in her eight years of "solitary happiness" at nearby Sawrey (1905-1913), produced (by the time she was fifty) thirteen successfully published books. Six of them were intimately concerned with the very same neighborhood which had no charm for Rebekah Owen. Throughout the past fifty years the world has been delighting in the information about that neighborhood made available in the books of Beatrix Potter. The illustrations were done "on the spot." On page 62 of *The Tale of Jemima Puddle-Duck,* Rebekah Owen could have immediately recognized the little inn called the Tower Bank Arms which stood (and still stands) at one end of Sawrey village. In *The Tale of Tom Kitten* she could easily have identified the high wall and the long, sloping garden-path that led up to the Hill Top Farm which Miss Potter had bought through Heelis & Co. in 1905, six years after the Owens had acquired Belmount Hall through the services of the same firm. Rebekah Owen had had an eye for the cats she had seen at Max Gate— she even recalled their names*—but she had no eye for the Lakeland cats. It remained for Beatrix Potter to immortalize the feline who drove Mr. Samuel Wiskers away: "Once upon a time there was an old cat called Mrs. Tabitha Twitchit, who was an

---

* Hardy had named four of the cats after the fairies in *A Midsummer Night's Dream:* Cobweb, Peaseblossom, Moth, and Mustardseed. Rebekah also remembered a roaming white cat called Marco [Polo].

anxious parent," and two generations of children have learned to take delight in Tabitha Twitchit's activities. "Once upon a time there was a frog called Mr. Jeremy Fisher," and children in nurseries throughout the world have listened over and over again to his tale, read according to the true Rebekah Owen formula of endless and patient repetition.

Meanwhile, in Belmount Hall, repetition of another kind was going on. In December, 1917, the London *Times Literary Supplement* informed Miss Owen of the publication of Hardy's *Moments of Vision*. She promptly ordered a copy, read it when it came, and checked twenty-two of the poems. That accomplished, there was little for her to do but wait for the chief event of the day—the arrival of the postman. In mid-January, 1918, Rebekah received a letter from Mrs. Hardy which informed her that

dear Mrs. Sheridan [of Frampton] passed away yesterday afternoon [Jan. 13]. . . . She paid us a New Year visit. . . . Before leaving, while my husband was out of the room (he ran upstairs to find her a book), she clasped my hand in both of hers and . . . said that I had made my husband's life happy. She said the title of his book, *A Changed Man,* applied to him, for she remembered his *careworn* look and knew what his life *used* to be.

On February 6 Rebekah was sixty years old. (She admitted to only fifty.) Her birthday reminded her of another date close at hand. It was now four years since Hardy's second marriage. As wedding-anniversary presents, she mailed Hardy a costly book on Dorset, and she sent "an expensive weeping Standard rose-tree, extra size," to Florence. A few days later, Miss Owen followed up these gifts by sending her copy of *Moments of Vision* to Max Gate, so that it might receive the usual benediction of the poet's autograph.

Hardy had, however, become increasingly annoyed by such requests for his autograph. Rebekah had been poking her books under his pen now for more than twenty-five years: to her it was a dignified old habit; to him it was an ever-growing nuisance.

Rebekah had, of course, no way of knowing how many other persons—total strangers—were presenting *their* copies of the books for the author to sign. Hardy was now nearly seventy-eight years old. If he had not been receiving Florence's solicitous care, his tired old body might have given up the fight long ago. When a man is seventy-seven, "it is time to be old, to take in sails." Hardy decided to take in at least one sail. "Why do I go on doing these things?" That is the question he asked himself in a recently composed poem. (It later appeared as the last poem in *Human Shows,* 1925.) "Why not cease?" Very well, he *would* cease. He would stop at least one annoyance: he would autograph no more books. He announced his decision to his wife, and left it to her to draft some sort of statement that could be sent in response to future autograph-hunters. And in February Rebekah Owen's request came a-knocking at the door.

Mrs. Hardy was now faced with a painful and unwelcome duty. On February 18, however, she took apologetic pen in hand and sent Rebekah

a statement which I much hesitate to make. It seems so very unkind and ingracious, more especially after your kind gift of that delightful book, which I hope my husband will write and thank you for. It is this: that he has ceased altogether to give autographs. He will not even autograph a book of poems for *me.* Lately the requests have become absolutely overwhelming. . . . I am returning yours [*Moments of Vision*] with a *sad* heart. . . . But you know, Betty dear, it is impossible to make him do things. At his age—77—there is sometimes (what shall we call it?) fixity of purpose. He refuses to give *any* autographs or to be made to write letters. . . . I am so sorry. I do so dislike doing this.

The receipt of this letter shocked and stunned Rebekah. She was furious. It brought her correspondence with Florence Hardy to an abrupt halt. For the rest of this year, and throughout the whole of 1919, and for the first four months of 1920, the flow of messages back and forth between Belmount and Max Gate experienced an almost complete stoppage. Not until the approach of

Hardy's eightieth birthday, in June, 1920, was there any attempt at *rapprochement*, and by that date, though wounds had somewhat healed, the scars were there to stay. Rebekah never wholly recovered from that affront to her vanity. When Florence's "statement" of February 18, 1918, reached her, Miss Owen wrote on the envelope that it was "another evidence of the peasant origin which I noted in my journal in 1892," and that long before this she had had proof of Hardy's being "receptive but not responsive."

But that retort discourteous did not satisfy Rebekah. She had lost her sense of humor. In 1900 she had boasted of making every one in Dorchester laugh. She knew how to laugh herself, but she couldn't laugh *at* herself. She and Catharine had laughed over Hardy's faults, but Rebekah couldn't laugh at her own. After brooding for ten days over the slight she had suffered at the hands of the adored one, she could not resist the desire to blow off steam by making a "statement" of her own. She did not send it to Florence; I do not know that she sent it to any one; but she wrote it all out, carefully and fully, and dated it and signed it as if it were a legal document. If she intended it for posterity, here it is for posterity to read:

"A very long friendly intercourse comes to an end with this. I am deeply—well, less hurt than disgusted. Mr. Hardy has always, since 1892, written his name in his books for me, probably began doing so before other people asked the same favour, for I think the request for this sort of autograph is very recent. I bought the books, sent them with return postage, and I may say, have given generously to both his wives,—*very* generously to this one. Not only did I give her a very charming and uncommon piece of silver as a wedding present, [but] I have [also] kept each anniversary since by another. In 1915 I remember I gave her a cheque for £2. 2. 0. Another year I gave her a two-guinea book (new copy) about Botticelli. This year I sent an expensive weeping Standard rose-tree, extra size, of a rather scarce rose which I knew she wanted. A few days later I sent him my copy of *Moments of Vision* with a nice note asking him to write in it; and with it, as a special present for himself, a very lovely book, never cheap and now out of print, and one which he was *bound* to like: *Where Dorset Meets Devon*. I almost grudged giving it. After undue delay, I got a letter from Florence Hardy, enclosing this type-written one which she *says* he dictated, refusing to autograph any more books for me or for any one, that as his autograph enhances the value [of the book] from five shillings (six *I* paid) to five pounds, and people have sold them, he must reserve the autographing of his books as his contribution to the Red Cross Fund 'and other charities, as alas! it is all he can now give.' This I feel sure is her language, he would not say 'Alas,' and I believe few, if any, ever knew him [to] give any money to any charity. I have heard him inveigh against bazaars, Missions and other charities. Also, it is not true that his signature is all he, 'alas,' has to give. He must have made a fortune, and be roping in lots from the sale of his books every year. The thing is he *hates* giving anything. I noted this years ago, and can recall many instances. One, considering his own origin, is amusing. Once during a walk beyond Herrington, a little lad at a cottage opened a gate for us, leading out upon Came Down. I had no money. Mr. Hardy felt for some, put it back and said it was not necessary, that children liked the fun of opening gates for people. (I have never told this to anyone but my sister. She knew he was close with money and his first wife openly said so, and the second hints it.) I wondered if *he* used to open the gate by his birthplace to let people onto Bockhampton Moor and think the 'fun' sufficient reward.

"It isn't so much the refusal to autograph this book—though an exception might have been made to one of the oldest of his real devotees—as the way it was done, and *much* worse, the total

ignoring of my gift, which makes me feel I have done with that
friendship. Not so much as the *slightest* message of thanks, of
mere acknowledgement was sent me. I wish I had the book back.
But here his peasant origin tells, as his first wife was fond of saying. The same thing came out in his brother, whom we never met
till 1914. Mrs. T. H. took us there, in our motor, to see him and
his sisters and their garden. He had some pretty single mauve
primroses and some geraniums which he had raised from seed. I
said if he would give me one little seedling primrose and a geranium cutting I would give him a double mauve and a double
white primrose and some special geranium and fuchsia cuttings.
He promised gladly. I sent stout plants and good cuttings and
got nothing in exchange. The Hardys are like their class in the
North Country, receptive but not responsive. [Rebekah liked
that phrase!] I have known too much warm-hearted and spon-
taneous generosity among Dorset peasants and farmers not to
think the Hardys are unworthy of their country folk whose mot-
to is 'Use 'em well they'll use 'ee better.'

"I think Florence is sorry, or affects to be, but she can do nothing. I admit he is justified in refusing autographs for people he
does not know or knows only slightly; but he has given them to
me (in books only, I never asked for others) since 1892 and no
one was ever more genuinely and loyally devoted to his genius.
I saw his faults and talked and laughed over them with my
sister. My diary and letters to her noted them, but I would never admit them when his first wife dissected his character, nor
ever gossip about them to anyone. I shall certainly tell Margie
(Moule) Leslie, for she knew his parsimony and said last year
he was very mean never to have given me one of his books. He
gave her one when she married, he gave one to Miss Teresa Fetherstonhaugh. It is the keeping my gift (without thanking me
even by message) and at the same time sending a brutally worded
refusal which hurts and alienates. Yet he *always* seems so particularly glad to see me.

"Peasant blood! How the Old Testament and Shakespeare despise a churl!

R. Owen

Belmount Hall,
   Outgate, Ambleside.   February 28, 1918."

Poor lady, poor lady! To discover, after twenty-six years, that in Thomas Hardy's eyes, she was just one in a crowd; that although "no one was ever more genuinely and loyally devoted to his genius," he was unwilling any longer to take orders from her; that although she was "one of the oldest of his real devotees," he would make no exception even of her: *that* was what hurt. She unfortunately had no way of knowing how very serious the problem had become for him. After her death there appeared in the *Dorset County Chronicle* (May 30, 1940) an article by T. H. Rogers on "How Hardy Solved the Autograph Nuisance." It is too bad that Rebekah Owen could not have read it. Instead of sympathizing with the plight of the weary, hard-pressed author who found that his mounting reputation and spreading fame brought down upon him an avalanche of letters and requests that was "absolutely overwhelming," Rebekah could think only of herself. "The total ignoring of *my* gift!" Poor self-centered soul! How she shrinks in our estimation as we read the outpouring of her wounded ego! Whatever Hardy's faults, whatever his limitations, whatever his impoliteness if not his "brutality," he had at least learned how to turn his thoughts outward, and not to center them upon himself. He may never have sent Rebekah Owen a book, but he *did* give books away. Mrs. Hardy once reported that, during the war, her husband

paid a visit to the Commandant of the Prison Camp here who took him to see the German prisoners. T.H.'s kind heart melted at the sight of the wounded and he expressed his sympathy with them by eloquent gestures to which they responded in a most friendly manner; and also he wished many of the *well* prisoners "good-day" to which they replied with alacrity, and now he is sending them some of his books, in German, for their library.

What an opportunity Rebekah Owen had, especially during the war, to lose herself in similar fashion and forget her wounds in rendering public-spirited service! But with all her giving, she had never learned to give without an eye to some return.

Her neighbor Mrs. Heelis, on the other hand, was active up to the very year of her death with projects and undertakings that looked far beyond her own immediate and personal interests. She became President of the Herdwick Sheep-Breeders' Association while Rebekah was brooding over a few "single mauve primroses." Mrs. Heelis labored long and ardently in the service of the National Trust, hoping thereby to preserve the natural beauties of the Lake District. Rebekah liked to boast to her friends, especially to those Dorset people who were "so pleasant as well as of superior birth and fashion to Lake District people," that she owned a beauty spot in the North. "Such a view and such a garden!" But it was Mrs. Heelis, not Rebekah Owen, who helped to preserve the beauty of that region. She—Beatrix Heelis—helped the National Trust to acquire a strip of wooded land near the Windermere Ferry; and she, not Rebekah Owen, acquired the large estate just to the north of the village of Coniston and turned it over to the National Trust, thereby preserving for posterity the beauty of the landscape one looks out on, to the North, when one visits the graves of Catharine Owen and Caroline Ash. By the will of Beatrix Heelis, the Lake District holdings of the National Trust were increased by four thousand acres. At the death of Rebekah Owen, there was, behind the high wall at Belmount,

> an unweeded garden grown to seed:
> Things rank and gross in nature possessed it merely.

There are persons who, after having been hurt, lick their wounds, get a good night's sleep, and rise to go about their business. In the course of a few days they have almost forgotten the affront that so smarted when the wound was fresh. And there are others, equipped with what Hardy called "pachydermatous hides" (*Tess*, Chapter 25), who do not feel the injury in the first place. James Boswell had such a hide. One day in the spring of 1772, he attempted to defend drinking by saying to Johnson: "You know, Sir, drinking makes us forget whatever is disagreeable. Would not you allow a man to drink for that reason?" Dr. Johnson (who had now known Boswell for nine years) replied: "Yes, Sir, if he sat next *you*." Boswell lost no sleep over the insult.

But Miss Rebekah Owen was made of more vulnerable stuff. For twelve months she sat like Tam O'Shanter's wife, nursing her wrath to keep it warm. On the first anniversary of the Great Rebuff, Rebekah's blood was still at boiling temperature, and to ease the pressure she wrote a further "statement," dated February 1919:

A year ago a very long friendly intercourse came to an end. . . . The commercial spirit which feared to advance the value of my copy of *Moments of Vision* painfully bears out what his first wife said of him. . . . I am reminded of much which I am too loyal to write here.

There is a saving grace as well as an admirable reticence about that clause: "much which I am too loyal to write here." In spite of her pain and disillusionment at the man's "churlishness," she was still loyal to the author's genius. We can take pleasure in recognizing the fact that she was *not* one of the common crowd —including some writers of biographies—who take great delight in knocking noses off of statues. Hardy himself had observed the signs of this delight. In *The Mayor of Casterbridge* (Chapter 21) he described the keystone of an arch, carved like a mask which "originally . . . exhibited a comic leer, . . . but generations of Casterbridge boys had thrown stones at the mask . . . and the . . . appearance was [now] ghastly." How often Betty

Owen had read that description! Even though she had no brother, she had doubtless observed that the instinct to throw stones is almost universal among boys; but in her own make-up there was a gentler and kindlier element which saved her from taking any delight in tearing the statue of Hardy from its pedestal. Just as Boswell came to recognize Johnson's faults and eccentricities without allowing them to obscure his merits and virtues, so Rebekah Owen recognized Hardy's genius and greatness as an author, at the same time that she saw his defects as a man. She did not jeer at these faults, as the Roman crowds of old were allowed (so we are told) to jeer at generals on their Day of Triumph. "Every hero becomes a bore at last," Emerson remarks somewhere or other; but it is quite clear, I think, that this assertion does not hold true for Rebekah Owen and her hero. He did *not* become a bore, even when she spoke most scornfully of his peasant blood. Her interest in his books survived and thereby provided the food with which to nourish her battle-scarred loyalty to his memory.

Her slow and timid resumption—not of normal relations, but of a cooler and more disciplined correspondence with Max Gate—was possibly the result of Florence Hardy's initiative. After twenty months of silence, Florence wrote (November 8, 1919) to announce that there were hopes of a "Hardy play" in the spring—not at Dorchester but at Oxford. The Oxford University Dramatic Society was to give a performance of *The Dynasts* and perhaps Rebekah would care to see it. Yes, perhaps she would.

The Oxford performance was, however, *not* given "in the spring" but in mid-winter, on February 10, 1920. Hardy himself was in the audience. He had come to Oxford, and in the afternoon was presented for the honorary degree of Doctor of Letters by the university which had (according to Hardy's fiction of twenty-five years before) refused admission to one Jude Fawley; and in the evening *The Dynasts* was presented. The manager of the Dramatic Society afterwards reported that, although the epic-drama was copyrighted, Hardy "*gave* his play to us, not grudgingly nor with any air of patronage but with ... gracious ... courtesy." This comment by Charles Morgan, who in 1920 was the manager of the O.U.D.S., did not get into print until ten years after the event, and by that time it was powerless to effect any change in Rebekah Owen's fixation regarding Hardy's "commercial spirit." One can only regret that she was denied this opportunity to adjust her impression of the man. Her astigmatism was never corrected.

Rebekah Owen did not get to Oxford to see *The Dynasts*, and there is no clear evidence that she even tried to get there. She had ordered a copy of Hardy's *Collected Poems*, published in 1919, but the book (when it came) remained to brood with her at Belmount Hall. Three months after the performance of *The Dynasts*, she wrote to Mrs. Hardy to ask how it had gone and—doubtless with much greater timidity and uncertainty—to ask whether Florence thought that her husband would welcome a birthday greeting from an old friend. Hardy would be eighty on June 2, 1920.

On May 25 Mrs. Hardy replied briefly: "*The Dynasts* was very good at Oxford. We quite expected to see you there. .... I am sure that any message from you on his birthday will gratify my husband." Accordingly, on the second of June, Rebekah telegraphed her congratulations to Hardy, and then she waited. Ten days passed. Florence Hardy eventually responded: "I write for my husband to thank you so much for your kind telegram of congratulations. ... Of course he ought to reply to it himself, but he seems absolutely dazed by the number he has received—over 200. .... We think so much of you at this season, as the two rose trees you gave us are covered with bloom."

That at least was pleasant to know, and the news gave Rebekah an idea. She would send a further supply of flowers, something that might grow at Max Gate and remind Hardy of his New

York friend—"one of the oldest of his real devotees"—and remind him, too, at some season other than July. Rebekah decided
on daffodils. When she wrote to say what she was sending, she
reported having heard that the Dorchester Dramatic Society
was planning to give a new "Hardy play" in the fall and that she
was hoping to attend. The flowers were sent but they failed to
thaw the ice in Hardy's pen. On July 23 Mrs. Hardy replied:
"Thank you so much for your lovely gift of daffodil bulbs to my
husband. . . . The play this autumn will be a great success. I am
glad that you are coming."

Rebekah replied immediately. She had, she said, been re-reading the Hardy books. Had she been looking over the volumes of
his poems, and had she (near her favorite "Middle-Age Enthusiasms") come again upon the lines "To a Lady offended by
a Book of the Writer's," and did she, at this late date, wonder
whether *he* had taken offence at her own earlier ill-concealed
coolness over *Jude the Obscure?* One would like to know. At any
rate, she had recently taken down her long-neglected copy of
Jude and had read it with more experienced eyes than she had
possessed a quarter of a century before; and at this chastened
period in her life *Jude* had seemed a greater work than she had
at first thought it to be. All of this she now reported to Max Gate.
The writing of her letter gave her a chance to put a new question
to Hardy: the old habit of quizzing him had not yet been wholly
subdued. Under date of August 1, 1920, Mrs. Hardy replied:
"I am sorry that I cannot find the passage to which you refer. . . .
He cannot remember either. . . . Lately so many *reliable* critics
have told T.H. that they prefer *Jude* to all of his other novels,
so I am glad that you like it better."

Rebekah proceeded with her plans. In 1920 the new Hardy
play was to be *The Return of the Native* as adapted by T. H. Tilley.
This would be the first post-war undertaking at Dorchester, and
Rebekah wanted, as usual, to be present on the first night. When
information about her plans was received at Max Gate, Florence

promptly wrote (on October 15) to give Miss Owen some inti-
mation as to what had been going on there during her long absence: "I am glad that you will be able to come to the play. ...
My husband has altered very much of late. ... He cannot stand
a long conversation." So—Rebekah had better be prepared.

The Return of the Native was given five times at the Corn Exchange in Dorchester, between November 17 and 20. Rebekah
arrived and saw the performance on the seventeenth. She again
had a chance to meet the cast after the play and sat at a small table
to take tea with the actress who played "Eustacia." In this fine-
looking, mature woman Miss Owen recognized the same actress
who, as a seventeen-year-old girl, had played "Marty South" so
successfully in the 1913 performance of *The Woodlanders*. Gertrude Bugler, now a twenty-four-year-old beauty, was so much
sought after that the elderly lady from America was not allowed
to monopolize her at the tea-table. Every bystander could tell
which of the two women was of greater interest to Hardy. In a
poem he was shortly to write, he let the whole world know what
he thought of ladies like Rebekah Owen (a poem he published
in *Winter Words*, 1928):

> "I'm a lofty lovely woman,"
>   Says the lady in the furs
> In the glance she throws around her
>   On the poorer dames and sirs. ...
> "True, my money did not buy it,
>   But my [father's], from the trade. ..."

Hardy's preference for the unspoiled country maidenhood represented by Gertrude Bugler was clear enough. He obviously
had no desire to talk to Rebekah Owen. His eyes were on "Eustacia." Many years later, Gertrude Bugler was able to recall
how Florence Hardy had asked Dr. E. W. Smerdon (who had
played the part of "Clym Yeobright") to tell Miss Bugler that
Hardy would like to have a few words with her. Dr. Smerdon
thereupon escorted her away from Miss Owen's table, explaining

as they went that Mrs. Hardy had sent him "to rescue her from being bored by that tiresome old woman"—the same old woman who only a few years before had been "best and belovedest Betty" to Florence.

. Rebekah Owen doubtless had her own thoughts at this time, but she did not record them. She perhaps knew of another novelist whose interest shifted. In earlier years, when the great Turgeniev had been asked who was his favorite heroine, he had answered: "Madame Roland." In 1880, three years before his death, he was asked the very same question. He then replied: "Any dark-complexioned maiden." It was probably just as well that Rebekah Owen did not know that this was the last time but one that she would ever see her Distinguished Author. She signed no "statement" on Hardy's obvious indifference to her, but when she got back to Belmount Hall there was none of the effusiveness and high spirits about her that had once marked her speech and her letters. After Christmas she sent a post-card to carry her New Year greetings to Max Gate, and on December 31, 1920, Florence Hardy replied with similar economy of words and postage: "Many thanks for your post-card." Seven months passed in eloquent silence.

On July 23, 1921, when the London *Times* printed a poem by Hardy on an old and familiar hymn, Rebekah clipped it from the paper. She was then entertaining a visitor named Ella—some unidentified American friend (perhaps a former member of the T.H.B.L. now touring Europe)—and the two talked of Hardy. Since her friend was going to visit Cornwall, Rebekah urged her to go to Boscastle and hunt up the church at St. Juliot's, not far away. The visitor obviously lacked Miss Owen's close acquaintance with *A Pair of Blue Eyes*, and on August 2, 1921, when "Ella" got to Cornwall, she bought a picture post-card of St. Juliot's church and wrote: "We visited this spot but could not find any of the names you mentioned. Many thanks. ... We leave here tomorrow. ... Ella." On August 4 Rebekah added her own note to this card: "I am certain Mr. Hardy put a tablet to his first wife in this church, which was the church he, as architect, went to restore and where he first met her." Rebekah was correct in all of these statements.

Soon after her visitor had departed, Betty Owen wrote to Florence Hardy to tell her that she liked the poem "On the Tune Called the Old-Hundred-and-Fourth" (afterwards published in *Late Lyrics*, 1922), and asked whether there was to be another Hardy play in the autumn. If so—pointed question!—would Miss Bugler appear in it? On August 7 Mrs. Hardy replied: "It was so good of you to send that postcard, saying that you liked the poem. I did like it very much myself. That old hymn has a peculiar fascination for my husband. I am sorry to say he has not been at all well this past week. He has been seeing far too many people. . . . I do not know when the next Hardy play will be given. . . . Miss Bugler is to be married, but will still be leading lady."

As it turned out, there was *no* Hardy play in the fall of 1921, and there is no record of Miss Owen's having ventured away from home during that year. Another fourteen months dragged by, and not until October, 1922, are there signs of life among the gathering ghosts of Betty's Hardiana. On October 22 she found an item she thought worth clipping from a newspaper for insertion in her copy of *Far from the Madding Crowd*. She ordered a copy of *Late Lyrics*—of course *not* to send to Max Gate to be autographed, but just for her own perusal. When it came, she read the poems attentively enough to check some and annotate several. The poem "Last Words to a Dumb Friend"—Hardy's cat—led Miss Owen to recall that "This was Peaseblossom." And Hardy's lines "On a Discovered Curl of Hair" led Rebekah to record the fact that "Mr. Hardy showed me this curl once in his first wife's presence. Also a miniature of her. I should call the colour more golden than brown—not red-golden."

When Rebekah heard that a new Hardy play was afoot for

November of 1922, she wrote to Max Gate to sound Florence Hardy out. A week or more followed without any reply. At last, on October 29, Mrs. Hardy broke the silence: "I am sorry not to have replied before this to your letter but . . . I did not know if we should be at Max Gate at the time of the play. . . . We shall be so glad to see you when you come down. . . . I hope you won't be disappointed in the play. Personally I think it very poor."

That was not very encouraging but Rebekah went anyway. On November 15-17, 1922, "A Desperate Remedy" was given at the Corn Exchange with Miss Owen present in the audience but with Hardy (apparently) absent. The adaptation from *Desperate Remedies* had been made by T. H. Tilley and aroused (I gather) no great interest. Hardy himself had, just at this time, other thoughts on his mind: it was ten years since Emma Lavinia had died, and on the anniversary of her death, Hardy went to the Stinsford churchyard with flowers for her grave. If Rebekah Owen remembered the day of the funeral, she left no record to tell us so.

She sent her customary New Year's greeting to Max Gate, and on December 29 Florence responded: "Just a line to wish you a very happy and prosperous New Year. . . . We have had a quiet Christmas all alone." But "just a line" was not enough to suit the lonely lady at Belmount Hall. If that was to be all that was forthcoming from the receptive but not responsive occupant of Max Gate, Rebekah would turn elsewhere. Now that Mussolini had made the Italian railroads run on time, to Italy she would go. The year 1923 is therefore a complete blank in the Hardiana records from Belmount Hall. When Hardy published *The Famous Tragedy of the Queen of Cornwall* in that year, Rebekah Owen bought no copy (unless, by chance, it was one of the two books lost at sea in the 1942 shipment from England). When the *Queen of Cornwall* was given at Dorchester in November of 1923, Hardy attended, but Miss Owen was obviously not there. When, in February, 1924, the play was repeated in King George's Hall, London, Miss Owen was not there.

Meanwhile, the "Hardy Players" at Dorchester had embarked upon a most ambitious undertaking. In 1923 an American company had made a film-version of *Tess of the D'Urbervilles* with Blanche Sweet in the rôle of Tess. This film was shown in Dorchester in 1924 and some of the odd mistakes made in the filming provided great amusement for the "Casterbridge" natives who went to see the picture. Some of the Hardy players went and afterwards spoke to Hardy about this American film-version of his novel, and in this way they came to learn of his own attempt, thirty years before, to dramatize *Tess of the D'Urbervilles* for the London stage. They now persuaded him to hunt up his old manuscript with a view to their performing the play in Dorchester. Hardy not only found the manuscript and agreed to its use, but (at the age of eighty-four) took an active part in the production of the play—attending many of the rehearsals. Gertrude Bugler was now Mrs. Ernest Bugler, having married her cousin; she was cast for the part of "Tess," and Dr. E. W. Smerdon who had played "Clym" in 1920 was assigned the rôle of "Angel Clare." In the programs of both these plays, Dr. Smerdon's name appears first on the list of the actors.

Some of the cast had not even been born when the novel first appeared in 1891 and were therefore unacquainted with the notoriety which *Tess* had conferred on some spots not very far from Dorchester. Hardy offered to try to get these actors into the spirit of the play by taking them on a *Tess* tour. Many years later, Gertrude Bugler was able to recall motoring out to Wool in the most luxurious automobile that Dorchester could then provide; she recalled how the party of actors had picked Hardy up at Max Gate—"a happy, smiling, and almost excited little man"—and how he had sat beside her on the ride. On their arrival at Wool, Hardy showed them the old manor-house to which

Tess went on her honeymoon and then helped the actors rehearse the confession-scene in the back room of the house. After the rehearsal Hardy showed "Tess" the wall-paintings on the landing and professed to see some resemblance between the D'Urberville women and Gertrude Bugler. Mrs. Bugler, however, "did not feel particularly flattered" by Hardy's remark!

Rebekah Owen, meanwhile, had returned to England from Italy in time to learn of what was going on at Dorchester. She wrote to Florence Hardy from Bath, to ask for further information about the projected performance of *Tess*. In reply came a typed letter:

MAX GATE, DORCHESTER.

6 October 1924

Dear Miss Owen:

I am sorry to say that Mrs. Hardy is in London at a nursing home recovering from an operation which, though serious, was not dangerous. She is hoping to get home again in a week or so, but matters being uncertain, and Mr. Hardy not being sure of keeping an engagement, it seems to be doubtful if you would see him here if you were to come. No doubt Mrs. Hardy will write herself later on.

Yours truly,

M. O. R.

Secretary

Rebekah's letter having been forwarded to Mrs. Hardy in London, Florence herself wrote on October 9 to say: "Hope to be home tomorrow . . . and we could see you on Saturday (11th), if you let us know." But Rebekah was by this time occupied at Bath; she decided to wait a month and come to Dorchester just in time for the play. She wrote to Mr. Tilley, the adapter of previous Hardy plays, and asked about dates, but she found him a different source of information from Mr. H. A. Martin.

Tess of the D'Urbervilles, Thomas Hardy's own adaptation somewhat revised, was given at Dorchester November 26-29, 1924, with Gertrude Bugler climaxing her previous successes by her performance in the rôle of Tess. Miss Owen (still at Bath) did not learn about the schedule until the last minute, when there was all too little time to arrange for a call at Max Gate; and on this occasion Rebekah did so want to make satisfactory arrangements, for she wished to bring a friend with her. Under date of November 24, Mrs. Hardy wrote to Miss Owen: "I am so sorry you did not hear from Mr. Tilley. . . . I shall be in on Thursday morning [27th] and glad to see you and your friend for a few minutes. . . ." How that phrase "for a few minutes" must have made Rebekah cringe, as if she had been flicked by a whip.

Rebekah Owen came and saw the play. Hardy was either unable to attend, or—if he *was* there on the same day as Miss Owen —he was in the company of James M. Barrie and closely guarded against all approach by the alert Florence. The play was not at all the same thing the Owens had seen in New York twenty-seven years before, when Mrs. Fiske had brought the house down. Lorimer Stoddard's version was a much more effective piece of work for the theatre than Hardy's own adaptation. The Dorchester version tried to crowd too much of the novel into its five acts, and it lacked the concentration of the American version. Miss Owen may have done her own contrasting of the two versions, but if so, her comment failed to get attached to her copy of *Tess* or to her program of the play.

There was a certain poignant appropriateness for Rebekah about this final—for it was to be final—contact with *Tess of the D'Urbervilles*. In the last scene of the play, Gertrude Bugler as Tess asked Angel Clare: "Do you think we shall meet again. . . ?" He made no reply. The constable came to arrest her, and Tess's last speech was: "It is as it should be. I am glad—yes, glad. This happiness with you could not have lasted. . . . I am ready." And when the curtain came down, it descended not only on a play called *Tess* but also on the drama of Rebekah Owen.

These past few years of her life—in fact the entire decade since the death of her sister Catharine—had marked the slow decay of her friendship with Thomas Hardy. In his tired eyes she had become a nuisance and he made little effort to conceal the fact. On this, her last, visit to Dorchester, she was even denied the dignity of a dramatic departure. There was some misunderstanding with Mrs. Hardy, who was busy playing hostess to Barrie. Result: there was either an unsatisfactory call at Max Gate (with no Hardy to be seen) or no call at all. Rebekah's vigorous and long-lived enthusiasm for the Wessex tales and novels thus straggled to a miserable end in the sandy delta of Hardy's indifference. There isn't anything of dramatic interest even about her exit. If this book were a book of fiction, its heroine would deserve (and get) a final scene in keeping with the impressive rôle she had played in the earlier scenes of the drama. But real life is not like fiction, as Mark Twain's biographer, A. B. Paine, once pointed out to Hamlin Garland. The latter had been reading the *Life of Mark Twain* and thought that the fourth volume was "a tragic story." When he remarked on its gloom, Paine replied: "The man who writes biography has *got* to be tragic, unless he is a liar. The novelist may shift the scenery and lighten the drama; the biographer must stick to the facts, and the facts of life are tragic." In the case of Rebekah Owen they are not even tragic; perhaps not even pathetic. They come perilously near to becoming trivial.

As soon as the performance of *Tess* was over, Rebekah and her friend hurried off to Italy. There she spent two and a half months, admiring the American efficiency with which Mussolini was making things click. By mid-February, 1925, she had returned to the dreariness of Belmount Hall and from that unhappy abode she wrote to Florence Hardy. Back came a reply, dated February 16: "I hope you had a good time in Italy. I do so wish we had seen more of you at the play, and had a talk, as I feel a misunderstanding might have been cleared up."

Rebekah relapsed into silence, but she was unable to stay long at Belmount. In June, she was back again in Bath, and from her friend's address she wrote to Mrs. Hardy to explore once again the possibility of a call at Max Gate. Mrs. Hardy's reply left nothing in doubt. On June 18 she wrote: "I am so sorry but my husband has been so upset by the heat and too many callers that the doctor has imperatively ordered, in writing, a complete rest. . . . I am so sorry, as I should like to have seen you, and could, if you cared to come for that; but I fear that T. H. will be invisible. . . . I hope that you are having a good time at Bath."

That was the end. Obviously, Rebekah did *not* "care to come for that"—i.e., just to see Florence. If T. H. would be, as the French say, "invisible" (not available to callers), who'd care to see Max Gate? Perhaps Rebekah was able to quote Hardy's poem on "Beeny Cliff":

O the opal and the sapphire of that wandering western sea,
And the woman riding high above with bright hair flapping free—
The woman whom I loved so, and who loyally loved me. . . .

What if still in chasmal beauty looms that wild weird western shore,
The woman now is—elsewhere—whom the ambling pony bore,
And nor knows nor cares for Beeny, and will laugh there nevermore.

Similarly, Rebekah could say to herself that, if Hardy was not at Max Gate, or was "invisible," who knows or cares for Max Gate? She would laugh there nevermore.

But in the fall of 1925 Rebekah Owen showed how strong old habits were with her: she bought a copy of *Human Shows,* when this latest collection of Hardy's poems came from the press, even though it was left to stagnate on her shelf. There is nothing to show that she ever reached the last poem, in which Hardy asked: "Why do I go on doing these things? Why not cease?" When *Tess* was given at the Barnes Theatre in London in September, 1925, Rebekah was not present. When *The Mayor of Casterbridge,* as dramatized by John Drinkwater, was given at the Pavilion Theatre in Weymouth a year later, Hardy attended, but he did not see Miss Owen in the audience. She had apparently moved to Italy to stay.

When the news finally came, in January, 1928, that Thomas Hardy had died, Miss Owen was residing in a hotel in Rome. Her thoughts went back to that day in 1913, when she had called at Max Gate and had found Florence Dugdale in charge, as it were, for the first time. How "Wessie" had barked at her! Rebekah now wrote to Mrs. Hardy and did her formal best to express sympathy: once before, she had written to Max Gate to express sympathy, when the first Mrs. Hardy had died; now she wrote to her successor when Hardy himself had died.

Florence Hardy's reply reached Miss Owen in Rome:

MAX GATE,
Jan. 26, 1928.

My dear Betty:

It is all too terrible, like a dreadful nightmare. I thank you so much for your kind words of sympathy. Life seems absolutely at an end for me, and I wish it actually were.

Poor Wessie died a year before his master, Dec. 27th, 1926. He never quite got over the loss. He had been growing weaker for some months, and was very *very* tired.

I hope you are well, and I send my loving thanks.

FLORENCE.

The rest is silence. Shortly before his death Hardy had written a poem entitled "He Resolves To Say No More." In it he declared that

From now alway
Till my last day
What I discern I will not say.

This poem was given last place in a posthumous volume of his verse. Hardy was not the only one who resolved to say no more. After Florence and Rebekah had sent and received those messages in January, 1928, neither ever wrote to the other again. Their fifteen-year exchange of letters was ended; their interest in each other had died with Hardy.

Chapter XI

——————◆——————

Débâcle

AT the time of Hardy's death, he had partly completed the preparation of the sheets of manuscript for his last volume of poetry. It was published before the end of the year 1928 with the appropriate title *Winter Words*. I do not know whether Rebekah Owen bought a copy or not. If she did, it may have been one of the two (or more) volumes lost at sea in 1942. In any case, there is no copy of *Winter Words* in the Owen Collection now in the Colby College Library.

It is regrettable that we do not know (and doubtless never can know) whether Miss Owen read *Winter Words*. One would like to be able to state with assurance that this last harvest of her author did come to her attention, particularly because there were in this book two poems that dealt with a question which she must often have asked herself. Miss Owen must have been puzzled by Hardy's conduct on more than one occasion. He was delighted to see her when she called, "saying so twice over." Yet he would allow her letters to go unanswered. He wished she would settle in Dorset, yet he refused to autograph her book. He wanted her to go cycling with him, yet he was not at all sure of being "at home" when she planned to call at Max Gate. Was there ever a man of such unpredictability? What manner of man was he? and why was he so?

If Rebekah Owen ever read *Winter Words*, she found the answer to these questions. Hardy was a man of moods. He says so himself. In the poem "Concerning His Old Home," there are four stanzas, each one of which describes a mood of the poet. In Mood I, he wants never again to see the "dismal place" where he was born. "I would forget it ever!" In Mood II, he would be "faintly glad" to see it "just once more." In Mood III, he is quite willing to revisit "that friendly place" any time and often. And in Mood IV, he promises to haunt "that loveable place" night and day!

In the poem called "So Various" Hardy describes a jury of twelve men. There is no need to quote his descriptions of them in full, but the men are worth identifying. This dozen is made up of the following: 1. a brisk-eyed man, quite young; 2. a stiff old man of cold manner; 3. a staunch, robust man; 4. a fickle man; 5. a dunce; 6. a learned seer; 7. a man of sadness; 8. "a man so glad, you never could conceive him sad"; 9. an unadventurous, slow man; 10. a man of enterprise, shrewd and swift; 11. a poor fellow who forgets anything said to him; and 12. a vindictive man who forgets nothing. And then Hardy adds, in a concluding stanza:

> All these specimens of men. . . .
> Curious to say
> Were *one* man. Yea,
> *I* was all they.

If Rebekah Owen ever read "So Various," she must have found in it the answer to her question as to why Hardy's conduct with regard to her had been so inconsistent, so unpredictable, and—"so various."

There is, of course, nothing really freakish about such a plural personality. Just a year ago James Thurber, in writing about F. Scott Fitzgerald and his wife Zelda, declared (in *The Reporter* —"a fortnightly of facts and ideas"—on April 17, 1951): "There were four or five Zeldas and at least eight Scotts, so that their living room was forever tense with the presence of a dozen disparate personalities." If Rebekah Owen found Hardy to be one man one day and a different man the next day, it merely meant that he had moved from Mood No. I into Mood No. II.

Miss Owen was sixty-nine years old at the time of Hardy's

death. She was to survive him by eleven years. Boswell survived
Samuel Johnson by eleven years. That fact serves to remind us
that, if she had been determined and persevering, eleven years
would have been long enough for her to get a literary work done.
Her book might yet have been written. Boswell, however, was
only forty-four when Johnson died. Rebekah Owen—almost
seventy—was too old to begin a new life. She had reached an
age when even an experienced writer is often glad to put his pen
aside. When Wordsworth attained the very same age which Rebekah Owen had reached by the time of Hardy's death, Wordsworth wrote to his American correspondent, Professor Henry
Reed of the University of Pennsylvania, to say:

I am standing on the brink of that vast ocean I must sail so soon—I must
speedily lose sight of the shore, and I could not once have conceived how
little I now am troubled by the thought of how long or short a time they
who remain upon that shore may have sight of me. . . . I feel . . . justified
in attaching comparatively small importance to any literary monument
that I may be enabled to leave behind. It is well, however, I am convinced,
that men think otherwise in the earlier part of their lives. . . .

In the earlier part of her life, Miss Owen may have had vague
ambitions to leave some sort of literary monument behind. But
like Mrs. Emma Lavinia Hardy, who had confessed that she
lacked the energy and perseverance needed to get her literary
inspirations into words and down on paper, Rebekah Owen had
never subjected herself to the discipline and drudgery of organ-
izing and systematizing and developing her voluminous notes into a book. And now, at the age of seventy, what she chiefly wanted was peace and comfort. A hotel in Rome gave her both. As her
physical vigor declined, she found the English winters increasingly unattractive, and she eventually did what so many English
poets have done—she settled permanently in Italy and returned
to Belmount Hall only occasionally during the summer.

When Florence Emily Hardy's *The Early Life of Thomas Hardy* appeared at the end of 1928, Rebekah Owen obtained a copy,

and it cannot be doubted that there were few purchasers of the
book who were equipped as she was to read it and appraise its
portraiture of the man. True, this was only the first of Mrs.
Hardy's two biographical volumes, and the narrative of this first
volume conducted Hardy's life only to the publication of *Tess*
in November, 1891: that was eight or nine months before Rebekah turned up at the door of Max Gate. This first volume,
therefore, could not provide any comment on those years during which Miss Owen herself had known Hardy; but, even so,
it contained much to bring the past vividly back to her consciousness. The book was dedicated "To the Dear Memory," and Rebekah had in her possession letters from Florence that certainly
supplied a curious commentary on the word "dear." On page 96
occurred the transcript from the first Mrs. Hardy's "Recollec-
tions"—the diary which Florence had described, in her letter to
Rebekah, in language quite different from the circumspect account given in the book. Other pages recalled other memories.
On page 176 Hardy's letter to Handley Moule would remind
Rebekah of the time when she and Catharine were his guests at
Auckland Castle. At page 210, Hardy's note for July 22, 1883,
is given: "To Winterborne-Came Church with Gosse." Rebekah had a similar note in her own records, made a decade later,
when she and Hardy went *via* Came to Faringdon and sat there
a long time. The picture of Max Gate, at page 226 of *The Early
Life*, shows its appearance at the time when the Hardys first
moved in, in 1885. It was not very different from the way Rebekah saw it seven years later.

But it is at page 235 that Miss Owen would find her chief
cause for dissatisfaction with the *Early Life of Thomas Hardy*, for
at this point Florence told of the publication of *The Mayor of
Casterbridge*. "It was a story which Hardy fancied he had damaged more recklessly than perhaps any other of his novels." But
who saved it from further damage? Not one word about those

"good judges across the Atlantic" who had stepped into the arena and fought for the discarded episodes in the novel. On page 243 Hardy is quoted as having "often said that in some respects *The Woodlanders* was his best novel," but not one word about his dissatisfaction with Grace Melbury, or about the revision of the text which Miss Owen had prompted at the end of the story. Rebekah put her copy of *The Early Life* aside, unannotated and unloved. She had too much reason to perceive its defects, its reticences, and its suppressions.

When *The Later Years of Thomas Hardy* appeared in 1930, Miss Owen was in Italy, and I have been unable to learn whether she ever acquired a copy of the book. When her Hardy Collection was eventually re-assembled in America, there was no copy of the *Later Years* in it; but in view of the loss of several volumes at sea—a loss which has already been referred to—one cannot be sure. One would like to know whether Betty Owen ever saw page 154 of the *Later Years*—the page on which Florence Hardy reported that "two ladies called" on Mrs. Emma Lavinia Hardy a few hours before her death. But the ladies are not named in the book, and Rebekah Owen would doubtless have had as much reason for dissatisfaction with *Later Years*, if she ever saw it, as she had for dissatisfaction with the *Early Life*.

Living in Italy most of the time, Miss Owen had less opportunity than ever for lying like a trout in the stream, ready to snap up whatever tempting morsels floated past her. In 1934 she spotted two little items she thought worth salvaging for her copy of *Under the Greenwood Tree;* one she clipped on September 17 and the other only six days later. This was her last labor in the Hardy vineyard—labor which she had begun more than fifty years before. She had certainly earned her retirement.

During her occasional visits to England, Miss Owen found pleasure in the friendship which developed between her and her Sawrey neighbor, Mrs. Heelis. The latter had so effectively put an end to her life as Beatrix Potter that there were people who did not know that Mrs. William Heelis and Miss Potter were one and the same person. I think there can be no doubt, however, that Miss Owen was admitted to knowledge of the secret. This led, not only to interesting talk about books, but also to Miss Owen's giving at least one of her prized volumes to "Miss Potter." Among the Belmount Hardiana there was a copy of the *Poems* of William Barnes. This book had been edited by Thomas Hardy at the suggestion and by the persuasion and encouragement of Sir Walter Raleigh of Oxford University. Miss Owen presented it to Beatrix Potter Heelis—an act which accounts for the better state of preservation of this book than of some others in the Owen Collection. For the long-continued neglect of Belmount Hall was having its effect on the books. The dampness began to mar the covers. The bindings grew limp. Some of the copies which Rebekah had bought at Dorchester were cheap editions, with the sheets clipped together by metal wire, not sewn. The dampness of Belmount Hall penetrated these books and rusted the wire clips. Perhaps the only things that were helped by the cold, wet climate of Hawkshead were the dessicated flowers that Betty Owen had tucked into the pages of her books— sentimental souvenirs of her visits to one or another of the Dorset shrines.

During the summer of 1938, when she motored to England for the last time, Miss Owen reached the painful decision that her library had to be disposed of. She was now eighty and, when Mr. and Mrs. Heelis agreed to purchase the Belmount property, Rebekah decided to sell what books were saleable. Many of the volumes had by this date been so damaged by the dampness that few purchasers would want them; and as Rebekah handled the old familiar covers and glanced inside at the records of her readings to "dearest Tat" and to "dear Ashy," she doubtless did not wish to part with these old friends anyway. And who can doubt that the ghosts of Catharine Owen and of Caroline Ash hovered nostalgically around the drawing-room hearth, where Rebekah had so often read to them?

What makes ghosts walk the earth? That question has often been asked—and answered. Horatio gives three reasons in *Hamlet*, but none of the three is as good as the reason that Browning gives in "De Gustibus":

> Your ghost will walk, you lover of trees,
>   (If our loves remain)
>   In an English lane,
> By a cornfield side . . . if the good fates please.

And if loves remain, there was certainly another ghost a-haunting that Belmount neighborhood in the summer of 1938—the ghost of William Wordsworth. And his is an insistent ghost that will not let us go on with our account of Rebekah Owen until we have lent him an ear for a moment. Having left the Hawkshead Grammar School in 1787, Wordsworth entered Cambridge that fall and soon discovered that he "did not love the timid course of her scholastic studies." Throughout his Freshman year at Cambridge he "played the loiterer" and "in submissive idleness" let

> Eight months roll pleasingly away; the ninth
> Came and returned him to his native hills.

Every student of English poetry remembers the delight with which, in the fourth book of *The Prelude*, Wordsworth described his "Summer Vacation" of 1788. With what exultation he got back to his native District! What joy there was for him in that first sight of Lake Windermere, "magnificent and beautiful"! How he bounded down the slope, shouting for the ferryman! What a cordial greeting he gave the old man! How he hurried up the familiar hill on the far side! With what "eager footsteps" he made his way past the future home of Beatrix Potter and on

into Hawkshead, "that sweet valley where he had been reared"!
What joy it was to see it all again!

The delight of that return of 1788 was certainly great enough
to justify our surmise that, "if loves remain," the poet's ghost
will have been haunting that region ever since, making annual
returns to "that sweet valley." In 1938 Wordsworth would have
had his Sesquicentennial Anniversary. But if his ghost had followed his old habits and had proceeded "up the familiar hill"
along the well-known road from Hawkshead to Ambleside, he
would, "if the good fates please," have been struck by one exotic
feature never seen in the Lake District during the poet's life-
time: a foreign automobile! Off the road a short distance to the
right, a mile and a half (or less) beyond Hawkshead, an Italian
motor-car stood in the driveway of the stone mansion known as
Belmount Hall. The Italian chauffeur was as much out of place
as the automobile. He refused to stay at Belmount, and no wonder! The paper was falling from the walls, the roof leaked, the
whole place had an air of dejection and decay. Yet there were
signs of life: something unusual was going on there. Throughout
the month of August, the books from New York and Boston,
from Philadelphia and London, were sorted and packed. In the
evenings, Rebekah sat alone and read—with what thoughts and
memories—there in the house that she and Catharine had bought
nearly forty years before, with the thought that there they would
be happy. Rebekah's emotions, as she brooded in her evening solitude, may be gauged from a poignant record that she made at
this time regarding "the débâcle of Belmount Hall." "Débâcle"
tells the story in one word.

The Owen books—that is, those that were deemed saleable
—were moved to London; and at an auction held at Sotheby's
on November 7, 1938, the library that Henry Owen and Mrs.
Owen and Catharine Owen and Rebekah Owen had been collect-
ing for seventy-five or eighty years was scattered to the winds;
and shortly thereafter seventeen volumes of Hardiana began

their last trip across the Atlantic, back to the land of Betty's birth.

She, meanwhile, had returned to Italy. There she passed her eighty-first birthday, living alone in the Hotel de la Ville in Rome. Who can doubt that she spent many hours there like the "sad man" in Hardy's *Interlopers at the Knap*—the man who enjoyed silent contemplation and "allowed his mind to be a quiet meeting-place for memories"? Rebekah Owen certainly had the memories. Now that her precious books were gone, she had one kind of reward for the many years she had spent with them. For she had lived too long in intimate and almost daily contact with the thoughts and emotions, the attitudes and sympathies of Thomas Hardy, to be able now to banish him from her thoughts. "Billy" Phelps once remarked (in his *Autobiography*): "I *live* with Goethe as I live with Shakespeare and with Browning. . . . Goethe's soul has been in my heart for fifty years. I think of him every day of my life." So it was with Rebekah Owen. Hardy's portrayal of human life had been in her heart for more than fifty years. She had read the novels and tales so often and so closely and with such devoted study, that they were now a part of her life. Even without his books physically before her eyes, she couldn't help thinking of Hardy every day of her life.

There had been a time in her youth when she had looked at Shakespeare's world through the romantic eyes of twenty-one and had found it good. Her vision of "stately old-time gardens with . . . many a fair pleasaunce"—"was not the picture exquisite?" Now, fifty years later, she was equally capable of responding with sympathetic imagination to Hardy's far-from-exquisite picture of human life. This was no little achievement, since Hardy's view of life was one for which the English novel contained no precedent. Victorian fiction was innocent of any depth of tragic perception until Thomas Hardy appeared upon the scene. He was the one who had showed English readers that the novel could do for them what the Greek drama had done for the fellow-countrymen of Aeschylus and Sophocles. In *Jude the Obscure* (as Rebekah Owen came, somewhat belatedly, to see) this aspect of Hardy's genius appears at its greatest. If Miss Owen had not substituted the fashionable world of southern England for the academic society in which she had previously moved when she was a resident of New York City, she might quite conceivably have followed up her letter to Longfellow with more scholarly and more perceptive compositions. She might have eventually come to write the sort of comment that was later on composed by a scholar not far from Rebekah's old home in New York. Professor Bruce McCullough (of New York University), writing on *Jude the Obscure,* asked:

What lies beneath the grim exterior of this sad and somber novel? Obviously it possesses great strength and passionate sincerity, an acute sense of reality, and a terrible cruelty. Out of its faithful record of the pathetic romance of youth there emerges a hero noble in resignation and fortitude. . . . Its dark picture of an unresolved conflict between human and natural forces is pessimism, if you will, but it is also the bracing refusal of an energetic temperament to be reconciled to the postulates of a mechanical universe, or to be trapped into the complacent assumption that reason can chart the way to happiness. It thrills with a sense of humanity and finds unquenchable zest in life, no matter how painful. Under its apparent cruelty there broods a tender, compassionate spirit so full of loving-kindness that it ceaselessly looks to see its own "genial germing purpose" mirrored in the will of the universe. Above all it emanates a thoughtfully idealistic sense of the possibility of life in which social law more nearly coincides with individual needs.

Even if Rebekah Owen never achieved an articulateness equal to that here shown by Professor McCullough, she would have followed all his remarks with ease and understanding. She had responded sympathetically to Hardy's quotation from Shakespeare on the title-page of *Tess:* "Poor wounded name! My bosom as a bed shall lodge thee," and she had now come into belated possession of a tragic perception that was fit companion for her other literary insights.

Not that everything in Hardy was tragedy or pathos. He knew how to laugh, and Rebekah's keen sense of fun had led her to take early delight in the humor of Hardy's pages—especially in the racy dialogue of the rustics who have been so often compared to Shakespeare's clowns that the comparison has by our own day become a stale commonplace of Hardy criticism. But Rebekah Owen knew good stories when she heard them, and those who listened as she read *Tess* can never have forgotten, for example, the anecdote related by Dairyman Crick. Rebekah must have known it by heart, and in the days of her Roman solitude, she must have been able to repeat it to herself. Who can object to hearing it once more?

Once there was an old aged man over at Mellstock—William Dewy by name. . . . Well, this man was a-coming home . . . from a wedding, where he had been playing his fiddle, one fine moonlight night, and for shortness' sake he took a cut across . . . a field . . . where a bull was out to grass. The bull seed William and took after him, horns aground. . . . Though William runned his best, and hadn't *much* drink in him (considering 'twas a wedding, and the folks well off), he found he'd never reach the fence and get over in time to save himself. Well, as a last thought, he pulled out his fiddle as he runned, and struck up a jig, turning to the bull, and backing towards the corner. The bull softened down, and stood still, looking hard at William Dewy, who fiddled on and on; till a sort of a smile stole over the bull's face. But no sooner did William stop his playing and turn to get over the hedge than the bull would stop his smiling and lower his horns towards the seat of William's breeches. Well, William had to turn about and play on, willy-nilly; and 'twas only three o'clock, and 'a knowed that nobody would come that way for hours. . . . When he had scraped [his fiddle] till about four o'clock he felt that he verily would have to give over soon, and he said to himself, "There's only this last tune between me and eternal welfare! . . ." Well, then he called to mind how he'd seen the cattle kneel o' Christmas Eves. . . . It was not Christmas Eve then, but it came into his head to play a trick upon the bull. So he broke into the Nativity Hymn; just as at Christmas carol-playing; when lo and behold, down went the bull on his bended knees, in his ignorance, just as if 'twere the true . . . night and hour. As soon as his horned friend were down, William turned, . . . jumped safe over hedge, before the praying bull had got on his feet again to take after him. William used to say that he'd seen a man look a fool a good many times, but never such a fool as that bull looked when he found his pious feelings had been played upon, and 'twas not Christmas Eve [after all]!

But beyond the tragedy and the pathos and above the humor of Hardy there was one other quality which must have had a vague and probably undefined attraction for the Catholic believer in Rebekah Owen. Hardy had an eye for nature equal to the eye of Beatrix Potter—an eye which she put to such splendid use in drawing the pictures for her animal stories; and Hardy had also a mind with which to meditate on nature—a mind superior to Wordsworth's stumbling and fumbling intellect. The result of this combination is seen in many of the most characteristic passages of Hardy's novels and poems. They are usually called descriptive passages, and they often refer to the seasons or the elements, but they are rarely *mere* description. They may begin, for example, with a toad laboring "humbly" along, but they never end there. Hardy had a power (and had it very early in life) of passing from the trivial to the cosmic, a power that he shares with no other novelist of his day; and one cannot read his books as often as Rebekah Owen had read them without being lifted and stretched and inspired by these passages. One example of this sort of thing may be pointed out in *Far from the Madding Crowd* (Chapter 2). Hardy was only thirty-three when he wrote this description of "midnight on the shortest day of the year":

A desolating wind wandered from the north over the hill, . . . covered on its northern side by . . . ancient and decaying . . . beeches. . . . To-night these trees sheltered the southern slope from the keenest blasts. . . . The dry leaves in the ditch simmered and boiled . . . , a tongue of air occasionally ferreting out a few, and sending them spinning across the grass. . . . The thin grasses, more or less coating the hill, were touched by the wind in breezes of differing powers, and almost of differing natures—one rubbing the blades heavily, another raking them piercingly, another brushing them like a soft broom. The instinctive act of humankind was to stand and listen, and learn how the trees on the right and the trees on the left wailed or chanted to each other in the regular antiphonies of a cathedral choir; how hedges and other shapes to leeward then caught the note, lowering it to the tenderest sob; and how the hurrying gust then plunged into the south, to be heard no more. The sky was clear—remarkably clear—and the twinkling of all the stars seemed to be but throbs of one body, timed by a common pulse. The North Star was directly in the wind's eye. . . . A difference of colour in the stars—oftener read of than seen in England— was really perceptible here. . . . To persons standing alone on a hill during a clear midnight such as this, the roll of the world eastward is almost a palpable movement. . . . The impression of riding along [with the stars] is vivid and abiding. The poetry of motion is a phrase much in use, and to enjoy the epic form of that gratification it is necessary to stand on a hill at a small hour of the night, and . . . long and quietly watch your stately progress through the stars. After such a nocturnal reconnoitre it is hard to get back to earth, and to believe that the consciousness of such majestic speeding is derived from a tiny human frame.

This artistic progression from the dry leaves in the ditch to the stately motion of the stars elevates and expands the reader's "tiny human frame" until it assumes a cosmic majesty. Rebekah Owen must have felt this. And as she "rode along" with the stars, she could congratulate herself on her possession of a religious faith which Hardy could only regret *not* being able himself to hold. He would have liked to share her creed, to know where Wordsworth got his authority for talking about "Nature's holy plan"; and if Rebekah or any one could have convinced Hardy that there *is* a plan, he would have been the happiest of men. In this respect Miss Owen was much more fortunate than her distinguished author.

Blessed with this consoling spiritual anchorage which fate had denied to Thomas Hardy, Rebekah Owen came in her solitude to the inevitable end at last. On Lincoln's birthday, Sunday, February 12, 1939, she died. Funeral services were held for her at the Roman Catholic church of Sant' Andrea delle Fratti on the following day, and she was buried in the Anglo-American section of the Catholic cemetery of Verano in Rome—far from her father and mother in New York, far from her sister in Coniston, far from Hardy's ashes in Westminster Abbey.

The stage of the drama which we have been following was thereafter quickly emptied. Florence Hardy had already died, in the fall of 1937, apparently without a word of comment on that event from Rebekah Owen. On November 13, 1940, Mary Drisler died in New York City. And on December 22, 1943, Beatrix Potter, at the age of seventy-seven, died in her beloved Lakeland. "Exeunt omnes." ("Exeunt Omnes" is the title of a poem which Hardy composed on his seventy-third birthday; it was published in *Satires of Circumstance* in 1915.)

Just a year before the present writer put these words down on paper, he stood beside the Hardy graves in the Stinsford churchyard. Inevitably, Hardy's instructions to his readers came to mind. In his poem entitled "A Poet," Hardy told us what to say if we ever find ourselves standing beside his grave:

> "Whatever his message—glad or grim—
> Two bright-souled women clave to him;"
> Stand and say that while day decays;
> It will be word enough of praise.

And as we stand, in imagination, beside that grave in the Verano cemetery in Rome, what word of praise are we to say? A dozen and more years have passed since Rebekah Owen was buried there, and one may well wonder whether anyone has ever gone to her grave, as Hardy went to the grave of Emma Lavinia, to leave flowers upon it. In the long run, Hardy himself may prove to be the one who erected the best kind of memorial tablet for Rebekah Owen—the one he put up in *The Mayor* nearly sixty years ago when he paid his tribute to "some good judges across the Atlantic." One may take pleasure, too, in the thought that Hardy acknowledged his indebtedness to Rebekah Owen in still another place. In the first and second editions of *Wessex Tales*, the woman "who assisted at the dairy" in *Interlopers at the Knap* was named Susannah. Then Hardy "fired" her, and installed Rebekah in her place. There she is to this day. "Rebekah was the woman who assisted. . . ." And in all truthfulness she did assist.

Chapter XII

The Belmount Books

O N the day of Hardy's death," wrote John Macy back in
1928, "the world knew, that is, everybody but the Nobel
Prize Committee knew, that the greatest man of letters
in the world had gone and that there was no one quite clearly
second to step into his place." The opinion was then quite widely
held that Thomas Hardy was indeed "the greatest man of letters
in the world," and when *The Early Life* and *The Later Years* were
published, many readers turned eagerly to those books to learn
more about the great author who had just gone. What was the reaction of these readers after perusing Florence Hardy's two volumes? Were they heard to quote Hardy's poem "His Heart"
(published in *Moments of Vision*, 1917), exclaiming:

> Yes, here at last, eyes opened, do I see
> His whole sincere symmetric history?

The truth is that, while there were some readers—a few—who
thought they had Hardy's whole history in these two volumes,
there were others who were far from satisfied. Like Rebekah
Owen, they saw the omissions, they sensed the suppressions, they
felt the lack of complete candor. They knew that the last word
on Thomas Hardy had *not* been written.

Sometimes the world has to wait a long time for a definitive
appraisal of an author. Two hundred years after the death of
Alexander Pope, Geoffrey Tillotson began his book *On the Poetry
of Pope* by remarking: "The time has not yet come for a proper estimate of Pope either as man or as poet. . . . Until the scholars and
critics have been at work on him for many more years, much of
the subtlety of his life and work must lie undistinguished." Har-

dy has been dead only twenty-four years and it is obvious that the time has not yet come for a proper and final estimate of *his* rank, either as man or as poet or as novelist. Scholars and critics have much more work to do before the subtleties of Hardy's life and writings stand fully revealed. Rebekah Owen's jottings and annotations, her records and letters, are therefore all the more welcome as useful contributions to the uncompleted project, that of making the final appraisal of an important literary figure. If Hardy's "whole sincere symmetric history" is ever to be achieved, its author will need the help of Rebekah Owen's Hardiana.

After the Sotheby auction in London in 1938, the already-mentioned seventeen books from the Belmount library crossed the ocean and in January, 1939, reached the library of Colby College. An examination of these books shortly led to the discovery that there was a large number of additional Hardy books still stored in Belmount Hall after its sale to Mrs. Heelis, together with allied and associated voumes. And, by the time that Beatrix Potter Heelis had been able to make a careful search in the mouldering Hall—an investigation which she carried out soon after Miss Owen's death—she learned that there were letters and scrapbooks, photograph albums and souvenirs, miscellaneous memorabilia about Hardy, all surviving as mute witnesses to Rebekah's long-continued and devoted service as a student of Thomas Hardy.

Arrangements were made with Beatrix Potter for the sale of all this material to Colby College, but before the books could be moved, World War II was under way. Hitler's bombers helped to speed things up. One night a German pilot flew his plane over the Lake District and, failing to find Glasgow or Wigan or whatever else he was looking for, he unloaded his bombs onto the field just in front of Belmount Hall. They killed a few sheep and broke some windows in Rebekah's old home. Beatrix Potter thereupon hastened the evacuation of the books. In order to minimize the risk to which they would be exposed in being shipped across the ocean, she dispatched the books in small quantities, two or three at a time. Then she would later report how many packages she had sent. She usually signed her letters to the present writer "H. B. Heelis" and not once did she mention her own books or allow the name "Beatrix Potter" to slip into the correspondence. Throughout the years 1940 and 1941 and during the first few months of 1942, the packages kept coming, until scores of books had safely reached the college library in spite of the German submarines. One package failed to arrive, and Mrs. Heelis thereupon decided to suspend operations until after the war.

Unfortunately she did not live to resume the shipments, but when her heir, Captain K. W. G. Duke, R.N. (retired), moved into the cottage on Castle Farm, he found that Mrs. Heelis had left packages carefully marked for Colby College, to be shipped after the war. This additional material was sent in 1946; one elusive item—Hardy's letter about the site of the Duchess of Richmond's ball on the eve of Waterloo—turned up in 1949; and in midsummer of the following year Captain Duke dispatched the last two stragglers. They presented themselves at Colby in July, 1950.

The re-assembly of Miss Owen's Hardiana in America now makes it possible to do what she probably never did for herself —to draw up a complete list of the collection. She had trusted her memory. In the list that follows, the books are arranged in two groups: in one the books *by* Hardy are listed in chronological order; and in the second group the books *about* Hardy and the books which Miss Owen (for one reason or another) associated with him are listed in alphabetical order.

In arranging the Hardy books in their chronological order, the date of first publication has been followed, even though Miss Owen did not always own a copy of the first edition. In each such case, however, the date of her copy is given in addition to the date of the first publication of the novel or story.

HARDY'S OWN WORKS

How I Built Myself a House. In *Chambers's Journal* for March 18, 1865, pages 161-164. Part XV of the *Journal* (dated March 31, 1865) containing the pages for March 18. Rebekah Owen's note written on her copy is a correct statement of the fact: "The first published writing of Mr. Hardy." She added: "Unearthed from our attic, October 17, 1894. R. Owen." It was a fortunate coincidence that Henry Owen apparently subscribed to *Chambers's Journal,* for Rebekah would have had to wait a long time for an American printing of this sketch. It appeared in print in New York for the first time in 1925, in *Life and Art* edited by Ernest Brennecke.

Desperate Remedies. (First published in London anonymously in 1871.) New York, Harper & Brothers, 1896. From the first American collected Uniform Edition; green ribbed cloth. A present to Rebekah Owen from Mrs. Allen H. Gangewer of Burlington, New Jersey, a frequent visitor to the sessions of the T.H.B.L. in New York. Miss Owen wrote no notes in this book, other than to record the fact that she had read it twice.

Under the Greenwood Tree. (First published in London anonymously in 1872.) London, Chatto & Windus, 1892. "A New Edition," red pebbled cloth (rebound). Autographed: "Faithfully yours, Thomas Hardy." This novel was published under Hardy's name by Henry Holt in New York in 1873. It is not only the first Hardy book to be published in America, but also the first to be pirated and the first to receive critical comment by an American reviewer. Professor William Hand Browne of The Johns Hopkins University, writing in the *Southern Magazine* for September, 1873, declared that *Under the Greenwood Tree* is "one of the brightest, freshest little stories that we have come across for many a day, full of sparkling bits of description, vivacious conversation, quaint sketches of character, and amusing incident." At this date, however, Rebekah Owen was only fifteen years old and had not yet discovered Hardy. Her copy of *Under the Greenwood Tree* was purchased nearly twenty years later, a publication (little-known in America) by Chatto & Windus. This London firm also published the *Belgravia* magazine in which *The Return of the Native* was serialized, and their satisfaction with this last-named novel is doubtless indicated by their purchase of the copyright of *Under the Greenwood Tree* from Hardy's first publisher, William Tinsley. Hardy's failure to retain copyright in this one title has resulted in its having a more complex publishing history than that exhibited by any other product of his pen. Miss Owen bought her copy of the Chatto & Windus edition at "Casterbridge" on August 14, 1892, and apparently wore out its binding from constant use, first in Dorchester and later in New York and at Belmount. She had the book rebound at E. G. Humphreys' in Worcester. Several of her marginal notes are worth transcribing. Regarding "Jim Woodward's brother" (Chapter III) she wrote: "I saw the name of Woodward in the [Stinsford] cemetery to-day (August 31, '92) when I walked there with Mr. Hardy." Regarding the interview with the Vicar (Part II, Chapter IV), Miss Owen's brief note is: "Actually true." Regarding the "choosing the psalms and hymns" (Part II, Chapter II) she wrote: "Mr. Hardy told me that it was always the custom for the choir to choose the psalms and hymns, and that 'Mr. Grinham' was especially indifferent to the music and words selected. Whereas the driving forth of the 'Dummerford' Choir by 'Parson Clare' was entirely owing to the choir refusing to play if he chose the hymns." Miss Owen read this novel aloud at least eleven times. It was the first one she read to Mary Drisler and the last one to which she added her harvest of clippings.

A PAIR OF BLUE EYES. (First published in London in 1873.) London, Sampson Low, Marston, Searle, & Rivington, 1890. Red cloth. In Chapter IV Miss Owen identifies "the church" thus: "St. Juliot's, Cornwall. Mr. Hardy told me." There is, of course, nothing new now about this information, for Hermann Lea and other literary topographers and geographers have long ago supplied charts, maps, and detailed descriptions, none of which were available to Rebekah Owen. There is no point in transcribing all her geographical identifications and I shall therefore pass silently over them hereafter, except in those instances where she detects something not found in other reference-works. Miss Owen wrote three brief notes on Chapter 26. Referring to Hardy's statement that "she was content to play plays with her husband," Miss Owen noted: "Lady Susan Strangways, who eloped with William O'Brien the actor." On "The old lord . . . gie'd 'em a house to live in," she wrote: "Lord Kingston lent them Stinsford House." And on "The poor thing died," Rebekah noted that "the great vault . . . under Stinsford Church . . . is described in this chapter. . . . A tablet to her memory is in Stinsford Church."

FAR FROM THE MADDING CROWD. (First published in London in 1874 after serialization in the *Cornhill*.) London, Sampson Low, Marston, Searle, & Rivington, 1889. Red cloth. Miss Owen clipped from various newspapers numerous illustrations of the loss of sheep "alarmed by some dogs" or "frightened by a dog" and of hay-ricks on fire. The Great Barn (of Chapter 22) was described (so she reports) after one at Cerne Abbas. Regarding "King Noah" (in Chapter 42): "Mr. Hardy told me that some reviewer, instancing the humour of a certain new book, cited the expression *King Noah,* which Mr. Hardy himself had written years before, and thoroughly well remembered inventing the term." Rebekah Owen photographed the Sheep Fair of Chapter 50 in September, 1893.

FAR FROM THE MADDING CROWD. London, Harper & Brothers, 1901. This salmon-colored paper-wrappered edition, received by Rebekah Owen at "Belmount Hall, September 4, 1901," differs from the preceding edition in several ways. It contains Hardy's preface dated February, 1895, which is of course not found in the Sampson Low edition. It prints the text in double columns. It represents an attempt by Harper & Brothers to introduce in England the cheaper format they had been successfully marketing in America through their Franklin Square Library series. The Harpers acted as Hardy's *London* publishers for only a very brief period, 1898-1902, during which this six-penny edition of *Far from the Madding Crowd* was published. It is the only authorized edition of the novel published during the forty-year span from 1895 to 1935 in which Jan Coggan's watch behaves properly. Throughout that period the famous old "pinchbeck repeater" of Chapter 32 "struck one" and then, an hour later, "struck one" again. The error crept into the text when the novel was first published by Osgood, McIlvaine & Co. in 1895, and thereafter all authorized editions, except this London edition of 1901 (for which the type had to be reset), repeated the error until it was finally detected by a Colby College student in 1935. The printed text was soon thereafter corrected.

THE HAND OF ETHELBERTA. (First published in 1876.) London, Sampson Low, Marston, Searle, & Rivington, 1888. Red cloth. One of the most enlightening remarks Rebekah Owen made on this novel provides an explanation of the curious character of this book. Miss Owen got her information from the first Mrs. Hardy. She explained Hardy's reason for attempting "something different" in this book thus: "*Far from the Madding Crowd* was his last-published book, and adverse criticism which called it an imitation of George Eliot discouraged him greatly, and [so he] went off at a tangent and wrote *The Hand of Ethelberta* by way of contrast while at Swanage." From *Munsey's Magazine* for April, 1897, Rebekah Owen clipped a note about a Miss Beatrice Herford's success in "reciting [stories] in [London] drawing rooms" exactly according to "Ethelberta's plan" in Chapter 16. Mary Drisler had previously noticed in the New York *Sun* (July, 1894) "a minute description of some English girl of good family but slender means, who was ... telling ghost stories at country houses. ... I wonder if Mr. Hardy's book gave [her] the hint."

THE RETURN OF THE NATIVE. (First published in 1878.) London, Sampson Low, Marston, Searle & Rivington, 1890. "New Edition," red cloth. Autographed on the half-title: "Faithfully yours Thomas Hardy." Subscribed, beneath Hardy's autograph, "Rebekah Owen, Casterbridge, August 6, 1892." She read this book aloud at least five times. Among her notes are these: "One day Mr. Hardy was proposing various walks that he wished to take [with] me. So I suggested Egdon Heath. 'But I have [just] been there with Miss Preston, and a very nice excursion we had,' he said. I submitted that I was willing to play second fiddle to Miss Preston, though I owned to a jealousy that I had not written ... her article (July *Century* 1893)." Regarding Eustacia Vye's saying (in Book I, Chapter 6) that she "was happy enough at Budmouth": "I told Mr. Hardy that I could not quite forgive Eustacia for liking Budmouth. He said: 'Ah! it was quite different in her day.' At Max Gate, Aug. 29, 1892." Regarding Clym's having been "a jeweller's manager" (II, I): "Mrs. Hardy said she did not like Yeobright having been a jeweller. I said it had struck me that he could not have retained his integrity after being a shopman in London and Paris and learning to tell falsehoods glibly as shopmen all do." This pen-merchant's daughter never had a good word for the commerce that had produced her wealth.

THE TRUMPET-MAJOR. (First published in 1880.) London, Sampson Low, Marston, Searle, & Rivington, 1889. "New and Cheaper Edition." Red cloth. Autographed: "Yrs faithfully Thomas Hardy." With a note in his hand at page 48, changing "printing" to read "printed." Miss Owen read this novel aloud at least six times. On "The Alarm" (of Chapter 26): "Mr. Hardy told me that he had never heard any one describe the entry of the King into Weymouth, or the flight of the people at the supposed approach of Buonaparte. Dorchester was just as frightened, he said. At any rate ... the flight was, to his delight, after the book was published, corroborated by an old gentleman who was a boy of six in 1805 and remembered it all and was so pleased to read of it in the novel. Major Hawkins of Martinstown also told me that his father was much charmed with *The Trumpet-Major*, having heard much about those times from his father, who was in the Yeomanry." A note on the Theatre Royal (in Chapter 30) Miss Owen owed to her correspondence with Mary Drisler in New York. After the Owens had turned their backs on Madison Square, Miss Drisler had to shoulder full responsibility for keeping the T.H.B.L. alive and active. That her enthusiastic interest survived Rebekah Owen's departure is clear enough from a letter she wrote shortly after her father's retirement: "Did you ever copy out anent *The Trumpet-Major* what Miss Kemble says about Weymouth and the little theatre there where Miss Johnson must have played. I hardly know if it is safe to take for granted you do not know it, but I will venture on a few lines. After describing Weymouth scenery Miss Kemble says:

When I got there [to the theatre] I was amused and amazed at its absurdly small proportions; it is a perfect doll's play-house, and until I saw that my father really could stand upon the stage I thought I should fill it entirely by myself. . . . My mother used to tell droll stories about old King George III and Queen Charlotte who had a passion for Weymouth. . . . I long possessed a very perfect coral necklace given my mother by the Princess Amelia.

. . . My father still remains a trustee [of the Public Library]. Give [my] love to the three. . . . Affectionately yours, M. D." Miss Owen added her own note on the "droll stories about Queen Charlotte." Said Rebekah: "Mr. Hardy told me . . . relations of his lived at Sutton Poyntz and Preston . . . [who] told him how Queen Caroline [*sic*], in an old red shawl, used to dodder about Weymouth." After Rebekah had told Hardy that she did not regard Anne Loveday as a wholly worthy heroine, "Mr. Hardy told me that Mrs. 'Barry Cornwall' used to sign her notes to him Anne Loveday, Anne being her Christian name. . . . He spoke of the different impressions conveyed to the mind by the two ways of spelling Anne." Rebekah had perhaps told Hardy that her mother's name was [Catherine] Ann—spelled without the terminal "e."

A LAODICEAN. (First published in 1881.) London, Harper & Brothers, 1898. Second issue of the first English collected Uniform Edition; green cloth. No notes; uncut.

TWO ON A TOWER. (First published in 1882.) Leipzig, Germany, Bernhard Tauchnitz, 1883. Two volumes, rebound in cloth and red imitation-calf. First Continental edition. Autographed on the title-page of Volume I: "Yours faithfully, Thomas Hardy." Subscribed by Rebekah Owen: "Max Gate, 1896." This novel was serialized in *The Atlantic Monthly*, where it failed to please its editor Thomas Bailey Aldrich. Rebekah Owen did not live long enough to read a report on Aldrich's displeasure with this novel when such a report appeared under the title "Thomas Hardy and his New England Editors" in the December 1942 *New England Quarterly*, but it is clear that she too shared some of Aldrich's feeling. In any case, she was satisfied to acquire no other edition of this novel than this Tauchnitz copy. It was given to her in March, 1894, by Mary Drisler, "in memory of many Hardy readings begun in 1887 with *Under the Greenwood Tree*."

THE THREE STRANGERS. (First published in *Longman's Magazine*, London, March, 1883.) Miss Owen's collection included two American appearances of this story: in the Supplement to the New York *Evening Post* for Saturday, March 10, 1883; and in the *Sunday News*, Charleston, South Carolina, April 1, 1883.

THE ROMANTIC ADVENTURES OF A MILKMAID. (First published in the London *Graphic*, June, 1883, and serialized in *Harper's Weekly*, New York, June 23 to August 4, 1883.) New York, George Munro's Sons, [1894]. The date printed on the cover of Miss Owen's copy reads: "No. 139, Seaside Library, Pocket Edition, Jan. 23, 1884"; but the advertising-matter inside this paper-backed and worthless piracy shows it to be an 1894 publication. Hardy was wise in refusing to autograph it. Why Miss Owen had to wait until 1894 to acquire a copy of the *Romantic Adventures* is not clear, for no work by Thomas Hardy was more scandalously pirated in New York City than this. It was published by Harpers in their Franklin Square Library on June 29, 1883; price: ten cents. George Munro seized upon it immediately and had a Seaside copy ready two weeks later. John W. Lovell issued his own pirated edition early in August. Munro issued it a second time in December, and a third in January, 1884. George Munro's brother, Norman L. Munro, also published *The Romantic Adventures*, and F. M. Lupton touched the bottom of depressed values when he offered his Leisure Hour copy of the *Milkmaid* for three cents! The copy acquired by Rebekah Owen is a specimen of the ninth American printing of this trivial by-product of Hardy's off-period of composition.

INTERLOPERS AT THE KNAP. In the May, 1884, *English Illustrated Magazine* (pages 501-514). In this printing of the tale, the name "Susannah" appears, later to be replaced by "Rebekah." It contains the episode in which Johns "with much puffing" climbed to the top of a signpost on a dark night, in order to read the road-directions, and discovered, when he reached the top, that the letters on the signpost were all obliterated. Rebekah Owen recorded the information that this episode was based on an actual incident and that Thomas Hardy's father had been the one who fruitlessly climbed the post.

THE MAYOR OF CASTERBRIDGE. (First published in 1886.) London, Sampson Low, Marston, Searle, & Rivington, 1887. Second edition, one volume, red cloth. Autographed by Hardy and with eight identificatons of Dorchester sites and streets in Hardy's hand. At least one of these may be here transcribed. Regarding the statement (in Chapter 22) that the Museum was "an old house in a back street," Hardy wrote: "From 1851 to 1871 the Museum was in Trinity Street; before that in Judge Jeffreys' lodgings in High West St., by no means a back street as Trinity Street is." Regarding the wife-sale in the first chapter, Miss Owen preserved ten clippings dealing with actual sales or attempted sales. Regarding the "mechanical improvements" (of Chapter 3), "Mr. Hardy told me that the musical steam merry-go-round, with horses that go up and down, cost eight hundred pounds." Regarding the chimes (in Chapter 4): "Mr. Hardy said that some one wrote to inform him that the chimes do not play at 8 o'clock [as stated in the novel] but at 6, 9, and 12!" In annotating Chapter 21, Rebekah Owen wrote that the "queer old door and ... leering mask" are in Shirehall Lane and that "the keystone mask is still a familiar sight in Dorchester." This remained true until as recently as 1938, but in 1950 the present writer found it gone. Thanks to the alert action of the curator of the Dorset Museum, the "leering keystone mask" is now preserved in the museum over which H. J. Moule once presided. Miss Owen's notes on this novel are the most detailed and the most extensive of all those that she compiled.

THE WOODLANDERS. (First published in 1887.) London, Macmillan & Co., 1887. Second edition, one volume, red pebbled cloth. Regarding Hardy's statement (in Chapter 8) that Mrs. Charmond "often thought of writing ... but could not find energy ...," Rebekah noted: "Exactly E.L.H.," i.e., Mrs. Emma Lavinia Hardy. Miss Owen also noticed that Calfhay Cross appears under its "real name," but that Bubb Down appears as "Rubdon Hill" and that "Delborough" (in Chapter 48) is really Chelborough. In this identification of the scene of Winterborne's tragic death, Rebekah Owen is alone; for while F. O. Saxelby lists the place in his *Thomas Hardy Dictionary* (1911), he does so without naming the actual spot, and B. C. A. Windle (*The Wessex of Thomas Hardy*, 1902) and Hermann Lea (*Thomas Hardy's Wessex*, 1913) and Donald Maxwell

(*The Landscape of Thomas Hardy*, 1928) ignore it altogether. Miss Owen can claim Chelborough as her exclusive possession.

WESSEX TALES. (First published in 1888.) London, Macmillan & Co., 1889. Second edition, one volume, red cloth. Miss Owen notes that "all the Wessex Tales are true." The tale of "The Three Strangers" is true, she says, "but the incidents did not all happen at one time, as in the story." Similarly, "The Withered Arm" is true, but "he learnt *all* the details and ending [only] after he had published the story; in some respects they were more gruesome than in his version." Davies was the real name of the hangman. "He was a friend of the Hardy family, Mr. Hardy told me." Regarding "Interlopers at the Knap," Hardy informed Miss Owen that "it was my father who rode along . . . and was obliged to climb the guide post and strike a light, finding nothing on the fingers of the post." Miss Owen asked: "And did he go for one wife and take another?" Hardy replied: "I cannot quite say as to that!" with a laugh. With regard to the village of "Verton" in this same tale, Miss Owen identified it as Long Burton, but noted that Hardy placed it in a wrong position with relation to King's Hintock for a man to pass through, plausibly, on arriving (say, at Southampton) from Australia. In the next edition of *Wessex Tales*, Hardy changed "Verton" to read "Evershead" (i.e., Evershot). At the same time he changed the name of "the woman who assisted at the dairy" from "Susannah" to "Rebekah."

THE MELANCHOLY HUSSAR. In *Three Notable Stories* (pages 153-211), London, Spencer Blackett, 1890. First Edition; rebound; pages trimmed. (Rebound with *A Group of Noble Dames*.)

A GROUP OF NOBLE DAMES. London, James R. Osgood, McIlvaine & Co., 1891. First Edition; rebound. (Bound with "The Melancholy Hussar.") Miss Owen noted that "All the *Group of Noble Dames* tales are true [except that] Mrs. Hardy says that 'Barbara of the House of Grebe' is not. Often Mr. Hardy has got traditions from old people who got them from old family servants of the great families, whose representatives now think that Mr. Hardy ought not to have published them. At least Lord Ilchester thought so of 'The First Countess of Wessex,' though Lady Pembroke and other descendants of Betty (he knows eight) are quite pleased. One Lord R— (I forget) [Rowton?] said to Mr. Hardy, 'It is all nonsense, you know, of Ilchester to feel so, and I shall tell him so.' Betty's father, the rough hunting Squire, was Squire Horner of Mells

Park; Mells was the plum picked out by Jack Horner from the pie in which the Glastonbury title-deeds were baked. The Abbot charged him with them, he picked out the deeds of Mells property and took the rest to King Henry VIII. . . . Mr. Hardy told me to-day, Nov. 12, 1896, that . . . Betty was so tiny she could not reach the door-knob of her husband's room. . . . Squire 'Dornell' is very true to life; he was just such a man. . . . Miss Teresa Charlotte Fetherstonhaugh of Moreton is the great-great-grand-daughter of Betty." Miss Owen makes the following identifications in the tale of "Anna, Lady Baxby" (Dame the Seventh): "A particular year: 1642. Sherton Castle: Sherborne. Earls of Severn: Bristol. A certain noble Marquis: of Hertford. Lord Baxby: Digby. A noble Lord: Earl of Bedford. An August evening: in 1645."

TESS OF THE D'URBERVILLES. (First published in three volumes in 1891.) London, James R. Osgood, McIlvaine & Co., 1892. Fifth edition, one volume, light brown cloth with gilt decorations. Regarding Durbeyfield's boast in Chapter 2, "Mr. Hardy told me that he heard a drunken man at the corner of Durngate and South Streets in Dorchester singing just such a boast." Regarding the statement in Chapter 14 that "a saner religion [than heliolatry] never prevailed," Miss Owen records: "I have twice heard Mr. Hardy say, 'I could worship the sun'." Regarding the praying bull in Chapter 17, "Mr. Hardy said: 'There was something like this once.' [I.e.,] Dewy and the hymn played to the bull are founded on fact." Regarding the Paridelles and Retty Priddle (in Chapter 19), Miss Owen noted that these names occur in Stubbs' account (I, 45-48) of Henry II's Partizans. Then she added: "Very curious, for I doubt Mr. Hardy having seen this. [Later:] He told me that he had not." Regarding the "little railway station" and the "neighbouring holly tree" (in Chapter 30), Miss Owen states: "The tree is really at Moreton Station. Mr. Hardy told me, and I afterwards noticed it." Miss Owen thus effectively disposes of B. C. A. Windle's claim that the station at Wool was meant. Hermann Lea omits all mention of the station. Regarding Tess's employment (in Chapter 47) in feeding the threshing machines, Rebekah Owen had been told that women were no longer so employed; "but we often saw them, in fact never saw *men* employed as feeders. One was *close* to Casterbridge, November 1892. . . . The title of *Tess* was to have been *The Valley of the Great Dairies,* and Tess's own name Rose Mary. Mrs. Hardy told me that she was called Rose Mary so long it was difficult to think of her as Tess."

TESS OF THE D'URBERVILLES. London, Harper & Brothers, 1900. The six-penny double-columned edition in salmon-colored paper wrappers. Signed: "Betty Owen, August 1, 1900." This edition was the only London edition of *Tess* published by Harpers. Hardy himself once owned a copy just like Rebekah Owen's; the two copies now stand side by side.

LIFE'S LITTLE IRONIES. (First published in 1894.) London, Osgood, McIlvaine & Co., 1894. Second edition, olive-green rough cloth, brown decorations, gilt lettering. Autographed on the half-title: "Yrs faithfully Thomas Hardy." and signed "Betty Owen. Written at Max Gate, November 23, 1896." She read this book aloud at least three times. "The Son's Veto" (which Hardy thought was his best story) had appeared in the Christmas 1891 issue of the *Illustrated London News*.

THE SPECTRE OF THE REAL, by Thomas Hardy and Florence Henniker; now known to be largely the work of Hardy. (See "Thomas Hardy and Florence Henniker," by Richard L. Purdy, in the *Colby Library Quarterly* for October, 1944.) In a book entitled *In Scarlet and Grey*, London, John Lane, n.d. [1894].

JUDE THE OBSCURE. London, Osgood, McIlvaine & Co., 1896. First Edition, green ribbed cloth. Barnes's poem (in IV, 4) is identified as "Shaftesbury Feair."

THE WELL-BELOVED. London, Osgood, McIlvaine & Co., 1897. First Edition, green ribbed cloth.

WESSEX POEMS. London, Harper & Brothers, 1898. First Edition, green ribbed cloth. Autographed on the title-page: "Yours truly, Thomas Hardy." In Rebekah Owen's hand: "Max Gate, November 24th, 1900. ... He wrote in my books and carried one of them home for me."

ENTER A DRAGOON. In the London edition of *Harper's Magazine* for December, 1900. Inscribed: "R.O.—Casterbridge, December 5, 1900."

THE DEAD QUIRE. In the Christmas Number of *The Graphic*, London, December, 1901; page 16.

POEMS OF THE PAST AND THE PRESENT. London, Harper & Brothers, 1902. First Edition, green ribbed cloth.

THE MARKET GIRL. In *The Venture:* an Annual of Art and Literature, edited by Laurence Housman and W. Somerset Maugham. London, John Baillie, 1903. Decorated boards; linen spine.

THE DYNASTS. London, Macmillan & Co., 1904-1908. First Editions. Part I: 1904; Part II: 1906; Part III: 1908. Three volumes, each autographed "Thomas Hardy" on the half-title. Volume I is signed: "Betty Owen. January, 1904."

SELECTED POEMS OF WILLIAM BARNES, chosen and edited by Thomas Hardy. London, Henry Frowde, 1908. First Edition. Given by Rebekah Owen to Mrs. Beatrix Potter Heelis.

TIME'S LAUGHINGSTOCKS. London, Macmillan, 1909. First Edition. Autographed on the half-title: "Thomas Hardy." On page 160 there is a correction in Hardy's hand.

A CHANGED MAN AND OTHER TALES. London, Macmillan, 1913. First Edition; green ribbed cloth.

SATIRES OF CIRCUMSTANCE. London, Macmillan, 1914. First Edition. Autographed on the half-title: "Thomas Hardy."

MOMENTS OF VISION. London, Macmillan, 1917. First Edition. Miss Owen checked twenty-two poems, including "The Oxen" and "Afterwards." This is the book which she submitted to the poet for his autograph and received it back unsigned.

AND THERE WAS A GREAT CALM. In the Armistice Day Section of the London *Times*, November 11, 1920; page iii.

LATE LYRICS AND EARLIER. London, Macmillan, 1922. First Edition. Miss Owen annotated only two of the poems.

HUMAN SHOWS. London, Macmillan, 1925. First Edition. No notes.

The reader who is already acquainted with the complete body of Thomas Hardy's writings will readily observe from the foregoing pages that Miss Owen owned the entire Works in one form or another, with the exception of *The Queen of Cornwall* (1923), *Winter Words* (1928), and a few *minuscula*. Her copy of the *Collected Poems* (1919) is missing.

BOOKS ABOUT HARDY

Shelved with her Hardy books, Miss Owen's Hardiana included not only critical and biographical works dealing directly with Hardy but also volumes which, for personal reasons, she associated with him. For example, the writings of H. J. Moule, the Dorchester curator, are there, even though they often do not refer to Hardy or his books; and the writings of George Oliver are there, even though his sole connection with Hardy—in Rebekah Owen's mind—may have been his urging her to do a book of her own on the Max Gate author. In some instances Miss Owen's reasons for associating certain books with Hardy seem irretrievably lost, and it is of course possible that some "Interlopers" have sneaked into the Hardiana fold. Her Italian chauffeur's lack of familiarity with English may have had something to do with the confusion.

ABERCROMBIE, Lascelles, *Thomas Hardy*. London, Martin Secker, 1912. This is the book which Rebekah Owen loaned to Hardy on November 26, 1912. The next morning Mrs. Hardy died. Hardy returned the book two days later.

ADCOCK, A. St. John, "Thomas Hardy, the Grand Old Man of English Literature," No. I of "Some Gods of Modern Grub Street," in the *Manchester Evening News*, March 17, 1923.

ANONYMOUS, *Architectural and Historical Notes of Lincoln Cathedral*, n.d. Paper. Autographed: "Rebekah Owen. August 21st, 1886."

ANON., *Illustrated Guide to Weymouth*. Weymouth, J. Sharron, n.d.

ANON., *The Oxford Visitor*, with 56 fine copper engravings by J. and H. S. Storer. London, Sherwood, Neely, & Jones, 1822.

ANON., *Rambles and Rides Around Oxford*. Oxford, A. T. Shrimpton & Son, n.d. Second edition; bought in 1892.

ANON., *Stowe*. London, J. Seeley, 1827.

ASHE, Thomas, *Songs of a Year*. London, Chiswick Press, 1888.

BRENNECKE, Ernest, "Thomas Hardy Today," page 12 in the *New York Times Book Review* for June 5, 1921. A review of the 21-volume Anniversary Edition (New York, 1920-21) of Hardy's Works.

CASE, M. and E., *Dorchester Almanack and Street Directory for 1893.* Dorchester, Cornhill Printing Works, 1892.

CASE, M. and E., *Dorchester Almanack and Street Directory for 1894.* Dorchester, Cornhill Printing Works, 1893.

CASE, M. and E., *Photographs of Dorchester,* n.d.

CHEW, Samuel C., *Thomas Hardy, Poet and Novelist.* Bryn Mawr Notes and Monographs III. New York, Longmans, Green & Co., 1921. First Edition.

CHILD, Harold, *Thomas Hardy.* London, Nisbet & Co., 1916. First Edition.

DORCHESTER DEBATING AND DRAMATIC SOCIETY. Four Programs: "The Mellstock Quire," November 16-17, 1910; "The Trumpet-Major," November 27-28, 1912; "The Return of the Native," November 17-18, 1920; and "A Desperate Remedy," November 15-17, 1922. Miss Owen's programs for "Far from the Madding Crowd," November 17-18, 1909; for "The Woodlanders," November 19-20, 1913; and for "Tess of the D'Urbervilles," November 26-29, 1924, seem not to have survived.

Dorset County Chronicle: "Henry Joseph Moule": a pamphlet reprinting the obituary notice in the *Chronicle* on March 17, 1904.

GROVE, Lady Agnes, "Women's Suffrage in Time of War," in the *Cornhill Magazine* for August, 1900. Lady Grove was often Hardy's hostess in London.

HARDY, Florence Emily, *The Early Life of Thomas Hardy.* London, Macmillan, 1928. First Edition.

HARPER, Charles G., *The Hardy Country.* London, Adam and Charles Black, 1904. A note by Rebekah Owen reads: "No mention of the particularly vivid Salisbury scenes in *The Hand of Ethelbelta.*"

HEATH, F. R. and Sidney, *Dorchester and its Surroundings.* Dorchester, F. G. Longman, 1905. Homeland Handbooks No. 46. First Edition.

HEATH, Sidney, *The Heart of Wessex*. London, Blackie & Son, 1910.

HOLLAND, Clive, "Thomas Hardy," in *The Bookman*, London, November, 1901.

HOLLAND, Clive, *Wessex*. London, Adam & Charles Black, 1906.

HOWELLS, William Dean, *Their Silver Wedding Journey*. London, Harpers, 1900. Autographed: "R. Owen. September 11, 1901. Belmount." Read at various times, and finally "in the nights of the débâcle of Belmount Hall."

HUTTON, Laurence, *Literary Landmarks of Oxford*. London, Grant Richards, 1903.

JOHNSON, Lionel, *The Art of Thomas Hardy*. London, Elkin Mathews & John Lane, 1894. First Edition.

LEA, Hermann, *Thomas Hardy's Wessex*. London, Macmillan, 1913. First Edition.

LING, Henry, *Dorchester Almanack and Street Directory for 1911*. Dorchester, Henry Ling, 1910.

LING, Henry, *Dorchester Almanack for 1913*. Dorchester, Ling, 1912.

MACDONELL, Annie, *Thomas Hardy*. London, Hodder and Stoughton, 1894.

MOULE, Handley C. G., *Memories of a Vicarage*. London, The Religious Tract Society, 1913. Note by R. O.: "This book contains 27 references to Thomas Hardy's mother."

MOULE, Handley, *The School of Suffering*. London, Society for Promoting Christian Knowledge, 1905.

MOULE, H. J., *Cerne Abbey Barn*. Dorchester, Dorset County Chronicle Printing Works, 1889.

MOULE, H. J., *Dorchester Antiquities*. Dorchester, Henry Ling, 1906. Second edition.

MOULE, H. J., *Notes on a Book Called Domesday*. Dorchester, Dorset County Chronicle Printing Works, 1890.

MOULE, H. J., *Notes on the Walls and Gates of Durnovaria*. Dorchester, Dorset County Chronicle Printing Works, 1893.

MOULE, H. J., *Old Dorset*. London, Cassell & Co., 1893.

OLIVER, George, *The Guesten Hall, Worcester*, n.d. Note in R. O.'s hand: "Worcester, April 30, 1888."

OLIVER, George, *Kilpeck Church, Herefordshire*. Worcester Diocesan Architectural and Archaeological Society, March 21, 1887.

OWEN, Rebekah, *Postcard Album*. With views of Dorset buildings and landscapes.

OWEN, Rebekah, *Scrap-book No. 3*, "made in February, 1894." This contains letters, clippings, programs, notes, souvenirs, cards, tickets, advertisements, bills, photographs, and other miscellanea. Information as to the fate of Scrap-books Numbers 2 and 4, etc., is lacking.

PARRISH, Gladys, *Carfrae's Comedy*. London, William Heinemann, 1915. Inscribed by Miss Owen: "R.O. from Florence Hardy. Max Gate, December 1915."

PRETOR, Alfred, *Ronald and I*. Cambridge, Deighton, Bell & Co., 1899. Dedicated "To Mrs. Thomas Hardy who suggested and encouraged the writing of these tales." Inscribed: "To Miss R. Owen from E. L. Hardy. July '99."

SKURRAY, Francis, *Shepherd's Garland*. London, Simpkin & Marshall, 1832.

SMITH, Samuel, *The Parish and Church of Leigh*. Worcester Architectural and Archaeological Society, n.d.

SPENDER, Harold, *The British Isles*. London, Cassell, n.d. [1903]. Contains "Mr. Thomas Hardy's Wessex," pages 17-29.

Sphere, The: "Printer's Pie": a Festival Souvenir of the Printers' Pension, Almshouse and Orphan Asylum Corporation, 1904. London, Office of The Sphere, 1904. This contains (at pages 59-60) a reproduction of "The Death of Nelson" from pages 168-169 of Hardy's manuscript of *The Dynasts*.

STEPHENS, James, *Five New Poems*. London, A. T. Stevens, 1913.

THOMPSON, A. H., "Thomas Hardy," in *The Eagle*, a magazine supported by members of St. John's College, Cambridge, December, 1895; pages 36-61.

YOUNG, Ernest W., *Dorchester: its Principal Buildings, Institutions, and Surroundings.* Dorchester, Henry Ling, 1886.

ZANGWILL, I., "Without Prejudice," pages 238-246 in *The Chap-Book*, Chicago, Stone & Kimball, January 15, 1896.

As one casts a retrospective glance over these old books, what do they all amount to?

First of all, we see Rebekah Owen's influence stamped upon the text of several of the Wessex Novels. Her major accomplishment lies in her persuading Hardy to restore to *The Mayor of Casterbridge* the caged goldfinch. In *Far from the Madding Crowd* she detected the erroneous "left" for "right," and after twenty years of error she brought about its correction in 1895. In 1892 she uttered a phrase which Hardy thought worth putting into *Jude the Obscure,* and in *The Well-Beloved* she may well have been responsible for the description of the exotic broad hat with "radiating folds." And in the *Interlopers at the Knap,* she transferred her name, *Rebekah,* spelling and all, to the woman who assisted at the dairy.

Second, we find Miss Owen anticipating the modern editor and scholar in numerous identifications of people, places, incidents, and allusions. She is the only one to detect Burke in *Far from the Madding Crowd,* and to detect Shakespeare in *The Withered Arm;* and in hearing echoes of Browning in Hardy's verse she played the part of a self-reliant pioneer. She has no rival in Chelborough, and she alone saw the little holly tree at the Moreton railway station. Even more valuable are her notes on people. She spots Lady Susan Strangways and Isaac West, John Amey and Mr. Burt, Mayor Davis and Hangman Davies, William Downe and Squire Horner, Lady Ilchester and Captain Mansel, the Earl of Bedford and Thomas Hardy Senior; and she thus brings corroborating evidence to support Hardy's statement, once made to Henry Arthur Jones, that he had never put a character into any of his books without having warranty for him in real life.

Third, we are indebted to Rebekah Owen for her preservation of Hardy's comments on his own work, for his reminiscences about the sources he drew on, in fact and fable, and for his explanations of his aims and purposes, sometimes successful and sometimes not, in his writings. Without Miss Owen's help, we would still be ignorant of what Mary Ellen Chase called Hardy's "line of reasoning" in deciding to change the ending of *The Mayor of Casterbridge*, we would be unaware that he had been "all along" provoked with Grace Melbury in *The Woodlanders*, and we would not know why he deliberately "went off at a tangent" in *The Hand of Ethelberta*.

Finally, without the help given us by Rebekah Owen, we would have to remain ignorant of many incidents and episodes in Hardy's life—not only his life when *she* was present, talking with him at Max Gate or biking or hiking with him, but also his life before she appeared upon the scene. He told her of many things which did not find their way into the pages of *The Early Life* or *The Later Years* and we are richer for this knowledge. In more ways than one, Rebekah Owen provides us with a more intimate picture of Hardy's home-life than we have as yet obtained from any other source. She enables us to look at the Max Gate menage through her spectacles and gives us a vividly drawn portrait of the first as well as of the second Mrs. Hardy. What we thus learn helps us a great deal in arriving at an understanding of the novels and the poems produced at Max Gate. Not a few of Hardy's poems, including some that have gained the world's acclaim, take on new meaning and are seen in a new light when they are set against the background of Thomas Hardy's acquaintance with the lady from New York.

Mention should be made, too, of the many letters which Miss Owen so carefully preserved for posterity. They mirror Victorian society for us with a vividness that brings New York and Oxford, as well as Belmount and Max Gate, clearly before our eyes and helps us the better to understand the society to which Thomas Hardy first addressed himself. As stated on the first page of Chapter One, Hardy's world was not our world, and anything that helps us to see it more clearly and more truthfully is welcome. If we are not in a position, even yet, to "see his whole sincere symmetric history," we are certainly much better off than we would have been, if Rebekah Owen had never heard the sound of Hardy's magic flute and had never followed it down the street, through the traffic of Madison Square, across the ocean and into his own drawing room.

INDEX

Index

Please notice that the numerous letters printed on the preceding pages are indexed under "LETTERS" and are listed under the names of both the writers and the recipients. Hardy's own letters are also indexed under "Hardy."

Moule, Horace, 75
Moule, Curator Henry J., 74, 75, 112,
114, 122, 132, 136, 137, 144, 146,
237, 242, 243, 244, 245
Moule, Mrs. H. J., 118, 132, 134, 137
Moule, Isabel, 75, 146
Moule, Margaret, 74, 75, 117, 131,
132, 134, 135, 141, 146, 152, 160,
172, 178, 187, 196
Moule, Mary, 75
Moulton, Louise C., 176
"Mountain View," 37, 81
Munro, George, 21, 33, 236
Munro, Norman L., 33, 34, 236
Munsey's Magazine, 111, 233
"Music in Hardy's Life & Work," 183
Mussolini, 206, 210

N

National Academy, 12
National Trust, 198
New England Quarterly, 236
New Forest, 84
New York City, 6, 73, 156, 222
New York Evening Post, 22, 26, 236
New York Herald, 10
New York Historical Society, 13
New York Journal, 119
New York Sun, 234
New York Times, 21, 35, 141, 243
New York Tribune, 20, 21, 119
Nicholas Nickleby, 36
Nisbet & Co., 243
Nobel Prize, 228
Northumberland, 42
Notes on a Book Called Domesday, 244
Notes on Durnovaria, 244
Novalis, 79
Nuneham, 36
Nutcracker Suite, 35

O

O'Brien, William, 232
Old Touraine, 144
Oliver, Emma, 30, 40, 105
Oliver, George, 30, 36, 38, 39, 42, 58,
64, 82, 94, 98, 179, 182, 242, 245

Olivia, 17
"On a Discovered Curl of Hair," 205
"On First Looking into Chapman's
Homer," 23
"On the Western Circuit," 102
Orlando, 17
Oseney, 31
Osgood, James R., 50, 51, 55, 125
Osgood, McIlvaine & Co., 50, 105, 123,
233, 238-240
Osmington, 70
Othello, 17
Outlook (London), 127
Overmoigne, 83
Owen, Catharine, 9, 16, 19, 25, 29, 36,
41, 42, 58, 69, 75, 76, 84, 109, 140,
144, 145, 151, 152, 154, 156, 172,
178, 226
Owen, Henry, 3, 7, 9, 10, 12-14, 19, 20,
47, 220, 231
Owen, Mrs. Henry, 19
Owen, Joseph, 5, 8, 14, 30
OWEN, Rebekah: acquires a motor-car,
148; advises Longfellow on sonnet-
revision, 17; arrives at Dorchester,
53; "assists," 227; begins reading
Hardy aloud, 34, 232; becomes "Betty," 110; calls at Max Gate, 56; calls
Hardy a churl, 197; ceases writing to
Max Gate, 212; conceals her age, 11,
12; cuts her last clipping, 217; cycles
with Hardy, 134; decides to leave
New York, 120-121; dies, 225; dines
at Max Gate, 63; discusses Tess, 108;
enjoys the proudest hour of her life,
44; goes alone to Dorchester, 133;
goes slumming with Hardy, 136, 137;
hankers after Oxford, 29, 38; has
her chance, 180-183; is admitted to
the Bodleian, 79; is born, 11; is disgusted with Hardy, 194-197; is "mad
at" Hardy, 126; is repelled by *Jude*,
101; learns to cycle, 105; learns to
lead, 20; makes a scrap-book, 245;
meets Hardy, 55-58; meets Hardy's
writing for the first time, 22; organ-
izes a Hardy Book League, 99; per-

Date Due

JAN 2 1 '66		
JAN 2 8 1986		
APR 1 5 1986		